I0625524

Living For Love:

Set Yourself Free from the Daily Stress, Worry, & Hurry that Wears You Down

Dr. Shawn Haywood

ISBN: 979-8-218-10708-6 (Paperback)

Any references to historical events, real people, or real places have been changed to protect the privacy of real clients of Reimagine Love.

Cover Design by Dani Lou Illustrates

Developmental & Line Editor:
Danielle Anderson, Ink Worthy Books

Copy and Proof Editor: Emily Reader

Printed in the United States of America.

First printing edition 2022.

www.ReimagineLove.com

DrHaywood@ReimagineLove.com

Living For Love:

Set Yourself Free from the Daily Stress, Worry, & Hurry that Wears You Down

Dedication

To God, Source, Truth, Divine Spark of all that IS, my undying gratitude for this divine-human experience. And for the constant Truth and Unconditional Love that is revealed each and every day. All glory belongs to You.

Acknowledgments

To my husband, Christopher Haywood, you are a Divine expression of the most unwavering, unconditional love I could ever hope for, pray for, or desire to experience. Thank you for being exactly who you are. I love you with every ounce of my heart and being. You are the most precious gift God could *give* me.

To the late Dr. David R. Hawkins and his wife, Susan, the love I carry within, share, and experience would not be possible without your teachings.

To my mother, Donna Jean Fugate, who taught me that anyone could be lonely at any moment and, therefore, might need my love, so give it freely. You have always been the wisest woman I know. Thank you for your love and guidance.

To my tribe of extraordinary warrior women who have shared countless lessons and unconditional support during my fifty years on this planet, my grandmother Barbara Schumm, my aunt Judy Acks, my longest and bestest friend Kim Gowanloch, my sister Jodi Parisot, my spiritual soulmate Julie Granger, and my aunt Pamela Van.

Last but certainly not least, to my three loving and spirited brothers, Shannon, Shane, and David Parisot, you are deeply loved and cherished. Thank you for your unwavering brotherly love and protection.

Table of Contents

Introduction: Getting Started!

What you hold in your hand is a step-by-step map to FREEDOM—freedom in time, money, relationships, and, of course, emotional and spiritual freedom. Such freedom is achieved by living for love, as you will learn throughout this book. I'm guessing you're likely questioning whether "love" is what you need to be living for right now. How can love help bring you what you really want—freedom from the heaviness and anxiety you feel each day?

I know how hard it can be. I know that some days, you labor over what to make your family for dinner while feeling exhausted and just wanting to fall into a heap on your bed at seven o'clock. Other days you stay up late trying to finish that important work project when you would rather be watching a Netflix show and snuggling with your sweetie. And then there are the days where your sweetie, or children, seem to be the source of your frustration and anxiety, and you feel like making a prison break. Or maybe you got up early for another work meeting when you promised yourself—again—that you would not miss another yoga class. Or you find yourself face-deep in a pint of Ben & Jerry's ice cream or a bottle of wine (again) after another argument with your husband..., and it all just feels like too much to bear.

I hear from so many clients and women in our community that sometimes life just feels like "too much". They want to crawl back into bed until they feel less stressed, less overwhelmed, and have less conflict in their marriage. They want to have less on their plates and instead have more peace, time, space, joy, and *freedom.*

Believe me, I understand, and I see you.

Here's the truth. You *can* feel light every day. You *can* experience emotional, relational, and financial freedom. You *can* feel divinely connected all of the time—AND applying what you learn in this book to your life will take you the distance.

1

This is not a quick fix or a magic pill you can take that will transform your life. It is a collection of new practices and emotional skills that gain traction like a beautiful snowball gaining speed as it rolls down the hill—and with a commitment to these practices, so it will be for you.

Women today push themselves far too hard. They overdo it to the point of frequent frustration and resentment. They overcommit to the point of exhaustion, and instead of asking for help and support, they try to do it all and be it all—embodying the Super Woman persona to their detriment. They expect perfection, and instead of standing in their own innate perfection, they are led to feel as though they are not enough and will never be enough. They are led to a place of constant emotional, mental, physical, and spiritual burnout.

Perhaps you have identified as a perfectionist at one point in your life, as I did. The problem is that perfectionism as a *lifestyle*—not simply situational—creates a mental, emotional, and spiritual dynamic of NEVER feeling like enough for yourself and others. It leads to impossible expectations that inevitably end in frustration, disappointment, and disconnection. It robs you of your precious time, energy, and resources while leaving you feeling as if there is never enough and YOU are never enough.

When perfectionism is running the show, the sense of "not-enough-ness" tends to follow you everywhere, from business to the bedroom. And so does the heavy feeling of shame, as perfectionism and shame are a mated pair and never go anywhere without the other.

Here are a few examples of where the voice of not-enough-ness comes through like a megaphone: you are not doing enough; not accomplishing enough; not working long enough; not spending enough time with family, friends, or pets; not making enough money; not being a good enough mom; not feeling secure or confident enough; not being skinny enough, smart enough, successful enough, and any other place where you can possibly perceive of never being enough.

Do any of these sound familiar?

I'm willing to bet they do. And here's where the real trouble comes into the picture.

Most days, you vacillate between feigning a smile, fighting a meltdown, or actually full-on melting down. You wear a mask that says, "Everything is great," while slowly dying of soul-sickness on the inside.

Rarely feeling like enough plagues women of all walks of life—you are not alone in this struggle. This underpinning is a dominant unconscious driver behind all the "overdoing" you engage in. When living a life of constant "overdoing," you experience more emotional lows and exhaustion, lash out at the people you love, and, at the end of the day, you are left feeling totally depleted. When one does not feel good enough, overdoing of all kinds ensues.

Women endlessly beat themselves up for this core skewed perception (and falsity) of "not being good enough." That not-enough-ness yells loud and long and encourages women to feel wretched and overly emotional.

Additionally, despite your endless effort, most areas of your life feel frustrating, and you view them as either "not bad" or "not great." In relationships, you may have a strong tendency to bounce between "It's all my fault that I feel crummy," and "It's their fault that I feel crummy."

In the end, you often wind up feeling strained by the demands of balancing work, family, and friends, and though you might have people around you much of the time, you still feel alone. And the most unfortunate piece is that you have simply grown to believe that this is just how life is, which I am guessing does not encourage you to feel very loving or loved.

You go to bed fretting about what you did not get done, or angry at yourself for overeating or overdrinking, or not sticking to your workout plan, just to wake up in the morning with a belly full of anxiety, already feeling taxed by the day ahead. Before you've even begun, you just want to pull the covers back over your head and try again tomorrow. But "tomorrow" ends up being a repeat of yesterday; cue the movie *Groundhog Day*.

The thing is, you are actually a complete badass, superstar, Wonder Woman. Somewhere inside of you KNOWS THIS IS TRUE, but you have not yet determined how to live in this space, to feel in this space, or to live FROM this space. Instead, you lay in bed at night replaying all the ways you or others failed you that day or worrying about what you did not check off your to-do list.

The women I have worked with as a life and relationship coach over the past twenty-three years reached the point where they had had enough running around on this hamster wheel and felt ready to live a life they could adore. The women who call to work with me are ready to wake up every day completely rested and leaping out of bed with joy and inspiration. They are ready to live for love! They are ready to shed the perfectionistic habits, mindsets, and emotions that led them to overdo, over-try, over-extend, overwork, over-please, and be overly busy. That "lifestyle" has only served to the detriment of their bodies, minds, and spirits, and they are ready to claim joy and freedom without all the craziness, upset, and frustration!

That's where living for love delivers tenfold.

Living for love is the most beautiful and fulfilling way to live, shine, and radiate from your beautiful, precious heart. When you live for love, you live in service and stewardship to all—the great

Mother Earth, other humans, The Divine, and of course to your gorgeous self and every space in between.

When you live for love, life flows gently and powerfully; it's effortless and enjoyable, and there is no more space for depression, lashing out, strict (and punitive) perfectionism, overflowing anxiety, worry and fear, petty resentments, or anger.

Simply put, when you live for love, everything and everyone around you changes, softens, and amplifies. You learn to become deeply emotionally FREE; this is the kind of freedom that really matters.

Now is the time to make this shift. Women are becoming increasingly ready to let go of defining their value, worth, and status by how busy, stressed, burned out, and exhausted they are. They are ready to reclaim joy, calmness, and simplicity without sacrificing impact, contribution, and sanity!

Women are now ready to work smarter instead of harder, to ask for help and receive support, even if others do not do it the way *she* (mom, boss, wife) would do it (wink wink!), to slow down and literally stop to smell the roses as she takes long, soothing walks in nature just for the *soul* purpose of meandering, enjoying, and contemplating life instead of for the strict purpose of "burning calories."

I want this for you too! I want you to wake up inspired every day and so jazzed that you literally rip the covers back and leap out of bed!

I want you to know that you are not alone and that you can learn HOW to stop feeling isolated on your metaphorical desert island. I want you to feel relieved from the pressures and strict demands of yourself, to have plenty of time, energy, and resources, to get ALL the support you want and deserve (even if you hate asking for help), and lastly, to learn the joy of giving yourself and others true, unbridled, unconditional acceptance, kindness, care, and love.

This is what it means to live for love.

To embrace and LOVE the whole of you, your contribution, your tribe, your LIFE!

You can live for and within love.

You deserve to live for and within the deep depths of love.

Your willingness is all that is required!

As a disciplined practitioner of living for love, I know how powerful it can be.

I have seen so many miracles occur in my life and in the lives of our clients over the past twenty-three years of owning ReimagineLove.com and LiberateMyLife.com.

As a result of dedicating my life to love, I have gained a sense of peace—peace that, as a woman who has experienced nearly every form of abuse and trauma, I could not have possibly fathomed existed. As I endeavored on my journey to live for love, I went from being utterly soul-sick, depressed, and filled with fear, worry, and anxiety to living in deep, unbridled Divine love, joy, and happiness.

Through this book, I want to share how to live in the peace that you, too, are craving; I want to walk with you as you embark on a freeing journey of healing and growth.

Are you in?

Setting Yourself Up For Success To Create Sustainable Change

Because this book is a guide to change and transformation, which encompasses growth, expansion, and deep healing, you must first understand the anatomy of change. In this section, you will learn to work with the brain, mind/ego, emotional systems, and

Spirit / Divinity / God / Source / Allness to weave sustainable, fluid change throughout your life.

I want to enable you to make powerful changes with minimal back-sliding and optimal results—let's set you up to make lasting changes instead of beating yourself up when a change falls off the wagon.

Most people approach change with grit and willpower alone. And while these can be mildly supportive elements to creating change, they cannot alone lead to the sustainable change and healing your heart is craving. Grit and willpower are akin to one single muscle in one single finger. You can pick up a pen or pencil, but you will not be carrying logs with the strength of one finger. And so it is for grit and willpower; they fatigue quickly and easily, leaving you feeling like a failure when desired change does not persist.

Let's begin this journey by arming you with the knowledge to actually apply change in sustainable ways. First, you must befriend all the elements within you that play a role in making change happen, including your brain, intellect, mind/ego, heart, feelings, and spirit. Within a more holistic approach, change can unfold in the most fertile soil.

The Limbic System

Beware! A few nerdy paragraphs lie ahead! If you are into that, GREAT! If not, do not worry. I promise it's only a few paragraphs and not too painful.

The limbic system is the part of the brain in charge of our behavioral and emotional responses, especially when it comes to survival: feeding, reproduction, caring for our young, and the fight, flight, freeze, and fawn responses.

Let's look at how the limbic system supports or restricts change. The limbic system, in very rudimentary terms, is more than ready—

eager even—to press the internal panic button and yell through a megaphone, "STOP! NOT SAFE, NOT SAFE, NOT SAFE!" when you set out to make a change.

The limbic system is not really interested in change; it is interested in sameness. To the limbic system, which is designed to protect you, change seems like a threat. It figures, "We've survived this long; why rock the boat?!" So, in some ways, you are wired for sameness, even when it is a destructive habit like alcoholism, self-loathing, or yelling at your children or spouse. On the other hand, the brain is magically and miraculously plastic and capable of absolutely profound change! This is truly a marvel of the human condition.

These two elements might seem in competition with each other, yet they are a perfect team! The limbic system keeps you safe and lets you know when you need to fight, flee, freeze, or fawn. And the plasticity of your brain allows you to do, well, anything else! Isn't that cool?!

In response to the way our brain works, I have developed nine elements to support sustainable change. You may choose to utilize one of these ideas for things like adding more green foods to your diet, perhaps a different tool for learning to be kinder to yourself, and another yet for creating a habit of reading for ten minutes a day. Or perhaps you might choose one or two and use them for every change!

Regardless, there is no right or wrong way to apply the elements of sustainable change, so use what is supportive and discard the rest.

Nine Elements of Sustainable Change

Think of the last time you went on a diet or tried to begin a new exercise routine. You started with excitement, motivation, and sound resolve to make the desired changes and stick to the plan.

And then… thirty to ninety days later (maybe less!), you abandoned your diet and traded salads and gym time for burgers, chocolate, and wine.

Sound familiar?

Even seemingly small changes can seem insurmountable. Take, for example, wanting to be more patient with your children, co-workers, spouse, or even other drivers. Yet, the next time your children do that "thing" that drives you crazy, or a driver is moving too slowly for your taste, or your mother-in-law makes that same old remark about your parenting, you lose your patience and lash out, marking the moment you, once again, fall off the "desired change" wagon and feel like an utter failure.

So, before you embark on learning about all the juicy tools to help you live for love, let's set you up for success and ensure you're able to apply this material in ways that are truly sustainable.

Start by joining our Reimagine Love Facebook group: www.facebook.com/groups/ReimagineLove.

This inspiring community of like-minded women is packed full of support; this is where I answer all of your questions and cheer you on, and it's where our members share wins and "fall on your face" moments so that we can be in one another's corner through thick and thin! And most of all, it's where we support each other in making the beautiful desired changes to transform your life bit by bit into the life of your dreams.

Once you're squared away with support through this journey, jump into the nine elements of change listed on the following pages. These elements have been identified and developed over twenty-three years of coaching individuals, business owners, professionals, and couples and have the power to support you in making your desired changes last for a lifetime.

1. **Decision & Commitment**

   Making a decision for change is about making a defiant commitment to your desired outcome, result, habit, mindset shift, or a new way of being in the world. All sustainable changes begin with your decision and a defiant commitment to that decision. So, to take action here is to simply decide to create a specific change in your life and then follow that with an ironclad commitment to your decision. To further support this, you might want to grab your courage and share your decision and commitment verbally to a trusted person, say it out loud in the mirror, and write it down ten times every single day. These actions allow for the commitment to be all-inclusive.

2. **Envision Your Desired Change As Already Complete**

   Visioneering is a powerful change agent! Because the brain/body connection does not know the difference between what is real and what is vividly imagined, as you envision your goals and changes as reality, you are propelled toward them in beautiful ways. There is much research on envisioning from schools like MIT, Harvard, Stanford, and the like. Feel free to do some googling if you would like to geek out!

   In the meantime, do yourself a solid, and as you read this book and identify changes you would enjoy adopting into your life, give yourself two to five minutes each day to envision how you will feel, who you will be, how you will relate to others, and how others will relate to you once you have made your desired changes.

3. **Know Your Why**

   It is vital to any sustainable change to know WHY you are making it. This is a wonderful way to work with the limbic system. A crystal clear WHY tells the limbic system, "This is important to our survival; we better get on board!"

Additionally, crystal clarity encourages the emotional system to get on board as well because there is an emotional connection to the desired change.

And lastly, when you have a heart-centered reason to make a change, the spirit jumps on the bandwagon to support the change as well.

Conversely, not having a heart-centered WHY makes it difficult to make a change last. For example, losing weight for a wedding is the type of change made for vanity, which is completely fine but not super sustainable!

Simon Sinek has written multiple books about understanding your "why" if you are interested in learning more about this powerful change agent.

4. **Let Go Of Willpower**
When desired changes do not stick, the first thing blamed is willpower. People lament, "I failed again. I just don't have any willpower."

But the thing is, willpower fatigues easily. It is not designed to drag you up the hill day after day after day when sticking to your commitment becomes challenging.

Instead, I encourage you to let go of the idea that wielding willpower is the holy grail of making change sustainable. There are other skills that are far more useful.

5. **Create Habit Systems To Support Desired Change**
Instead of relying on willpower, you can engage habit systems! I LOVE habit systems; we teach our clients to apply habit systems ALL the time. Habit systems make new habit formations and sustainable changes super simple.

Habits can form intentionally (daily meditation) or unintentionally (too many daily cocktails or low nutrition, quick food. When working to create change, forming new and desired habits is nearly always essential, and habit systems catapult your efforts.

For example, if you have a goal of learning to be or sit still, meditate or adopt a breathing practice to change from being high-stress to calm. You can engage in your new habit for change for two to five minutes each morning to get centered and start your day from a place of calm and peace. But most people have trouble sticking to this or even *remembering* to engage the new habit to ensure the desired change. So, this is where you can create a habit system to facilitate.

For this application, I recommend habit-stacking as one habit system. This calls for stacking a new habit with an already ingrained habit, like drinking your morning coffee. You begin by placing a sticky note on your coffee mug that says something like, "2 minutes." This way, you will be reminded to sit in stillness and breathe in loving calmness for two minutes before you allow yourself to pour your first cup of coffee.

For more information on habit stacking, please reach out to our team and me with your questions at drhaywood@reimaginelove.com.

6. **No Change Happens Without Emotional Preparedness**
This is arguably the most important element of sustainable change. Without being emotionally prepared to make a specific change, you will likely fail. Let's go back to the diet example. When a person decides to go on a diet (for any number of reasons, such as weight loss, longevity, health, wedding, class reunion, etc.), the dieter expects to completely change their eating and fitness in one fell swoop!

People expect (with the use of willpower) that they can wake up one day and eat only veggies and lean meats (or whatever the diet entails), plus workout every day after only working out sporadically for years or not at all for the past three years.

Coincidentally, these completely unreasonable expectations are the reason why ninety percent of New Year's resolutions fail by January thirtieth!

The hidden issue here is emotional preparedness. One must be emotionally prepared to make desired changes, and the mental and emotional body can only reach so far at one time. Said another way, if you have never run a day in your life, you will not likely be running the Boston marathon next week.

And so it is for all changes.

I eat a big salad for breakfast six days a week and a big omelet or scramble the other day. Yet, I did not start out this way. I made this transition systematically over a period of six months or so. People have become so used to things happening fast (i.e., Amazon's two-day delivery) that people have come to expect that a two-day transformation is realistic.

Sorry gang, our neurology is not set up for this. And as I mentioned earlier, brains do not like change in the first place. This is where emotional preparedness comes into play. When you are considering making any kind of change, from business to the bedroom, you must begin with a tiny fraction of that change. Literally, ask yourself what you are one thousand percent emotionally prepared to shift or change. For example, I ate one salad every Monday for thirty days, and then a second salad every Tuesday for another thirty days, and so on until it was a new and cherished habit that encouraged me to feel so healthy and proud.

These micro changes need to be easy. Change need not be a huge and heavy lift. In fact, the heavier the lift, the less sustainable change is. Change can be easy. Make micro changes bit by bit until the full change is implemented. And remember, making one sustainable change broken into fifty bite-sized pieces that you are *emotionally prepared* for that takes you a full year to complete is far superior to trying to make twenty changes that you try and fail at repeatedly.

Again, if you have questions about emotional preparedness, do not hesitate to reach out to our team at drhaywood@reimaginelove.com.

7. **Progress Over Perfection!**

Perfectionism will be elaborated on in Chapter Three, but for now, as you are setting yourself up for successful, sustainable change, it is incredibly important to keep your mind and heart set on making small gains, literally teeny, tiny steps forward (steps that you are one thousand percent sure you are emotionally prepared to make and sustain). Making even one microscopic step forward and sustaining it is better than concentrating your efforts on making great big, perfect changes that last only a day, week, or month.

The more perfectly you attempt to make a given change, the quicker you will revert back. It's better to eat five fewer French fries each time you order for thirty days and then five fewer again the second thirty days than not to be emotionally prepared to ditch fries altogether and then binge on three orders of fries for another two months!

Slow and steady wins the race!

8. **Eliminate Temptation**

Any time you are making a change, there will inevitably be a temptation to "stay the same." Whether it is cutting out French fries, letting go of self-recrimination, or working to outgrow the need for anger, there will be ample temptation to eat fries, be mean to yourself, or lash out angrily toward your spouse, kids, or a workmate.

Thus, as you are implementing change, work to mitigate temptation whenever possible. Steer totally clear of places that serve French fries for sixty days. Or you could repeat an affirmation or mantra so there is less mental space to indulge in self-recrimination, and so on.

Temptation is ready to thwart your positive efforts at the first sign of weakness, so keep it at bay as much as you possibly can.

9. **Include Only People Who 100% Have Your Back!**
   This idea is a sneaky one. Often the people who we think are in our corner are not always emotionally safe or emotionally trustworthy. And a key reason we built our Reimagine Love Community Facebook group is to ensure that you have a completely safe place to land, to make changes, and to feel one hundred percent accepted, cared for, and held accountable!

   It is, unfortunately, common for people closest to us to be the biggest challengers or nay-sayers of our heart's deepest desires. Not because they do not believe in you but because they do not believe in themselves and project their fears and doubts onto you as if they are about you. I remember when I wanted to start my own business back in 1999, three of the closest people in my life told me all the ways it would fail. I did not realize at the time that their concerns were their own fears being projected onto me, so I took it very personally, and it almost stopped me dead in my tracks. Not only did I feel hurt by these nay-sayers that I loved, adored, and respected, but I almost threw away my dream because of it. I shudder to think about how this all nearly did not happen—all the lives that have been forever and powerfully changed because of my work and my Reimagine Love company's work would have been non-existent! So, take it from me, whether your decision is to start a business, eliminate a limiting belief that has been holding you back, or eliminate anxiety or depression, be sure that you share your decisions with people you one hundred percent know will ONLY cheer you on!

In the end, living for love is a transformation. Eliminate all that is non-essential and detracts from your life, and focus with discipline and devotion on that which is inspiring, joyful, and life-giving.

Paulo said it best, *"Because ever since your goal found out that you were traveling toward it, it has been running to meet you - The Copt"*

— Paulo Coelho, Manuscript Found in Accra

Your goals for change are within your grasp, you simply need to honor how change becomes sustainable, stable, and permanent.

How To Use This Book

Now that you're armed with tools to help you sustain the changes you seek to make, it's time to jump in and get started! Here's how you can use this book to extract maximum value:

1. **Take Loving Action.** This book is chock-a-block full of practical and emotionally, and spiritually liberating concepts, tools, and actions—USE THEM! The number one reason people's lives do not change is that people LEARN ABOUT ideas instead of implementing and practicing ideas. The second reason is that people expect joy and happiness to show up as quickly as your Amazon Prime order. Living in freedom is a lifestyle to be *practiced* with commitment, day after day, even when you do not feel like it!

   You can use the tools in this book strategically. Instead of trying to apply *all* of the tools immediately, determine first which ones best suit you and will facilitate the results you are currently looking for. You can always go back and try additional tools later, but steer clear of starting off overwhelmed (you are already overwhelmed enough!) or thinking you need to apply everything all at once! One powerful new practice is more impactful than ten great ideas that sit on a neglected shelf.

2. **Get A Buddy!** In any new endeavor, it can be highly valuable to enlist others in your vision. I encourage you to find a buddy. Your partner or spouse might be a great choice, or a friend is fantastic too! Read this book together or alongside one another and experience the transformation as a team. There IS strength in numbers. Thriving together, achieving together, growing together, and healing together is wildly impactful and can accelerate progress.

3. **Goals.** Throughout this book, you will be encouraged to "Take Loving Action." Keep a journal or notebook handy as you navigate this book since you will want to take notes and create goals for yourself along the way. Goals can follow the traditional SMART method: Specific, Measurable, Action-oriented, Reasonable, and with a Time schedule. Goals are amazing, but they must have strong legs underneath to be executed! There will be more functional and useful goal-setting later. For now, keep your notebook handy and jot down any goals you may have currently. This is your first opportunity to STOP reading for a moment and take down a few objectives you might have for yourself.

Only love can return people to themselves and to spirit, and only love can facilitate joyful, peaceful living. I hope reading this book inspires you to take powerful action and to live fully, to live radically on the edge of each gorgeous moment that life has to offer—and most certainly, to Live For Love!

"It is time to stop acting
(or living) small.
You ARE the universe
in ecstatic motion."

Rumi

One Final Note Before You Dig In...

I adore hearing from readers like you!

Please take the time to share your wins, your struggles, your pain, and your victories inside our Facebook group, by private message on social media, or in an email at *drhaywood@reimaginelove.com*.

I always take the time to respond.

With deep love and gratitude, you are appreciated beyond measure.

Shawn Haywood, Ph.D.

CHAPTER 1

Self-Honor: A Prerequisite To Living For Love

Self-honor is the first step through the gateway to freedom. When you consistently honor yourself, you simultaneously honor everyone and everything. Self-honor is not about selfishness—it's not about putting yourself above all. In fact, the more experienced you become in self-honor, the more you can actually give of yourself without feeling exhausted, overwhelmed, overcommitted, or resentful. Self-honor is a prerequisite to consistently live for love and become deeply happy from the inside out.

To understand what self-honor looks like, let me share Janice's story. Janice came to me with what felt like a five-hundred-pound bag of worry, anxiety, and frustration that she metaphorically toted around and that served as a lens through which she saw most aspects of her life. Janice was married to a man she was absolutely crazy about, and they had a nine-year-old daughter.

Janice had a lot on her plate: mom, wife, president of the PTA, and she owned a successful physical therapy business. On our first call together, Janice said, "I feel like my life consists of one to-do after another. I sleep maybe six hours a night and have essentially zero downtime. In some ways, I feel like a prisoner to my own life." This was immediately followed by sobbing and sentiments of guilt.

"Shawn, on paper, I have a perfect life and truly a beautiful family—yet, I feel utterly alone." There it was—the truth she had bottled up for far too many years.

Her frustration had bent into almost daily bickering with her husband. She could not understand why she was so angry about all the little things her husband did or did not do that annoyed the shit out of her. And when I asked her about intimacy and sex, she let out a huge laugh and said, "Shawn, if I did have the time for sex, I'd probably use it to take a nap!"

Janice's experience is common among our clients. Based on our first conversation, I knew she was in the right place and that learning to live for love was the ideal journey for her to find happiness and fulfillment and truly live a joyful and inspiring life with her beautiful family.

And what is even more amazing, she knew it too and was ready to do whatever it took to feel light, carefree, and connected with herself and her family.

The first step for Janice was understanding self-honor and how to apply it to her daily life.

The practice of self-honor is a staple as one learns to reclaim joy, play, and happiness.

It is also a defiant act of courage.

Self-honor is an ongoing commitment to healing and growing to an ever-expanding consciousness and spiritual awakening. The commitment to honoring yourself by cultivating practices that involve self-love, self-trust, and self-compassion is among the most nurturing gifts you can bestow upon not only yourself but also the whole of humanity.

It is utterly true that we give to others what we give to ourselves. Thus, if you are not nurturing yourself with care, compassion, and kindness in increasingly unconditional ways, it is nearly impossible to share that with others without creating feelings of upset, anger, and resentment in return.

The marks of your efforts in practicing self-honor include becoming the most vibrant, sensual, connected, playful, calm, and enjoyable person *you* care to spend time with!

With all my heart, I wish I had understood this principle much, much earlier in my life. It would have saved me mountains of heartache, pain, and suffering (which I now understand to be quite optional!). I do not feel regret, however; I view my past, and the experience gained as a gift I have the privilege of now sharing with others. And it is my dream for humans of all ages to understand self-honor and embrace these powerful practices as early in life as possible. And for the record, young children and teens are very susceptible and open to practicing self-honor skills when they are taught and modeled by family.

I spent far too many years aggressively and cruelly abusing myself mentally, emotionally, spiritually, and physically. For me, these behaviors began at an early age.

For example, as a sixteen-year-old gymnast, I landed a tumbling pass in an awkward way and hurt my foot. I went to the doctor, had an x-ray, and found that I had a hairline fracture for which they put me in a boot—which I threw away immediately so that my mother would not find out and make me take time off from practice. I proceeded to go to my physical therapist the next day, told her the situation, and asked her to show me how to "tape it" so I could continue practicing. She told me all the risks, of course, and I simply responded, "I am not going to take time off, so you can either show me how to tape it up for the least amount of pain and least chances of further injury, or I'll just figure it out myself."

As you might be starting to see, not taking recovery time and allowing my body to heal was the complete opposite of honoring myself, my body, and certainly my beautiful spirit. The truth is, I did not actually care about my body. Enduring pain was just part of my M.O. at the time, and frankly, I thought I deserved pain and suffering.

In fact, anyone who continues to endure repetitive pain, suffering, and dishonoring habits believe they are deserving of the pain and suffering.

Another example of self-abuse (the complete opposite of self-honor) was the way in which I talked to myself—name-calling was the most common form of self-abuse I practiced for many years. I would say things to myself like, "You're worthless," "You're a fat-ass hog," "You're an idiot/stupid/dumbass," and, "No one could or will ever love you." Unfortunately, this was just the tip of the iceberg that continued for decades.

By practicing these self-abusive behaviors, I betrayed my beautiful essence and spirit for far too long, and I hear similar tales of self-torture from clients regularly. Thankfully, I eventually reclaimed my precious "Self" and am dedicated to helping others do the same.

My first introduction to the power of self-honor happened during graduate school while working toward my Ph.D. I had two professors who were wonderful mentors to me and who had just attended the very first coaching conference in the world! They brought back three hundred hours of cassette tapes (this was quite a few years ago, haha!) and offered to let me listen to them. I was hungry to learn and took them up on the offer. After listening to the tapes three times each, I found myself officially in love with the new and budding field of coaching and easily transitioned from being a traditional therapist to a life coach.

Truth be told, becoming a coach saved my life in many ways.

I remember a statement on one of the tapes that stopped me dead in my tracks; I must have rewound and played it about fifty times.

"You can only love others as much as you love yourself."

WOW!

My brain and emotions were totally thrown for a loop—I had never heard such impactful words.

This lesson was so important to me because I really wanted to be able to love my husband better, to be more patient with him, to show him more compassion, and to be one thousand percent less angry toward him. And I sincerely wanted to be more loving, patient, and compassionate toward others as well.

And all of a sudden, my entire paradigm flipped on its ear. Here this tape was saying that I had to LOVE MYSELF first!

Translation: I had to learn how to love myself better, be patient with myself, have compassion for myself, and become one thousand percent less angry toward myself FIRST, and then I would be able to transfer that type of love, patience, compassion, and grace onto others.

Holy shit, I thought to myself, *this is going to be really hard!*

But simultaneously, I knew wholeheartedly that it was true and that it was the pathway to true freedom.

And so it began with me. Now, let's begin with you.

There are three main components of self-honor that we'll review quickly and then dig into individually in greater detail.

Components Of Self-Honor

- Self-love
- Self-trust
- Self-compassion

In short, the art and practice of self-honor means to love yourself, trust yourself and be unconditionally compassionate to yourself.

These wildly wonderful life practices are dedicated to YOU! And what is super bomb-diggity is that everyone you cherish will benefit tenfold from your investment into deep self-love.

Self-honor is a reflection of your higher Self, Divinity, God, Source, and divine connection that is your birthright. In this way, self-honor consists of the above three elements set in motion by intentionality, courage, and devotion to ceaseless inner happiness.

The most authentic, empowered, and impactful women and men I have met along my journey thus far are dedicated practitioners of love, trust, and compassion toward themselves and others; they embody living for love.

These three elements require great perseverance and devotion and are needed to have the energy and time to truly live in inner happiness.

Let's look at each interconnected puzzle piece one at a time.

SELF-LOVE: Learn to Love Yourself With Unconditional, Unbridled Abandonment

Self-love embodies the opportunity to see yourself as a complete and divine entity, which in truth, is what you are. Unconditional self-love holds the ability to recognize that you are not a mere physical body or brain or collection of accomplishments to judge, boast about, or condemn. You are not your weight. You are not your IQ. You are not your job. You are not the roles you play.

You are divine perfection.

Stepping into self-love requires great courage and serves as a foundation for shifting the whole of your life.

The whole of you is total and complete, perfect, <u>and</u> in progress!

To live for love means embodying self-love, which is to radiate love toward yourself and, as a result, toward every molecule on the planet and in the universe.

Love is the only thing that is real. Anything that is not love is an illusion.

The goal of self-love is to one day live inside a constant state of unconditional love that is continuously expressed inward and outward in every word, deed, thought, feeling, and action.

Unfortunately, instead of embracing all the goodness, beauty, and essence of self, mankind, and the planet as a whole, most people stand firmly rooted in "not-enoughness." Some spend a lifetime seeking the elusive and insatiable "more, bigger, better" as a replacement for self-love, which results in futile attempts to fill a void where self-love and acceptance belong.

Rather than *gifting* self-love and acceptance, we seek out and focus on flaws, wrinkles, squishy bellies, missteps, pet peeves, failures, wrong-doings, resentments, meanness, fear, failures, worries, and the like within ourselves and others. In addition to seeking out and focusing on perceived flaws, we look to others for the attention, approval, care, and kindness that we withhold from ourselves. In short, we hate, loathe, or detest our very humanness, which IS divine in nature and could never be anything else. We even foolishly expect perfection, unconscious of the fact that perfection already exists within, waiting to be noticed, recognized, and embraced.

Your divine essence has been fully intact all along. The illusion of disconnection or loneliness elicits trying and over-trying and serves as a foundation for the practiced weapon of viewing oneself as "never enough."

The inner betrayal of self-sets the foundation for a lifetime of anxiety, frustration, depression, fear, and a constant state of hypervigilance and makes it impossible to consistently experience the inner peace and tranquility that is your birthright. So, in place of stepping into the mental, emotional, and spiritual freedom you so deeply desire, inner betrayal keeps you stuck inside of a plaguing feeling of "never enough."

Here is a bit of gorgeous and inspiring news. You are doing the very best you can with your current toolset, consciousness, awareness, beliefs, positionalities, perceptions, and mindset.

And wherever you are, it is the PERFECT jumping-off point to begin loving yourself with wild abandon.

From Christ, Buddha, and Mother Teresa to Hitler, Saddam Hussein, and Ted Bundy, all are motivated by the current state and are all doing what is considered "right" or "best" for each—even if we cannot possibly fathom the internal motivations of the latter group of people in this list.

All are the reflection and embodiment of love.

Certainly, Christ, Buddha, and Mother Teresa's lives were divinely led and truly lived for love, while people like Hitler were led by delusion, violence, and the propagation of lies and harm. Every human has done, and will continue doing, the best they can with the tools and awareness they have in any given situation and moment; ALL are born from love, no matter how much one might prefer not to believe this truth.

Women are plagued by striving to be or feel like "enough" in the realm of physicality and motherhood (secondarily in work, business, or career, which tends to be the number one place where men measure their worthiness). This is, of course, a losing battle since "not being enough" is impossible. And there is no possible way to prove or earn worth. You are born complete, and you will die the same way. No one is better or worse, less or more, enough or not enough. Thus, trying to be or prove that you are enough is like spitting into the wind—it is messy and senseless.

Most women never feel good enough, valuable enough, lovable enough, skinny enough, pretty enough, boobs enough, tall enough, smart enough, bootylicious enough, mom or step-mom enough, happy enough, or successful enough on a sustainable basis (meaning every day during one's lifetime).

It is impossible for "skinny enough" to equate to worthiness. There is no way that being "mom enough" can make you a valuable human. And how could this ever be measured, anyway? YOU JUST ARE. You are enough. You are *love* and loved. You are worthy. This seems to be the best-kept secret! Repeat it to yourself one million times or until you believe it.

All thoughts attached to not-enough-ness are rooted in fear and block you from profound or impactful forward progress and freedom.

Questioning "enough-ness" is a fool's errand.

Yet, questioning one's value, worth, and enough-ness has become an all too common narrative—and a diabolical betrayal of self.

In place of beautiful self-love, people instead try many escapes to deal with *perceived* voids in their worthiness; people indulge in vices that further encourage the cycle of self-deprecation, including the following:

- Dieting and binging
- Overconsumption of alcohol
- Overworking to prove worthiness at the expense of self and family
- Perfectionism and the many challenges that accompany it
- Anger
- Control and manipulation tactics
- Drugs

- Overtrying
- Dating men who are not good for them or take far more than they give
- People-pleasing or approval seeking
- Overpromising
- Constant apologizing (especially when there is no fault)
- Self-neglect or abuse
- Enabling
- And everyone's favorite gateway escape ... chronic thinking!

These ways of escaping, or numbing out, are all cheap replacements for genuine, unconditional self-love.

You are light and love. The more you adopt, live into, and operate from this truth, the more effortlessly life evolves.

You are an illumination of all that is divine, pure, and innocent (and so is everyone else, even those you may judge, criticize, or condemn).

You are entirely deserving of love at all times and in every single situation, no matter what.

To believe anything else is a departure from your Higher Self (God, Source, Universe) and a turn toward falsehood and self-betrayal.

I have practiced conscious unconditional self-love for many years now and continue to make gains year after year. Even the times when I used to judge myself most cruelly are now shrouded in softness and love. This took me an incredibly long time to be willing to practice, as I did not find myself—or my actions—deserving of forgiveness, nor myself worthy of love, for far too long.

But oh my stars, had I been able to get even a glimpse inside a life of unconditional self-love earlier, I would have quit my job and dedicated every waking moment to this practice until mastery was achieved.

Yet, there are occasional moments where I catch myself giving a bit of judgment to my waistline or thinking that I did not surrender something "well enough," as if God is somehow making a note of how well or poorly I surrender on a given day or gives two hoots about my waistline—it's actually quite comical when you think about it.

Fortunately, catching myself not loving myself quickly shifts into a blissful state of unbridled love.

In the past, I was incredibly self-abusive in the realm of food, body shape, and fitness. Most days, as soon as I was out of bed, I'd be using the bathroom scale as a marker of whether or not I would eat that day or how much I would be "allowed" to eat. And the old inner perfectionist can still rear her ugly head in moments of exhaustion or overwhelm. And I, too, have to remind myself that the "whole of Shawn" is a gift far beyond measure and far beyond this body's shape, size, or weight.

This shift in thinking is a practice that you, too, can adopt in any facet where you are apt to self-abuse. It takes time and perseverance, but it is WELL worth the effort. Life can be wild appreciation, joy, peace, inspiration, aliveness, and calm all rolled into one juicy experience.

How to Practice Self-Love

The shift that can occur for self-love to enter your life is a vantage point, so to speak. It requires you to move from *looking* to *seeing*.

Looking (with the eyes or mind/thoughts/mentation) occurs on a purely surface level and is pure perception—looking creates polarized opinions, like good or bad, that are rarely rooted in lovingness or truth.

Looking happens with only the eyes or mind, and says...

- "Your sides are pudgier than they used to be. You're such a lazy piece of crap."
- "You only got half of your list accomplished today. You totally suck at life. What are you? Unfocused, slow, or a complete idiot?"
- "You were late to your kid's soccer tournament. What a bad dad/mom you are. You should feel ashamed and guilty."

Seeing (intuiting from the heart, experiencing the Divine essence of self and Allness, seeing through the lens of Divine Love), on the other hand, is the ability to experience yourself, others, and the whole of the planet as perfect and in progress and far beyond what could ever be viewed with just the human eye or mind/ego on the surface-level. Seeing sounds like this:

- "It was just a misstep, an error in judgment. You'll do better next time."
- "Everything and everyone IS perfect, regardless of flaws, faults, or failures. I think I'll give him/her/myself a break."
- "Everything will be fine; this is just part of life and the human experience."

Seeing recognizes that all things are one, that EVERYTHING stems from the same source, and that everything and everyone is doing his or her best in any given moment. Seeing sprouts from divinity and divine connection.

The practice for you to dig into is moving beyond looking to seeing within and outside. You can even stand in front of a mirror with your eyes closed so that you can practice seeing into yourself, into your heart, and into your divinity.

Your body does not define you. Productivity does not define you. Your faulty conditioned/programmed thoughts most certainly do not define you, nor are they even real. Nothing external could ever define you.

Looking is the world of perception and opinion. *Seeing* is the world of spirit, progress, transformation, and, of course, love for yourself and others. Seeing past the surface and INTO yourself, others, Mother Earth, and everything in between is a living for love skill.

And this skill takes time, focus, and practice.

In time, you will begin seeing the essence of life instead of focusing on the purely physical form. Essence is what is inside. Form is the physical vessel. For example, your body is that of form, and your spirit and heart are the essence.

Here are a couple of examples of seeing in action. You might look at a chair and take it for face value. It has a padded, rounded red seat, four legs that taper at the bottom, and a long wooden rectangular back piece with long vertical cutouts. Or, you might see into the chair and thank Mother Earth for sharing her trees, for the hands that were made of love and labor to create a beautiful piece of furniture for you to use, enjoy, and make beautiful memories around an equally "love-made" dining table.

You might also look in the mirror and take what you see for face value. Judging wrinkles, bulges, the size of your waistline, and hair that is too curly or too straight. You may look at, even stare and curse at, perceived blemishes. Or, you can choose to see past the surface into God/Divinity expressing as you. You might see love and essence and pure perfection as being expressed by the "*hand that wrote all,*" as Paulo Coelho says in *The Alchemist.*

You see, living for love and being filled with joy and happiness is a matter of perspective, of choosing to simply look or deeply *see.*

As you begin practicing self-love by shifting into seeing, challenges like insatiability, perfectionism, confusion, and self-abuse will start to fade. You will be open to higher energy, inspiration, and enthusiasm. You will begin to chip away at habits of judgment, gossip, comparisons, perfectionism, or other harsh, demeaning patterns of betraying yourself and others.

Self-love is expansive and inclusive and allows you to feel joy and gratitude even when challenges are afoot, even when things are not going as you wish, or even when others are not behaving with love, care, or integrity.

Unconditional self-love is just that—UNCONDITIONAL. It demands dedication and practice to gain mastery. This means that you not only share love when family, friends, work, and making decisions are easy and without friction, but even more importantly, you share love when you (or others) fall down, mess up, say nasty things, feel guilty or ashamed, make mistakes, or fail in glorious fashion—as WE ALL DO! This is what makes love unconditional.

SELF-TRUST: Learn to Trust Yourself So Mistrust of Anyone Fades Away

Most people I meet or coach are overly concerned with their ability to trust others or whether or not others are trustworthy. But the interesting thing is, you need not worry about trusting others or "their trustworthiness" when you learn to trust yourself fully.

Self-trust is key to your expanding happiness. You can never trust others more than you learn to trust yourself or more than you are trustworthy to yourself. As self-trust grows, so does your intuition and your ability to "see" essence and to "see" things coming that you would not want to be a part of your life.

Paradoxically, others will be no more trustworthy to you or of you than you are to yourself and, therefore themselves. Trust is like a revolving door. When you feel that someone in your life is being "untrustworthy," it is of great importance to ask yourself where you have been untrustworthy to yourself or another. Trust and lack thereof are projections.

For example, I had a boyfriend once whom I found had engaged in multiple encounters of infidelity. And while I was obviously quite upset, I had to ask myself, how had I gotten into this situation? What role had I played? And where had my self-trust faltered? Of course, his actions were completely inappropriate and were his own. Even so, I had played a role. In truth, I had no business dating that person to start with. The lack of self-trust was eroded by the fact that I had gotten a divorce nine months prior and ignored all the warning signs with this dude because I had not yet forgiven myself completely for the divorce. You see, for that, or any negative situation, to happen in my (or anyone's) life, there were, and are, at least a dozen (or ten dozen) warning signs I chose to overlook, make excuses for, and outright ignore. We do this under the guise of "but I love him." But love is never harmful or icky—never—never—never. When we choose to overlook situations, make excuses for bad behavior, and outright ignore the events that are so close they're slapping us in the face, we are practicing self-betrayal and self-trust, which diminishes and demonstrates a lack of self-love. When this happens, it invites negativity, drama, and chaos of all kinds into your life. We make the mistake of saying, "He (she, boss, friend, etc.) is untrustworthy," when in truth, we behaved untrustworthy to ourselves—we engaged in SELF-betrayal instead of taking a stand for ourselves by setting boundaries, speaking up, or even leaving when it was appropriate.

Self-trust is a practice of self-integrity, thus deep self-honor. We can take an opportunity to look back and see where we have strayed from self-trust, not for the purpose of self-abuse or self-deprecation, but to look for patterns of lacking self-trust and self-honor. Open your eyes to where you have made compromises or just plain sold yourself out! When you are willing to be courageous and tell yourself the truth, you can make empowered choices and advocate for yourself, thus learning to engage in increasingly expansive self-trusting behaviors like setting boundaries and speaking up to advocate for yourself. This is a beautiful pathway to living free.

You must claim responsibility for what goes on in your life. Most of the time, even in the most challenging circumstances, you have played a part in the situation, and you must claim ownership so you can make empowered changes. Otherwise, you may end up bullying others with anger, frustration, guilt, or shame in a feeble attempt to forcefully take back power or shut down completely. This is never a winning combination.

As in all things, trustworthiness in and of others is but a mirror, a projection of your own bag of tricks–or poo, as the case may be at times!

Your ability to trust others lies solely on your level of trust in and of YOURSELF and your willingness to SEE and acknowledge, take ownership, live with integrity, and make choices that are truly great for you, even when it seems very difficult.

In the previous example, my excuse for choosing to overlook situations, make excuses for his crappy behaviors, and outright ignore a mountain of problems was, "but I love him." But it was not love; it was addiction. Love is never at the expense of another. Love is love, and it has no opposite.

How to Practice Self-Trust

To start examining how you trust yourself, here are some questions to ask:

- How am I doing with keeping consistent commitments? Commitments to myself regarding body movement–

assuming you are emotionally prepared to keep these commitments (wink, wink)? Do these commitments feel deeply loving and honoring, or like play? And how about commitments to myself regarding timelines, food intake, friends, work, or a marriage/relationship?

- Do I trust in my ability to handle ANYTHING that comes my way, no matter how difficult it may seem (losing a job, business or relationship failing, or even the death of a loved one)?
- Do I keep commitments to others, and when it is necessary to break commitments, do I do so with integrity and honesty?
- Do I practice asking clearly for what I want and need and give others loving emotional freedom to say "yes" or "no" to my requests in order to build trust (and emotional safety) in myself and others?
- Do I trust in myself to take courageous action and to stand lovingly for what I believe in?
- Do I trust in myself to take bold ownership of my role in every situation that unfolds, even when I would rather play the victim and blame others for my experience of life?

As you gain trust in yourself, keep an increasing number of commitments to yourself, ask for what you need and want, practice courage, and believe in your ability to handle all that comes your way, others will trust you and act accordingly in return. You will soon find it easier to trust while simultaneously becoming less attached when others behave in untrustworthy ways or do not keep their word.

After all, others' words, deeds, or actions are none of your concern—you cannot change others; you can only change yourself—and what a tremendous gift.

Dedicate yourself to building *your* inner resources, and let the rest go.

SELF-COMPASSION: A Personal Embrace

Holy cow, I was so darn resistant to infusing self-compassion into my life for so many years, even though I had a deep *knowing* that it was a wellspring of healing, spiritual evolution, and love.

Why did I resist? I think it was because I was just so darn good and practiced mentally and emotionally beating the crap out of myself and withholding compassion! And, maybe I had serious doubts about deserving compassion.

I also did not know how the heck to "do it" or really even what self-compassion meant.

I remember one time, many years ago when I felt so frustrated with my dog because she was running toward the road and not heeding her commands. When she finally stopped, I went to her and paddled her on the behind—it wasn't even hard, but I no longer believed in hitting anything or anyone EVER—under any circumstances. We train our pets with one hundred percent positive reinforcement, and it works great...sometimes dogs act like animals, and so do their owners.

I was so horrified by the behavior that I held it over my own head for months. I would write it in my journal each day as a way to remember and shame myself relentlessly, day after day, week after week, month after month.

It was horrible. The guilt was unbearable. I am literally tearing up as I write, just thinking about it all these years later. I would tell myself, "Some kind of spiritual devotee you are! You hit a tiny, helpless dog—you must feel so proud and strong to overpower a small dog." On and on it went. This was the only way I knew how to be. And I actually thought this self-torture would make me a better person—oh, the follies of the human mind and ego.

This stopped when I read in one of Dr. David R. Hawkins's books, my dearest and most beloved spiritual teacher where he said, "You cannot grow spiritually without self-compassion." And there it was, directly on the heels of this thing I had done to the dog that I had labeled as *horrific*, which I actually internalized as having made me a horrific human. I believed I needed to punish myself forever to make amends. The truth was, if I wanted to move forward, grow from this experience, and be free from guilt and shame, to continue the spiritual journey I had committed to, I would have to lay down this weapon. I would have to stop punishing and shaming myself. And I would have to give myself the gift of self-compassion.

So I did.

The moment I read this, I began sobbing uncontrollably and crying for all the years of unbelievable self-cruelty and punishment and withholding of love and compassion.

And then, all of a sudden, new freedom emerged from the ashes.

It took some time to truly forgive myself. To admit that I had acted out of fear and adrenaline, and frustration and that I, too, was doing my best at that moment. But I did it. And I have been practicing self-forgiveness and compassion ever since, even when I did not feel deserving. Remember, at every moment in life, we are all doing our best with the tools, awareness, and spiritual consciousness we have at any given moment.

I realized that punishing myself for this mistake, and any other perceived mistake, was a form of cruel perfectionism and denial of my innate humanness and was propagated by the ego. I have not completely transcended being hard on myself yet, but it shrinks bit by bit every year, and now the self-punishment usually lasts for just a moment or two before I shift into compassion and then love.

This is your opportunity to begin sharing self-compassion with yourself; forgiveness and grace might be your path.

When my coaching team or I are working with clients, we teach them to repeat one hundred times a day and place one hundred sticky notes around the house, car, and office with the words, "Give yourself only forgiveness, grace, and compassion. You did your best, and you're doing your best, even if the mind/ego is telling you otherwise."

It is a gorgeous practice, I invite you to try it. (Oh, and send me an email to let me know how it works at drhaywood@reimaginelove.com.)

Withholding, punishing, and self-abuse are well-worn paths for so many. Like me, you might feel like these habits are a necessary part of you, that you do not know how to break up with them or even who you are without them. It honestly felt scary to think about what it would be like to treat myself any other way. And unfortunately, fear of that kind of unknown can easily trick you into staying stuck in anything, from self-abuse to a crappy relationship, just like a mirage in the desert tricks you into thinking there is a watering hole ahead and encourages you to behave desperately to get to it. This is a wonderful time to connect with your "why" you want to change these habits.

Thankfully, I found something greater to live for. I wanted to be happy, to feel loved, and to finally feel at peace–I wanted to live for love–this became my incredibly powerful "why."

Self-compassion is a real challenge for many of my clients and other strong, independent, perfectionistic ladies. Women wrongly believe that if they are soft or compassionate with themselves or others, they will be taken advantage of or become lazy and unmotivated.

What the hell?!

How did this belief come to be?

Women resist incorporating self-compassion for the same reasons they resist parting with perfectionism: the fear of losing their edge, getting too soft, becoming lazy procrastinators, gaining weight, being a bad mom or business owner, or not being "successful," whatever that means!

The exact opposite is true.

For myself and most of my clients, we have achieved tenfold in *every* possible category of life since we began sharing self-love, trust, and compassion with ourselves.

The amazing thing is that self-compassion catalyzes the MOST beautiful transformations in all facets of life: from eating habits and body movement to friendships and family, from career and business building to connection and sex, and everything in between. As you grow these skills, you can SEE beyond the muck, lethargy, busy work, and time and energy wasters to that which is truly meaningful and inspired.

How to Practice Self-Compassion

Self-compassion is the practice of embracing your humanness AS divinity. It means demonstrating *unconditional* kindness to yourself at ALL times, even when you feel you have royally messed up and do not deserve care or compassion!

Practicing self-compassion sometimes means trading criticism for playfulness and having a gentle laugh and acknowledgment of the human condition and your innate fallibility! And to embrace that you are still absolutely perfect!

Self-compassion is to be given freely and fully, especially during the times when you really, really do not want to, for these are the times when you direly NEED it most.

Depriving yourself or others of compassion, kindness, and care is unnecessary and a departure from love. Would you deprive a child who is in pain or in need of medical attention? Of course not. We would see a wounded child and run to his or her aid out of compassion.

Just because we have grown to become an older human version does not make it okay to withhold love, compassion, kindness, and care when we are emotionally wounded, in emotional need, suffering, frustrated, anxious, depressed, angry, ashamed, or in any other sort of pain.

Sayings like, "Well, he had it coming," "What goes around comes around," "Karma's a real bitch," "Ha, you deserve what you get," "You should be punished," or "He's such an A-hole anyway," are, as stated before, projections of what you feel YOU deserve. Sentiments like these are always a reflection of self-perception and never about another person.

The tone of each of these statements is that of seeming to want others to suffer (meaning you believe you should suffer). That is a serious divergence from love and compassion, eh?

Always remember that you are completely deserving and worthy of compassion at ALL times.

Practice listening to your words as they reveal who you believe you are and what you believe you deserve; your words have nothing to do with others. Your words are always one hundred percent a projection of *your* inner world. Everything expressed outwardly is first expressed inwardly.

Thus, all efforts you make to love, trust, forgive, accept, and support within yourself will simultaneously extend to the outside world as well.

What a profound and beautiful gift!

Sharing unconditional self-compassion with yourself can *seem* difficult. But it is merely a matter of practicing a new skill, of replacing thoughts, beliefs, and mental programs that block you from soaring! You can retrain, refocus, and replace that which does not support you or that which is a departure from self-love, trust, and compassion.

Here's an example of replacing an old pattern of thought that I wanted to "eject" because it no longer served me and certainly was a departure from self-love and compassion.

I often give talks to audiences of women. Like everything in life, sometimes they don't always go as planned. A past version of me might have been self-punishing in response, saying a statement such as, "Geez Shawn, you are such an idiot. You looked like a complete fool. They probably think you are a complete bonehead."

Instead, as I began to practice self-compassion regularly, when I would "mess up" during a talk, I began saying and thinking statements such as, "I did my best. It may not have been my most flawless talk ever, but it was heartfelt and came from a place of love and care. Perhaps next time I can make the following changes to improve...."

Do you see the difference between self-punishment and self-compassion? It is not a subtle difference, is it?

The latter statement enables me to move forward and make corrections to my next talk easily and creatively. The former keeps me stuck in the past, lamenting and abusing me, and impedes improvement and progress.

Honestly, I could still be beating myself up today about many things that happened twenty years ago had I not chosen a compassionate and joyful path—like that time I made a series of mistakes and was swindled out of $50,000 in a past relationship. The old Shawn would have berated herself and this past boyfriend for the rest of my days—criticizing, belittling, judging, condemning, complaining, and so on.

But, at the time this happened, I was far enough along on the self-compassion journey to be at least a blend of gentle and loving with only blips of self-condemnation. I was—primarily at first and then fully within a few months—able to own my part (remember, we always play a role in negative experiences). I was able to forgive myself for being incredibly naïve and turning a blind eye when I should have acted on my suspicions instead of telling myself that "I am crazy," "Don't rock the boat," or "You're just looking for trouble." I was able to let go of and forgive both of us and could then move on without carrying the emotional baggage of this relationship into the next.

I have yet to meet a results-driven, perfection-seeking, super go-getter lady who did not need to learn how to *make mistakes and fail with grace, gentleness, love, trust, and compassion.*

The first step to learning how to do this is choosing to connect with the truth that ideas like "failure" are simply perceptions seen through your lens; they are a result of *looking instead of seeing.*

Making mistakes is an unavoidable part of life and an invaluable way to learn. Falling down is guaranteed. However, suffering and punishment in response are <u>optional</u>. Self-compassion is the loving path and provides the emotional space to accomplish meaningful endeavors. Compassion puts an end to holding grudges, keeping score, and looking to be justified when you fail. It allows you to spend less time beating yourself up and more time reveling in the lessons learned so you can move forward quickly with confidence, inner knowing, and empowerment!

Take Loving Action!

Let us take a look at how to begin practicing self-honor. The overall impact of practicing self-honor in life, marriage, career, and spiritual evolution is beyond description, and I hope you are feeling inspired to elevate your self-honor practices. The following action steps will support you in taking all three self-honor skills and tying them up with a pretty bow as you add them to your life.

1) Take a few moments to jot down the single most impacting idea you have learned about self-honor from this chapter and why it is valuable to you and your life moving forward.

2) Next, get crystal clear about one specific change you would like to make to elevate your self-honor practices. Which would you like to practice first? Self-love, self-trust, or self-compassion? And why?

3) What is one specific action you are willing to take so you can begin standing firmly in self-love, self-trust, and self-compassion (written reminders on post-it notes, forgiveness, seeing)?

Key Takeaways

- Self-honor is a gateway to freedom. It is not selfish; rather, it's your first step in consistently living for love and becoming deeply happy from the inside out.
- If you are not nurturing yourself with care, compassion, and kindness, it is nearly impossible to share that with others without feeling anger and resentment.
- The art and practice of self-honor means you must love yourself, trust yourself, and be unconditionally compassionate to yourself.
- All thoughts attached to not-enoughness are rooted in fear and block you from profound and impactful forward progress and ultimate freedom.
- Self-trust is key to your expanding happiness. You can never trust others more than you trust yourself.
- Self-compassion sometimes means trading criticism for playfulness and acknowledging your innate humanness, and embracing that you are still absolutely perfect.
- Embrace mistakes just as you would celebrate successes. Find the lessons and own your part.

CHAPTER 2

Value-Driven Living & Loving

"I'm digging for treasure!"

This quote is from *The Alchemist* by Paulo Coelho, one of my all-time favorite books. It's a beautiful love story that embodies all versions of love—spiritual, self, friends, family, romantic, and contribution. In this book, a person's values are symbolized as "treasures" to be discovered and carried with them on the journey of life.

Coelho was onto something big because values are truly treasures that have the ability to serve you well. In fact, in order for life to flow smoothly from day to day and year to year, one must create and commit to values that are intentionally selected to guide your decisions. Values should operate as active guideposts to serve all facets of your life.

Values are meant to inspire and keep individuals, relationships, families, and businesses on a specific—and loving—trajectory. When you are clear about your values, you lead an increasingly fulfilling life. Living with clear, heart-centered values is what it means to dig for or seek your treasure.

Without intentionally selecting values that serve you, your life will be infused with what I call "accidental values" that function in your life whether you are aware or not. Accidental values, when gone unchecked, wreak havoc on your life. This can be turned around by mindfully choosing values by which to live, love, work, play, and interact with others. This is an invitation to begin questioning every single thought and belief that crosses through your mind to ensure it is something you want to align with and that it is aligned with the values you genuinely want to guide your life.

This chapter is lovingly dedicated to taking a stand for that which your heart is most closely and naturally aligned with. The heart is your most powerful guide. Though more often than not, people have learned to steer away from the perfection of the heart's inner guidance and instead lean toward valuing thoughts, thinking, and logic streaming from the mind.

Over time, people forget to listen to the divine voice inside; they ignore it because its urging seems inconvenient or does not match with a craving, want, or desire. Or people quell its calls when the heart is perceived as having been broken or hurt too many times. In short, instead of learning to lean into the heart, we are taught not to trust it. Identifying your values and aligning with them will support you in returning home to your beautiful heart.

So you might be wondering... how can you rearrange life so it can flow smoothly? How can you learn to deeply honor yourself, your family, your career, your business, and your partner *simultaneously*?

The answer is simple: it starts with knowing and living by a *single* value. And while you might end up selecting two or three values (which you will learn how to do shortly), you will want to have one value that is at the top of the food chain for you—a single value to lean most heavily on for making any and all decisions.

How Does Value-Driven Life Navigation Work?

What people value most shows up in everyday life, whether deliberate or accidental. Values are illuminated in how you go about life in each and every moment of each hour, day, experience, and interaction, and in the words and deeds, you practice.

For example, you might intentionally practice setting strong, self-loving boundaries and, therefore, value self- and other-honor.

Or, you may regularly practice anger, silent treatments, resentment, yelling, frustration, or bitterness, and therefore *accidentally* value various practices of aggression (like I used to).

You might practice fearless loving candor, kind truth-telling, and open-hearted living, and therefore intentionally value practices of vulnerability.

Or perhaps you practice hiding your true self behind pleasing, performing, and perfectionism, and therefore accidentally value selling yourself out or other forms of self-betrayal.

Regardless of what you *say* you value, what you practice ultimately functions as what you *actually* value most in your life.

Maybe you have neither stopped to think about what your highest value is nor defined it clearly so that you can, indeed, design your life in accordance.

This is where there are two basic directions you can take: an intentional path or a haphazard path.\

For example, I used to accidentally value *essentially all forms of aggression*. This was not because I deliberately chose it, but simply because I learned to practice it frequently and well. For me, aggression looked like yelling, slamming doors, silent treatments, flipping drivers the bird (*blush!*), and shaming or guilt-tripping others, especially my husband. This aggression functioned as an accidental value because it drove and colored multiple facets of my life.

This accidental value showed up everywhere; in fact, it sadly ruled my home and relationships in many ways for decades. When I began to understand heart-centered value living, I began practicing a great deal of self-forgiveness to move beyond practicing this "accidental but prevalent" value of aggression.

Anger was an easy value for me to adopt because it was an ingrained part of my growing-up story.

That is the thing about values—we can easily adopt them from a place of innocence and naiveté as children, teens, and adults. Then we get to adulthood and do not realize or question the various ways we show up in life or feel powerless to change it, lamenting, "that's just the way I am." As innocent children, adults whom we loved and admired (parents or extensions of parental role models, like babysitters, siblings, teachers, coaches, etc.) modeled intentional and accidental values for us. We trusted and loved them and, as a result, innocently took on their values (positive and negative) and related habits and practices without question, which we then continue to practice into adulthood, as well as accidentally teach them to others.

Unintentional Programming In Action

Here is an illustration of unintentional value programming in action.

I struggled with reading as a child, especially reading comprehension, and staying focused on the task at hand. When I was in the first grade—mind you, this was the second of two times I would be in first grade—the teacher stood at the front of the class while I was in the back, trying to be invisible. Suddenly, the teacher called my name and asked a question. I had no idea what the heck she had asked or what she was even teaching. I was likely busy biting my nails, doodling in a notebook, or simply bored to tears—a frequent issue for me throughout my education.

I looked up at the chalkboard and mustered up the best guess I could without having a single clue as to what the heck was being discussed.

All at once, the entire class broke out into laughter; even the teacher pointed and laughed at me. I was crushed. It was all I could do to fight back a rush of tears.

The teacher even asked me if I was stupid.

I know, right?!

I felt utterly humiliated. I wanted to run away and never come back.

Worst of all—saddest of all—this became a critical defining moment in my very young life. This was the moment when I determined that I *was indeed stupid.*

This limiting belief colored my entire academic career until my last year of undergraduate school.

Until then, I did not even bother trying...ever.

I was resolved to the *fact* that I was stupid, and as a result, I didn't bother studying and instead became comfortable being an "average C" student, which in hindsight wasn't awful considering I almost never took a book home. I believed that all I could hope for was to be a good athlete, so I poured every ounce of my heart and effort into gymnastics.

Isn't it fascinating that one defining moment for this precious seven-year-old girl translated into more than two decades of practicing the unintentional values of learned helplessness and hopelessness regarding learning and intelligence? It took me seven years to complete an undergraduate degree.

Fortunately, this belief and associated practices did not stay with me forever.

I was twenty-six or so when I finally began to realize that just maybe I was NOT stupid.

That year, I was reading a book about different types of intelligence. I learned that all the ways I thought I "should" be intelligent perhaps did not apply to me. And the traditional ways of learning did not work great for me either.

Most importantly, I remember thinking, "Huh, maybe I'm just not the traditional type of smart!" And that, in fact, I was quite brilliant in beautifully unique ways. At that moment, a seed of belief in my divine uniqueness and intelligence was perfectly planted.

From that moment forward, everything changed.

A long-standing limiting belief had cracked open a portal to untold and unimaginable freedom. I decided to go to graduate school, start a business, dig deeper into great spiritual texts and ideas of the world, create programs, and give talks around the country. Even this book is a product of that moment and so much more.

This was the beginning of an increasingly intentional journey of letting go of crippling limiting beliefs and haphazard values that kept me in states of fear, anxiety, anger, victimhood, and self-pity.

Thus, the value of "lifetime learning" was born.

Today, I have read hundreds upon hundreds of books when previously I had not read an entire book in my life. My love and adoration for learning turned into a heart-centered value that would last many more decades than the ones born of powerlessness and fear. What had once been one of my greatest wounds had transformed into a new treasure—a grand inner victory.

Dedication to learning has functioned as a core value now in my life for more than two decades.

The payoffs for the new, transformed value are fourfold:

1) The more I learn, the more deliciously curious and inspired I become.
2) The more I learn, the more I grow toward spiritual evolution, positive emotions, a quiet mind, and intentional and meaningful goals and aspirations.
3) The more I learn, the more loving, vulnerable, and skilled I become as a coach, partner, and human.
4) And lastly, I just frickin' LOVE learning because it elicits unbridled joy!

Because I have intentionally defined learning as a value, I have created the daily practice of spending at least one hour reading or listening to an audiobook and journaling alongside, a practice that my husband has also adopted and that we share together each morning. And because this value supports vision and purpose in my life, the practice instills contentment, empowerment, happiness, and flourishing fulfillment.

This practice also promotes greater peace, surrender, and slow-paced living—which are intentional living for love ideals for myself and my family.

The daily habits and practices that accompany this and other core values keep me sound as a pound AND jacked up on life!

The Purpose Of Intentional Values

Do you see from "Little Girl Shawn" how easy it can be for values (positive or negative) to become unconsciously programmed and for habits like pleasing, lying, drinking, and perfectionism to crop up as accidental? And then to become dominant accidental values that we carry into adulthood? The scary thing with accidental values is that they are often practiced to eventual *accidental mastery* along the way.

The beautiful news, however, is that any accidental value can be replaced with one that serves and honors your very best life. For example, Little Shawn's accidental value of learned helplessness was eventually replaced with a heart-centered value of lifelong learning.

Whether practiced as accidental or intentional, values are in the driver's seat, directing your daily efforts, mood, career, family, and so on, whether you want them to or not!

Values take a bit of time to identify, which is perfectly okay. You will continue to gain clarity as you read.

Here is an example. If you say that family is most important, yet in practice, you work late most evenings and are away from your family most weekends because you practice workaholism and find your worth in your job, then work is functioning as a higher value than family in the way it presents practically in your life. Mind you, there is no judgment or shame here. Some parents have to work nights and weekends to feed their families. So, depending upon the context, working nights and weekends could be a positive or a negative value.

Practicing *accidental* values is reflective of self-doubt, fears, and insecurities. Accidental values often result from past hurt and serve as ways in which people attempt to cope with their past wounds by pleasing, avoiding disappointing others, or proving their value and worth, instead of embracing what is already perfectly intact within themselves.

The key is to become aware of accidental values and commit to shifting to intentional, heart-centered values. As beautiful, heart-centered values are defined and practiced, haphazard or accidental values begin to diminish—it is a natural process of elimination. Mind you, shifting your values requires work and commitment. It took me nearly twenty years to eliminate essentially all anger and anger-related habits.

Values are intended to be strong, sturdy, well-designed legs upon which your life stands day to day and year to year. Currently, the values that are functioning in your life (what I refer to as "functioning values") may be partly intentional and useful and partly haphazard or accidental. Everyone has heart-centered values that they live by and values that drive them forward and aid in decision-making. It is the accidental values rooted in lack and fear that we must strive to rearrange.

Most are not consciously aware, much less want to admit out loud, that they value ideas and practices associated with things like greed, overworking, alcoholism, neglecting family, overeating, seething resentment, overspending, anxiety, loneliness, meanness, gossiping, sarcasm, passive aggression, control or manipulation tactics, seeking approval, or other unflattering habits.

Yet, like it or not, accidental values appear as haphazard habits and ways of navigating life.

PLEASE, if you align with any items on the above list, do not use this as an opportunity to beat yourself up—remember to practice compassionate self-honor. You learned and adopted behaviors and thought patterns that were modeled for you.

Oy vey! My life used to be completely dominated by haphazard values. So if you are gritting your teeth a little, know that I see you, and I will walk you through how to select a value or two to guide your life later in this chapter.

Heart-Centered Values

Heart-centered intentional values are an essential difference between your *old life* and your *current life*. Before the age of twenty-seven(ish), there were essentially zero intentional values operating in my life. Aside from my dedication to gymnastics as a teen athlete, I was lost and directionless, and my heart felt broken during much of my young life. I existed with my head barely above water and lived in an almost constant state of some combination of emotional overwhelm, stress, victim mindset, self-loathing, resentment, worry, anger, fear, grief, or anxiety.

I was adrift. I had no idea what I wanted, how I wanted to feel, or what was even available as to what I could feel, nor did I know what the hell I wanted to be when I "grew up" or what I was capable of doing or being.

My life lacked the vital clarity that living in accordance with heart-centered values could provide as a piece of living for love. Clear, heart-centered values help you grow deep roots of clear direction so you can live from inspiration in areas like inner well-being, spiritual connection, career success, relationship closeness, positive body image, and professional contribution. My lack of clear, heart-centered values led to a complete lack of deliberate focus and intentional direction for too many years—but nothing is to be regretted in life, just learned from so we may be better and serve others better.

Here are some ways that lack of clear, heart-centered values showed up for me. See if you can relate:

- I was driven by perfectionism and a cruel intolerance for my own humanness, failures, mistakes, or missteps.
- I felt a chronic need to be liked, thus hustled feverishly to gain (or avoid losing) the approval of others.
- I grotesquely sold myself out to please others and be liked.
- I lived in a chronic state of anger (even when it was being denied or suppressed, it was always lurking just under the surface).
- I avoided conflict and had no idea how to say the magic word "no" (much like many of our clients when they first begin working with our coaching team).

- I starved and binged to punish and numb myself.
- I mothered and smothered men in romantic relationships.
- I was overly attached to striving, achieving, winning, competing, gaining, and getting results.
- I was wildly self-abusive and self-critical, and nothing I did was ever good enough for *me*. And sadly, I often led others to feel as though they, too, were never good enough.
- I did not like to make waves, yet I was a complete rebel. (The rebel piece I kept!)
- I pretended to be happy and feigned compliance when I could.
- I did what I thought would make others happy, to the detriment of my own happiness.
- I took on the role of being "the life of every party," meanwhile bubbling anxiety, frustration, and deep loneliness waged war inside of me, nearly enveloping me—mind, body, heart, and spirit.

In the end, I was doing "nice things" or the "right things" for all the *wrong* reasons. I had some fun, too, of course, but it was rarely heart-centered, joy-filled, or soul-singing fun. *Fun* was usually reserved for weekend nights and was usually combined with escapes like drinking too much alcohol and binge eating before bed, prefacing hours of laboring over the "right" outfit to get the "right" amount of attention. This could easily send me into an overly emotional tailspin, which usually ended in picking a fight with my husband (*blush*).

And when morning came, I would wake with a monumental amount of self-loathing, guilt, and shame. I traded honoring myself for doing what I *thought* others would like. Honestly, a big part of me thought I was being a kind, good person as I sold myself out bit by bit, a true reflection of not understanding living by sacred, heart-centered values.

The truth was, I was not doing anyone any favors. And certainly not with any semblance of authenticity, as if I had any comprehension of authenticity in those days. That expression of life was not healthy nor authentic, and it did not serve anyone's highest good, least of all mine.

All the chaos showed up in my body as well. My health was compromised with multiple autoimmune disorders, I barely slept, and I was exhausted to the point of literally falling asleep while standing during the day.

The values that had been functioning in my life were accidental at best and self-abusive and destructive at worst.

I felt soul-sick and utterly alone. No matter how many people I had howling with my self-deprecating "fat" jokes, which stemmed from significant body dysmorphia, or wooing at how much alcohol a one hundred and twelve-pound girl could consume, I still woke up each morning with the same suitcase overflowing with shame, anxiety, and overwhelm.

What can I say? I had a loving family and loving friends, yet I was a sad, hot mess for a lot of years!

Spoiler alert: I now wake up every single morning with love shining from my heart, a genuine smirk on my face (as if I have a secret, which I do!), and I am brimming with love, inspiration, and gratitude to kick off every single glorious day that God gifts me!

If you resonate with any of this soul-sickness, here is the good news—just like I eventually did, you, too, now, in this very moment, can create intentional values that set your course toward healing, joy, love, and inspiration; then you can practice those values to proficiency and live the accompanying totally bitchin' life! Your values can be exactly what YOU choose, and they will help you begin to overflow with meaning and joy.

Belong To Yourself First

Amidst that hot mess, I started to do a bit of learning, growing, and healing. After devouring tons of books, I began to uncover the truth that there was indeed a more self-honoring way to live. Plus, I knew I didn't want to feel so damn awful anymore, and I was committed to doing whatever it took to learn how to be happy—and not just moments of popcorn happiness, but genuinely happy ALL the time.

So, I made a single brave, crystal clear decision: I would begin to navigate life, business, and *all* decisions from a place of love, which is still my most prevalent value. I had begun to believe that I was worth it, and I finally inched toward loving myself enough to *belong to myself first.*

This is an incredibly clear value and directive. Leading life from a position of love (and eventually self-honor) was easy when life "felt" easy for me. But what about when others behaved rudely or offensively? If your highest value is love, the door must learn to swing both ways. So, what about sharing love when a truck full of teen boys intentionally swerved toward me when I was riding my bicycle and smacked me on the back? What about when I heard others say or do cruel things or I saw someone strike their child or pet in public?

At first, it felt extremely difficult to share love under these types of circumstances. In fact, I really did not even want to share love in these cases and continued feeling righteously justified to be nasty back (remember the anger I used to carry?). Practicing the deeply heart-centered value of love has been an evolving value that took many, many years to master and required great depths of dedication to the Divine, and the consistent practice of surrender (a skill you will learn later in the book). Yet this guiding value is one that has sprouted inner treasures that are second to none.

In my *old life*, however, before selecting love as the first value for which to run my life, how do you think I might have acted in situations that I perceived as distressing or upsetting?

If you guessed some version of snotty, mean, rude, shut down, prideful, lashing out, judgy, giving the silent treatment, arguing, shouting, slamming doors, or flipping other drivers the bird, you would be right! I used to be a real handful! And a saucy, saucy minx!

Don't get me wrong, I am still a saucy, saucy minx. You cannot take the stripe off a zebra. But now my sauce has transformed and stems from love and play, not anger and resentment.

When I first chose this particular value (operating from love), I messed up a lot and defaulted to undesirable and negative behaviors like anger, judgment, and nastiness. It was (and, on occasion, still is) especially entertaining when I do not *feel* like behaving lovingly! Practically speaking, I had a great deal more practice navigating life led by accidental values, thus in destructive, victimized, aggressive, blaming, or self-pitying ways, than I did in loving ways.

This is the human condition, and we have more practice supporting negativity (believe it or not) until we decide to reach for heart-centered values and live them with wild abandon.

Trust me, my little inner rebel (i.e., ego/mind) is alive and well—she is just no longer allowed to hop in the driver's seat and take me for wild, dramatic rides! There are still moments when it *seems* sweetly justified and I am tempted to whip out the old sass and zing another person. Beautifully, though, *I never regret responding with love.* Nor do I regret stopping and taking time to breathe and remember how this deep-seated, heart-centered value of love—and now a way of life—allows me to feel unbridled joy and universal connection without fail or disruption. I grew to understand that everything I do, think, say, or believe is either love or not—there is

NO third direction, just as it is for all intentionally chosen, heart-centered values.

As with most new habits or practices, when seeking to guide your life by clarity and intentional dedication to values, you begin clumsily at first, gain a bit of balance over time, then progress to novice level, then expert, and finally, mastery. Dedication to the value of love (and, more recently, unconditional love) has been a growing practice for nearly twenty-three years. And in recent years, I am beginning to live a significant level of mastery.

That which is most meaningful takes time to acquire mastery.

Remember, your habits or that with which you align most, or perhaps you are known as an (i.e., workaholic, control freak, rage monster, etc.), tend to be the *values* that guide your life. Some are intentional, others were accidentally picked up from loved ones along the way. To be super clear, let us look at a few more examples of accidental and intentionally chosen values.

- If you have a habit of criticizing, judging, or gossiping, you are practicing and highlighting the inner values of being critical, judgmental, or gossipy.
- If you are angry, resentful, frustrated, or nasty toward yourself or others, the aggression serves as a guiding value.
- If you volunteer with animal rescues, perhaps protecting and stewarding animals is one of your values.
- If you are nearly always on time, maybe timeliness is a value.
- If you choose your family consistently over extra work or cleaning to the point of wild perfectionism, perhaps your family is a heart-centered value.
- If you choose to close your heart or shut down emotionally with your partner, perhaps emotional unavailability is functioning as one of your values.

- If you practice stewarding your family, spouse, career, or the planet, perhaps stewardship is a value that is functioning well in your life.
- If you act in loving service toward others much or most of the time, perhaps service and love are your values.

Get the idea? That which we practice, choose or demonstrate most functions as a value. To start uncovering your functioning value, you might ask yourself, "What is my reputation? What am I known for? How do others view me?"

Heart-centered values are related to your most fundamental beliefs and dictate behavior, feelings, choices, and ultimately the experiences and results that show up in your life. Essentially *anything* can serve or function as life, love, family, spiritual, or career value.

If you still need to clearly define your values and create habits and systems to support them to ensure that they do indeed guide your daily life and decisions in intentional ways, no problem! You will soon receive specific instructions to do so.

Value-Driven Decisions

The main purpose of selecting heart-centered values is to serve as personal guideposts to make life, career, family, and relationship decisions that are wildly meaningful, effortless, and conflict-free.

So, on a very practical level, intentional values are designed to be decision-making parameters. And, as it goes with any decision, there will be consequences—positive or negative.

Consequences can be favorable or unfavorable, but they do accompany every decision we make. And when you shift into navigating your life with heart-centered values, whether they are intentional or accidental, consequences flow.

For example, early in our marriage, Chris and I intentionally chose to dedicate two full years to the value of fearless, unbridled, raw vulnerability. That dedication resulted from our desire to turn our plummeting marriage around so we could build a collaborative and joyful marriage together. We knew in our hearts that a truly great marriage was possible, though neither of us had witnessed what we would consider a great marriage. We also knew that the problems we were experiencing could be turned around and did not have to lead us to divorce. We had an abundance of hope, grit, and inner knowing. And through our dedicated research, we came to believe that a key component to a truly great marriage was the art of vulnerability.

We were right!

In the end, we realized that the very best marriages do indeed include mastering the art of radical vulnerability.

As we made daily, weekly, and monthly decisions rooted in the value of vulnerability, our marriage turned, bit by bit, toward loving and serving one another, putting the other's needs before our own, sharing the deepest spaces of our hearts, fears, and dreams—and we systematically removed every single ounce of blame toward the other, which requires an extraordinary amount of vulnerability and tenacity. From then on, our relationship, connection, sacred time together, talking, going on dates, playing, lovemaking, adventuring, etc., started coming before anything and everything else—barring emergencies. This was a natural consequence of practicing and mastering the value of radical vulnerability.

You see, most people try for surface changes, like implementing "date night." This is not necessarily a value-driven decision. More often than not, it is an attempt to grasp for straws. But when we seek to identify the real changes to be made in life, love, and business, we need to dig deep, look beyond the symptoms, and identify what value, if selected and devoted to, would clear out the clutter and provide amazing, loving, joyful consequences.

This is what it means to live for love.

What does this look like in our real, day-to-day life?

If Chris or I have been out of town traveling for work and return to invitations to hang with the ladies or dudes, our response is very simple:

Thanks, but no thanks; we will be spending the next couple of days together!

If we find ourselves in a week that has become overly busy, then the choice is simple: we take off a couple of extra days the following week to be together.

Nothing beyond a family or client emergency or death comes before the value of honoring our marriage. This means our relationship comes before work, money, friends, and family. Period!

What might happen in your life, marriage, career, or wellness if you had a value like vulnerability that you were wholeheartedly dedicated to and that you used to make any and every decision? What would change, how would you grow, and what would be the short- and long-term benefits?

This is one reason that Chris and I have such a strong, joyful bond and a piece of how we created a completely fight-free marriage for the past four years. There is absolutely never a question that our relationship and one another are at the top of the list. This has promoted a kind of relationship that I did not previously know existed or knew was possible. We have trust, vulnerability, care, joy, play, intimacy, passion, and a deep unwavering desire to serve one another with love and devotion. This value is further deepened by our number one heart-centered value of dedication to God and unconditional love for all of humanity.

Over time, we were able to release vulnerability as our number one value because it became a natural daily practice. Once that occurs, you can create a new value to live and make decisions by. Over time, values can change and shift based on how your life is evolving. Generally, you will dedicate yourself to a given value for at least twelve months.

Client Case Study: Jennifer

A lovely client of ours, Jennifer, has a story that perfectly illustrates the consequences that come with practicing accidental values.

When we spoke the first time, she shared with me an all-too-familiar story. Jennifer was a very high achiever in all of her endeavors. In high school, Jennifer was a track star and an 'A' student, and a self-proclaimed pleaser. She claimed to be "a little nerdy," but had plenty of friends.

Somewhere around age eleven or twelve, she recalls experiencing her first feelings of anxiety, which grew into anxiety attacks in her twenties, and finally panic attacks at age thirty-two. The panic attacks ultimately became the catalyst for reaching out to me.

At the time of her first feelings of anxiety and worry, she did not think much of it. She brushed it off and said, "most everyone in my family struggles with anxiety, nervousness, and constant worry, right?"

Jennifer reported being a proud, successful business owner of a 50-million-dollar software company. She slept only six hours per night and worked ten to twelve-hour days.

Jennifer was married, had a young daughter, and loved to run— that is when she could find time for running, which had become incredibly rare.

In the days leading up to our working together, Jennifer barely had time for sleep, let alone time for the self-honoring activities like healthy eating and the running that she so enjoyed.

She ate on the go (usually quick, low-nourishment food) and ran only about one to two times per month, which she reported as "not good since running is what keeps me sane!"

Jennifer claimed to be constantly apologizing to her husband for snipping at, blaming, and criticizing him, mostly because she was overly emotional from exhaustion and frustrated with not knowing how to "get her act together."

Her attitude and long work hours were taking a significant toll on her health, marriage, and daughter who had begun displaying several unfavorable behavior patterns, which had triggered a cascade of guilt and shame in Jennifer.

Jennifer was exhausted, irritable, and desperately missing connection and time with her family, friends, and HERSELF!

When I asked about intimacy, she laughed and said, "I don't even have the energy to launder my undies, let alone think about being sexy in them—which I feel guilty about seven days a week. I think my husband and I had sex on our last vacation...."

And then she burst into tears.

Eventually, Jennifer's anxiety became so overwhelming that she began taking medication to curb it, which, inevitably and unfortunately, triggered feelings of unworthiness and more guilt and shame for "needing" medication to manage day-to-day life.

Panic attacks were the final straw.

Jennifer did not know how she was going to change her life, but she knew she was ready to change it. She was ready to be done with the guilt and shame, missing out on her family, selling her soul to her business (which she loved, but needed a better balance), the exhaustion and frustration, and the medication!

She was prepared to be done practicing the many accidental values that resulted in anxiety, panic attacks, and an exhausting, low-quality life.

She had hit her rock bottom, which is a VERY powerful and often (eventually) empowering place to land. Frankly, I love it when people hit their rock bottom—and the sooner, the better—as this is where deep, heart-centered inspiration and motivation for change ignites.

Jennifer found it fascinating that behaviors and actions like progressively sleeping less, mounting frustration, lack of sex and sexual desire, and the very painful emotions like guilt and shame were the consequences of accidental values and the behaviors she had begun to practice as a result of those values.

She looked back and saw how she had been programmed—innocently—to believe that her worth was tied to her work, thus the accidental value of work above all was born. She lived a never-ending pursuit to find worthiness and love by constantly working.

And lo and behold, bit by bit, with each passing moment, these unwanted and unfortunate beliefs and behaviors became values that she practiced to proficiency.

Once we began working together, Jennifer quickly saw through the accidental practices. She had no idea she could choose to practice a different value and set her compass to point her life in a meaningful direction.

Jennifer was very encouraged by the idea of shifting her values to that which was deeply heart-centered for her, as well as designing practices that aligned with these values. She got on board quickly with the idea that if she practiced negative and unwanted habits, emotions, and decisions to proficiency, she could certainly do the same with all the things she INTENTIONALLY valued and wanted to create in her life, family, and business.

Jennifer began to shift her values toward "slow-paced, meaningful living," which specifically meant that she left work at 5:30 p.m. Monday through Thursday and 2 p.m. on Fridays. This one value-driven decision provided for family time and connection to flourish, peace to become a reality, and enough downtime to allow for running, yoga, reading, baths several times each week, and eight hours of sleep most nights.

By the time Jennifer was entering her last month of coaching, she was really in her groove. She was firmly rooted in several new practices that had set her and her family on a happier, healthier course together.

Eventually, literally all of Jennifer's concerns—including anxiety, panic attacks, exhaustion, lack of intimacy with her hubby, and lack of quality time with her daughter—were turned around.

She felt free for the first time in her life...

And what's more exciting, her business profitability grew right along with her emotional profitability!

Whether intentional or accidental, you are each practicing and adding permanence to functioning values every single moment. And, as a result, we will experience the consequences of all habits and practices.

Heart-Centered Values in Practice

Like Jennifer, when you choose to practice values like love, peace, surrender, slow-paced and meaningful living, inspiration, or patience, the natural consequences that accompany your values will flourish and intensify, leaving your heart and life overflowing with more meaning than you could possibly imagine.

Being clear with your heart-centered values and putting them intentionally into practice with specific actions that promote value-driven living allows most decisions to become very, very simple.

Here are some examples of possible heart-centered values that you might choose to adopt to guide a season of your life.

- Compassion
- Positivity
- Unconditional kindness
- Slow-paced, meaningful living
- Acceptance
- Stewardship
- Solutions-focused living (instead of cynical, victim, or problem-focused living)
- Joy
- Courage and bravery
- Love or unconditional love
- Vulnerability
- Radical self-responsibility (more on this later)
- Self-honor
- Empathy
- Service

Let me share a few values that have been on my list in past years. When I was focused on healing old wounds, I used to choose a specific value to dedicate to a twelve-month cycle. You are welcome to ignite a value for a season, four seasons, or a lifetime. This practice has been wildly beneficial. And honestly, I did not recognize it at the time, but for several years, healing myself—body, mind, and spirit—was a functioning value that served my life well.

- Deservingness (learning to believe that I was deserving of love, care, joy, peace, kindness, and goodness)
- Deep self-compassion (to remove and replace self-abusive habits with self-honoring ones)

- Life learning (the deep dedication and devotion of one to three hours every day to the intentional expansion of wisdom, knowledge, consciousness, and spiritual evolution)
- Play (moved me from "showing off" to receiving attention to genuine heart-felt playfulness—hula-hooping, bouncing on our mini-trampoline, roller skating, hiking, rock climbing, and playing all kinds of games with my sweet and extraordinary hubby, Chris)
- Service (seeking opportunities to serve the greater good of humanity and the planet)
- Surrender (learning to let go of the resistance and surrender that which keeps people stuck in mental turmoil, drama, anxiety, fear, anger, frustration, worry, and depression—more on how to surrender in a later chapter)
- Unconditional love (learning to truly love and be kind to the entirety of life in every single moment)

Heart-centered values can fairly easily become an ironclad part of life. But they must have strong legs for support. For heart-centered values to exist as more than stated ideals, they must have intentional practices, habits, and systems that function as strong support for at least one twelve-month cycle.

Heart-centered values help individuals, families, and companies determine whether they are on the intended path and fulfilling their goals spiritually, financially, interpersonally, relationally, and physically. Anytime you have a possible opportunity or decision to make, all you need to do is pull out your list of one to three values and make sure there is one hundred percent alignment with your top value(s). And POOF, the decision is made!

As you utilize your values, you can determine that there are ZERO yesses without one hundred percent alignment!

Sounds simple, right?

Intentional values are in place to help guide decisions, large and small.

We will go over the elements of creating and sustaining iron-clad practices in a later chapter, but for now, I will share some examples to give you a kickstart for how you can make decisions and start practicing habits that are firmly rooted in intentional values.

Let us take my client Janet for example. She is a C-suite-level executive with a big job and a great deal of responsibility. She and I had been working together for a while, and she already had numerous projects going on at work when this conversation happened:

- Thomas, Janet's boss, says to her: "Hey Janet, I really need you to stay late tonight to start on this new project."
- Janet's internal dialogue: *My highest heart-centered value is my family. My dedication to our family dinners is ironclad, and it is sacred connection time for our family.*
- Janet bravely responds: "Sorry, Thomas, I have a 6:30 p.m. family dinner commitment every day. It's our special time together, and I just can't miss it. But I can begin on this project first thing in the morning."

Can you imagine this situation? Have you ever been faced with a decision like this?

Because Janet was a recovering pleaser and perfectionist, sticking to her values and saying no to her boss required a great deal of courage, as well as a staggering amount of integrity and dedication to her family. As you can likely also imagine, staying committed and aligned with your values takes practice and dedication, just like anything that is valuable to you.

Just as with learning and practicing any new skill, you will need to be gentle with yourself when you first begin living and practicing value alignment. With consistency, the payoffs for upholding your values are truly fantastic and make life much easier and more meaningful.

Remember, if you live by strong values, you will arrive at your deathbed with no regrets, which is, unfortunately, a rare occurrence.

By creating an unwavering set of heart-centered values, life, work, family, and love can become simple, calm, slower-paced (if that is your desire), intentional, and a whole lot happier! I have even seen value alignment save dozens of marriages.

Values serve as your "treasure" because once defined, they effortlessly inform decisions, actions, to-do lists, and moods. Even your emotions will be impacted favorably. Heart-centered values and accompanying habits usually change over time as you grow and evolve, but creating an initial value(s) and supporting habits to enforce your value(s) is the key to success.

Take Loving Action!

1) The first step in defining heart-centered values is to get clear. Grab your journal, and let's answer a few questions to get this party started!

- What is the number one reason you want to define heart-centered values to guide your life and decision?
- What would the impact of living by clearly defined values have on your life, marriage, family, and career?
- What will having clearly defined values help to fix, remove, or solve in your life?
- What accidental values are currently operative in your life that you are ready to get rid of!?
- What intentional values are currently operative in your life that you would like to expand and capitalize on?

2) Define Your Values

Use the values listed a few pages back as a jumping-off point, and make a list of what you believe you would like your most heart-centered values to be. You are also welcome to look up examples of values on the internet or create your very own list if you'd like.

Feel free to make a list of ten or more values to begin with.

Next, whittle your list down to one, two, or three heart-centered values. Simplicity is key here. The more complex the list, the more work there is to do and the more you have to think when attempting to practice and make powerful decisions by utilizing your values. This encourages the brain to jump ship on the new habits because it feels too emotionally difficult. So, if you can get down to one core value to guide your life for the next twelve months, that is best. Next year, you can choose more than one if you'd like. Personally, I choose only one, practice it to mastery (however long it takes), and then choose another–this allows me to have a very tight focus.

Change is already challenging enough, so one great pro tip for making change permanent is to keep things simple. Please feel free to select just one single value to guide you over the next twelve months. If one really does not seem to encompass decision-making for all major pieces of your life (business, career, love, play, health, family, etc.), feel free to choose two or even three if you must. But be on the lookout for the desire to compartmentalize areas of your life. You are one being, and it is healthiest to be YOU authentically in the whole of your life.

When our team works with individuals, business owners, and couples, we have them choose ONE heart-centered value and use it for twelve months before expanding to two or three guiding values. This helps ensure that people are selecting the most important value to support them and their most pressing goals and needed changes.

3) Uncover The "Why" Of Your Values

Remember this one from the introduction and sustainable change model? It is important to understand WHY you want to choose a particular value to live by. You will be utilizing it for at least twelve months with the goal of turning your compass in a more fruitful and self-honoring direction. Once you have narrowed your value list to no more than three values, pull out your notebook or journal and answer the following questions to help you become *clear* about your top one, two, or three values and why you might choose them to guide your life.

- WHY is each chosen value important to you?
- How could this value help you turn old gunk, hurt, and haphazard or accidental values into powerful and empowered actions, thoughts, emotions, and overall positive life navigation?
- What kinds of decisions will be easier to make because you are living aligned with *this* value?
- What problems will be solved or avoided completely as a result of living in alignment with this value?

Pro Tip!

If you are married or in a committed relationship, feel free to do this exercise as a couple or family if you have children. Selecting a heart-centered value *with* your partner or spouse or your children is extremely useful and dramatically reduces conflict. After all, conflict is rooted in pride, wanting "my" way, or in wanting someone to do or be something *you* think they "should" do or be.

Thus, when you and your sweetie or children select a heart-centered, life-guiding value TOGETHER, you now have selected a decision-making model to help you both (all) lay down emotional weapons like pride, force, anger, bullying, competition, criticism, shaming, and blaming to get what you want. With a collaborative value, you will be able to make decisions for the highest good of the situation, instead of for purely self-serving motives.

4) Actions, Habits, and Practices To Ensure Value Alignment

Once you have your list of up to three values and you know why these values are best for supporting and guiding your life for the next twelve months, it is time to add daily, weekly, or monthly actions and practices to support and solidify each value. These actions will replace habits, thoughts, decisions, and practices that no longer serve you, or that trigger distress or suffering.

For example, this is what it might look like if you select "deep connection" as a guiding value:

- You may choose to move away from or end relationships or interactions that are predominately painful or unhealthy in some way.
- You may choose to have one deep, vulnerable conversation each day with people who are on a similar path as you.
- You may choose to spend more time in solitude in order to connect with your beautiful self.
- You might begin to serve and honor yourself and others in resentment-free ways (for example, ask three people each week how you might support or serve them).
- You can also use this value to make decisions on the fly. For example, perhaps your partner forgot to load the dishwasher, even though he promised to do it before he left for work. So, if "deep connection'" is your highest value, then you could choose to either accept that he forgot and love him anyway, remind him gently and kindly when he returns home, or just put the dishes in the dishwasher yourself as a loving act of kindness!

Get the idea?

Now, grab your journal and jot down each value and one or two specific habits, actions, thoughts, beliefs, or practices that will support you in living these values in a deeply devoted way.

You do not want these values and practices to just be "in theory" or something you write down but never use. Remember, one value is best, two are okay, and three is the absolute most—otherwise, your brain and emotions will be overwhelmed and resist the actions and shifts that your heart wants to make. We must work with—rather than against—our brains to promote effective change.

To get your wheels turning, here is a list of a few core values and practices many of my clients have selected:

Example Value 1): Meditation (working toward living in a meditative state for the whole of your life)

Why: To cultivate inner quiet

Practices: 1) formal sitting for fifteen minutes each day just before morning coffee, 2) "letting go" meditations—one minute at the top of each hour, 3) mindfulness practice five minutes each day just before lunch, with the added benefit of slowing down your eating and supporting healthy digestion!

Example Value 2): Spiritual Dedication and Evolution (living life as a prayer)

Why: To support and love others more fully.

Practices: 1) Pray for 2 minutes each morning just after opening your eyes, 2) read spiritual texts for thirty minutes just after cleaning up dinner and before the television is turned on, 3) attend one spiritual retreat each quarter for one year, 4) work with a coach for six months to further develop spiritual understanding.

Example Value 3): Great Health & Wellness

Why: To have an abundance of energy and fitness for the duration of my life.

Practices: 1) Rock climbing every Monday and Thursday after work, 2) walk one mile each day before breakfast, 3) hike five miles every Saturday, 4) do fifty squats and twenty push-ups just before lunch each day.

Example Value 4): Healthy, Self-Honoring Eating

Why: To look and feel great and to ward off illness

Practices: 1) Eat a salad every day for lunch, 2) Replace chips for nuts and seeds as snacks, 3) Cook organic meats and steamed veggies Monday, Wednesday, and Fridays for dinner, 4) Plan the coming week's meals each Sunday morning before grocery shopping, 5) Cut out refined sugar for twelve months with one exception per month

Example Value 5): Learning

Why: To gain valuable knowledge to help navigate life's path with confidence and know-how.

Practices: 1) Read or listen to a book for thirty minutes each morning while drinking coffee, 2) Watch one TED talk every Saturday morning, 3) Listen to one podcast during lunch on Tuesdays, 4) Hire a coach to help you grow and expand for six months.

Example Value 6): Marriage Success

Why: Be intentional about closeness and connection

Practices: 1) Friday night date night—take turns planning fun adventures, 2) Engage in three deeply vulnerable conversations each week, 3) Plan sacred time each Wednesday (go for a walk, have a glass of wine on the patio, and talk), 4) Work with a relationship coach for three to six months to gain additional connection skills, 5) Find house project to do once per quarter to practice working as a collaborative team, 6) Eradicate blame.

For more support with your relationship, see our Reimagine Love Master Class for relationship recovery, healing, and growth at https://www.liberatemylife.com/reimaginelove.

Example Value 7): Courage

Why: To break out of fear, anxiety, and worry

Practices: 1) Start a business—spend the first six months planning, setting it up, and getting it going. 2) Do one public speaking event each month, 3) Share vulnerably one time each day, 4) Find one fun, courageous action to take each week.

Example Value 8): Business Success

Why: To support yourself financially, feel purposeful, and make a contribution to the world/community.

Practices: 1) Create one excellent system each week to make business flow, 2) Lead from a place of love and abundance, 3) Cultivate amazing customer service from a place of a servant-heart, 4) Practice fiscal stewardship, 5) Delegate one thing to a virtual assistant each week to free up time for fun and play.

Are you getting the picture?

Be creative with your practices. They need not be at all traditional—they simply need to serve your highest, heartfelt objectives and support you in making decisions that allow you to live for love in ways that feel authentic to you. Values need to be highly effective, with their "why" and practices quite specific—think SMART goals as you flesh them out. The overall aim is to begin setting up yourself and your life for the kind of success you intentionally design and desire. Living aligned with your values should make you feel like you are wildly successful every single day!

Oh, and don't forget to give yourself loving grace when you forget to align with and make decisions rooted in your values. Remember, you must first be a beginner before becoming a novice and ultimately an expert and a master!

Now it is your turn—follow this template for each of your values:

Value 1:

Why:

Practices:

Remember, values can, will, and should change over time as you grow, heal, and evolve, so let this be a jumping-off point. You will want to revisit your values each year to re-evaluate. Chris and I have created a ritual of spending the month of December meditating, goal setting, and strategically planning for business and family. Thus, value evaluation is always a part of this exciting and inspiring series of couple-ship meetings!

Congratulations!

Are you feeling excited about designing a value-driven life?

Key Takeaways

- When you are clear about your values, you will lead an increasingly fulfilling life.
- What people value most shows up in everyday life, whether deliberate or accidental. Values are illuminated in how you live in each moment of each day, and in each experience, interaction, and in the words and deeds you do and practice.
- Practicing accidental values is not a reflection of one's love of others. They are usually reflective of self-doubt, fears, and insecurities.
- The main purpose of selecting heart-centered values is to serve as personal guideposts to make life, career, family, and relationship decisions that are wildly meaningful, effortless, and conflict-free.
- For heart-centered values to exist as more than stated ideals, they must have intentional practices, habits, and systems that function as strong supporting legs for at least twelve months.
- Just as with learning and practicing any new skill, you will need to be gentle with yourself when you first begin living and practicing value alignment. With consistency, the payoffs for upholding your values make life much easier and more meaningful.
- Be creative with your practices and ensure they serve your highest, heartfelt objectives and support you in making decisions that allow you to live for love in ways that feel authentic to you.
- Values need to be highly effective, with their "why" and practices quite specific—think SMART goals.

CHAPTER 3

Life As A Practice

Your current experience of life is the culmination of all that you have learned and practiced up to this point.

Life is a practice. Life is a series of practices. It could even be said that this life is a practice for the next life, stage, or season of life.

Most of life—your experiences, results, thoughts, beliefs, relationships, career, ability to connect, communication styles, habits, even addiction and numbing out habits—is the culmination of conditioning, programming, repetition, and education (formal and by observation) up to this very moment. In short, all that you experience currently is a culmination of all that you have consciously or unconsciously *practiced*.

Let me repeat that again because it is so stinking valuable. All that you experience currently is a culmination of all that you have consciously or unconsciously *practiced*.

You are basically a culmination of the whole of your history. This is, in effect, your "get out of jail free" card. Why a "get out of jail free" card? Because you have innocently adopted and absorbed what you are today. This provides a gorgeous opportunity for you to truly love, trust, and show compassion to yourself for all that you are and all that you have become. You can literally drop and forgive all self-harshness for any perceived faults, flaws, mistakes, and complete faceplants! You simply did not know any better. I hear you saying, "Well, Shawn, I should have known better with _ _ _ _ experience." To that, I say, if you had known better, you would have done something different.

You are a learning, absorbing creature, even when you do not mean to be learning and absorbing. Every habit you have, the way you speak, the way you connect with or do not connect with others, self-abuse, addictions, patterns of numbing, the way you love, and everything in between has been learned, adopted, and adapted—for better or worse!

This is what it means to understand life as a practice.

What's more, every moment you have been *practicing* life, you have been improving *something*.

For example, if you feel angry more often than you would like, it is a result of practicing various forms of anger—irritation, frustration, hatefulness, aggression, resentment, bitterness, impatience, etc.

This applies to thoughts, feelings, intentions, behaviors, and accidental values that have been observed, adopted, or programmed into your precious mind, body, and spirit, and then practiced to *proficiency*.

I invite you to begin considering each emotion, habit, thought process, belief, and spoken word as practices that have become proficient skills, so to speak. Because when you think of literally everything as a skill, the mind, body, and spirit will begin to depersonalize the things you consider as negative, or flaws, or mistakes, and they can then be recontextualized to "just something I innocently adopted along the way because I didn't know better but was doing my very best with the skill, knowledge, emotional awareness, and consciousness level at the time."

Isn't it wonderful?

Tada! Get out of jail free pass! You can stop beating yourself up now. But you must still take responsibility for discontinuing the practice of things that no longer serve your higher self, your excellence, your contribution, and your inner power. Dedicate yourself to practicing things that DO serve you, that are healthy, that allow you to eliminate all distractions and focus strictly on that which is in your highest good. You get out of jail free AND you get to step into a higher level of excellence and devotion to a high-value life.

What you practice every day is what you become increasingly skilled in. It is that simple. And, of course, at any time, you can stop or begin practicing anything.

Whatever is practiced most is made increasingly proficient. This is an incredibly important point to understand. This is how you understand that you are an innocent, learning being that simply sees, does, and repeats, often completely unconsciously. This is also where your personal power comes into play. You can, at any time, identify habits you no longer want to practice and begin to practice new habits that serve you at an increasingly higher level. Thus, there is no longer any need to personalize unwanted habits or beat yourself up—you can simply practice anew!

We are born as relatively clean slates, aside from some genetic propensities, temperament predictors, karma, and karmic proclivities. Human babies are born naïve, *ignorant*, and completely innocent and pure. They arrive with a few instincts toward survival. Most are not born stressed but rather born into stressful environments or perhaps developed in utero in a stressful environment, which data suggests predisposes infants to be more easily conditioned in the ways of stress, anxiety, fear, overwhelm, and worry. Yet, babies are born completely innocent.

Babies are not born unreasonably fearful, frantic, exhausted, cranky, argumentative, perfectionistic, mean, arrogant, stingy, rude, impatient, greedy, prideful, resentful, overly busy, overwhelmed, or bored. Nor, under most circumstances, are they born addicted to drugs, alcohol, work, sex, pornography, talking, thinking, social media, attention, romantic relationships, shopping, gossiping, or anything else. These negative or unwanted habits, feelings, patterns, emotions, and experiences we receive as lessons or programming *along the way*, and then they become ingrained (or entrained) with *practice*.

Sure, genetics play their part, but conditioning and practice are the pieces of the puzzle that matter most and that we can play with, shift, and change!

Gymnastics: A Practice Was Born

When I was six years old, my mother took me from our home in Grabill, Indiana, to Chicago, Illinois, to spend a couple of weeks with my darling aunt Pam, super cool uncle Obie, and cousin Debbie. Cousin Debbie was a whole year older than me, which I viewed as very cool and mysterious. She had long dark hair and was tall and thin, like a model. Oh, and did I mention, she was my idol?

I, on the other hand, was the cutest six-year-old (in my way of being cute, that is), with big, thick, goofy glasses and bright blonde toe-head hair. I was as scrawny as a grasshopper and as sassy as a Chihuahua (the type of dogs we have now, coincidentally)!

When we arrived, we barely had a moment to say our hellos before Cousin Debbie grabbed my hand and dragged me outside. She then proceeded to show me the most miraculous feat... a cartwheel. I was mesmerized. Starstruck. Dumbfounded. I thought to myself, *She's going to get to be in the circus someday, and I want in, too.*

Yes, I seriously dreamt of running away to the circus (um, still do!). Doesn't every young, fearless, tree-climbing, daredevil little girl?

As it turned out, Debbie had been taking gymnastics lessons. Her handstands, cartwheels, splits, and back bridges blew my mind and were the greatest things I had ever encountered. Her "cool" status skyrocketed right before my eyes. And for the next two weeks, Cousin Debbie taught me everything she could. I spent every moment possible trying to do my cartwheels, handstands, splits, and back bridges exactly as she demonstrated.

This summer trip was the dream of a lifetime—at the time.

Two weeks later, my mother arrived to retrieve me, and she could barely get out a "Hello, sweetie, have you had..." before I dramatically erupted with, "MOM, I have to take gymnastics lessons right away, or I will just *die!*" I then proceeded to drag her into the backyard to show her all my amazing feats of poise, agility, and acrobatics.

At that time, I likely more closely resembled a fish out of water, but she pretended to be impressed and amazed. Fortunately, my mother had been looking for something to keep me busy and burn off some of my never-ending energy!

And *voila!* Ten days later, I was enrolled in my first gymnastics class with Mr. Jim.

It was love at first flip! Gymnastics became essentially my whole world from six until my early twenties. There was little else I cared to do besides gymnastics—even boys paled in comparison to my true love!

Gymnastics was LIFE, and I loved every moment. It was the only place I felt like I truly belonged growing up.

What now stands out like a flaming sore thumb is how often I heard the old familiar saying, "practice makes perfect."

From my very first week as a gymnast, these words were echoed thousands of times. Since I was a *devout, addicted, perfectionistic, pleasing, approval-seeking* gymnast, loving this sport with the whole of my being, I took this idea very seriously.

I worked out longer hours than my peers, I took private lessons, and I had no regard for rest, for caring for injuries, or for wildly overtraining my young body. You get the point. I longed to be perfect, so I practiced every minute I could—I even had a make-shift gymnastics space, complete with a homemade balance beam, in our basement.

Practice Makes Permanence

It was not until my gymnastics career closed in my late twenties that I discovered a rather painful yet liberating truth.

By this time, I had completed my gymnastics career. I had also started my career as a life coach, was finishing graduate school, and was providing sports psychology training to teams, individual athletes, and coaches (which I still do on occasion, just for fun!).

One day, while working with a team of gymnasts who were eager to learn sport psychology skills, I heard the old familiar echo from a coach to an athlete: "Keep it up; practice makes perfect!"

As I gazed over at the athlete he was talking to, I did not see what would traditionally be considered a "perfect" gymnastics technique.

What I saw was a frustrated, upset, and overwhelmed girl who proceeded to repeat a technique that would no sooner lead her to a *perfected* skill than had she been practicing chewing gum and blowing bubbles instead.

Like young little Shawnie, she was practicing over and over and trying so hard—but she only succeeded in bringing *permanence* to

86

CHAPTER 3: Life As A Practice

her back handspring with four critical mistakes: bent arms, closed shoulders, fear, and frustration.

This athlete was literally not physically strong enough, flexible enough, nor emotionally prepared enough to perform the skill correctly, let alone add permanence or *perfection* to it in a favorable physical, mental, emotional, or spiritual manner. Her practicing was setting her up for failure.

The moment of this recognition was monumentally disheartening for my compassionate heart as an onlooker of this precious athlete who, through her own innocence, was simply doing what she had been instructed to do.

And this was one of the most liberating moments of my life.

I could see young gymnast Shawn in that same girl, and a lightbulb went off!

Both girls were more focused on practicing to work hard and achieve a perceived outcome rather than focusing on practicing correctly to build permanence to the correct skills.

Again, this was a habit of innocence—of not knowing any better—and blindly trusting those she loved and admired.

This is how we learn favorable and unfavorable beliefs, habits, emotions, and everything in between.

Something hit me like a ton of bricks that day, and thus, the beautiful concept of *practice makes permanent* was born.

The truth is, practice does *not* inherently make *perfect*.

Practice makes permanent.

Practice adds permanence to everything being practiced, and in the *way*, it is being practiced.

Both that little girl and little Shawnie had practiced, and practiced, and practiced... but did our gymnastics performance become *perfect* as a result of all the practice?

We had so many parallels—were both quite talented, and our bodies were suited *perfectly* for gymnastics. We worked our asses off, loved and trusted our coaches dearly, and the gym was the only place we felt any semblance of belonging as a kid and a teenager.

But were we the textbook definition of *perfect*?

Um, not so much.

While there were hundreds of fantastic, elegant, powerful, and beautiful details we each practiced seamlessly, we would also practice many haphazard gymnastics skills unknowingly with bent arms or incorrect technique—and with great repetition and passion and frustration and fear. Thus, we were adding permanence to haphazard problems like overuse injuries, poor technique, deep frustration, and, the saddest of all, the practice to permanence of harsh self-talk and mean self-perception for not being perfect enough, no matter how hard we work.

So, did the mere act of practicing gymnastics make it perfect? Sometimes no... and sometimes yes! It all depended upon how and what was being practiced.

Practice makes permanent is a matter of what is being practiced in any given moment. But permanence is a relative term. Something is only permanent for as long as it goes unaddressed—or as long as it is practiced. Even a permanent structure like a skyscraper will crumble over time or under extreme circumstances. Nothing in this world is actually permanent—this is where your freedom lies.

What Does Practice Makes Permanent Have To Do With YOU?

Whatever your life entails right NOW—whatever you are currently experiencing, whatever you have, feel, or do—is a consequence of all that you have practiced physically, mentally, emotionally, and spiritually.

What is really groovy is that you can change any practice at any time, so you can loosen and diminish permanence in any area that is less favorable while adding permanence to that which is genuinely preferred.

Thankfully, I did not only begin to incorporate this concept personally with my food, fitness, love, and relationships, but I also began using it in every facet of our coaching company, with individuals, businesses, families, and couples.

Looking at life through the lens of this concept, I realized that the enormous amount of anger I carried was simply a learned skill that I had practiced until it was permanent! AND I also realized—so joyfully—I could replace it by practicing love, patience, and kindness.

Additionally, my clients could do the same with fear, regret, worry, frustration, negative habits like binging and starving or over-exercising, overworking, perfectionism, self-criticism, arguing with a spouse about who is cooking dinner tonight, or with kids about cleaning their rooms and doing homework.

Literally any habit, any emotion, any experience can be whittled down or built up with intentional practice.

Looking at life through the lens of "everything is a practice, and practice makes permanent" adds ease to the brain and emotions.

The idea allows the brain to shift from personalizing habits, seeing the idea of change as daunting, and self-recrimination like telling victim stories ("I'm incompetent," "I'm not good enough," "I'm an idiot") to asking the more important question, "What can I specifically practice today—right this moment—that will add to my wisdom, intelligence, happiness, health, wealth, joy, compassion, career, marriage, emotional wellness, or spiritual evolution in ways that I adore?"

Can you imagine the freedom? A quick Google search will reveal that people spend between four and six hours EVERY DAY distracted and wasting time. Social media zoned out thinking about the most recent upset, stuck in painful or upsetting feelings or thoughts, mindless eating, drinking, gossiping, and last but arguably the biggest time stealer of all, technology. This includes zoning out for hours on Facebook, and Instagram, texting, playing games, shopping, or simply mindlessly roaming around on the internet. This behavior adds permanence to that which only takes from your energy stores, finances, emotional well-being, and health.

Practice Makes Permanent—Is it that simple?

When I learned that day that practice makes *permanence*, a huge light bulb went off! It was illuminated that I had been building permanence to accidental habits like anger, resentment, self-loathing, fear, road rage, being distracted, fighting with my husband, getting annoyed at what others did or did not do, worrying, and the like. These accidentally, innocently learned, and conditioned practices led me to feel alone and depressed in the world. I had been peppering my life with numerous haphazard practices and habits that would naturally lead to feeling crappy.

But here is the most gorgeous truth: we get to choose intentionally what we practice moving forward or at any juncture.

Sounds simple, right?

That's just the thing—it really *is* that simple!

But it may NOT be easy to remember what you prefer to practice...at first!

Regardless, it is extremely simple to identify behaviors, habits, feelings, beliefs, and reactions that you would like to stop practicing and replace with new, favorable practices that align with living for love. You will begin slowly and clumsily, but you WILL gain traction as you continue practicing.

The trick is to become aware of the haphazard practices and then be willing to shift and build permanence with that which is genuinely valuable to you.

Please remember, thought content, or what you think from moment to moment, is the most important practice with which to be intentional—what you hold in mind tends to manifest and make its way into fruition (i.e., permanence). Remember, permanence is a relative term. Something is only permanent for as long as it goes unaddressed.

If a runner practices running with knocked knees or flailing arms, she will build permanence into an inefficient and potentially painful running style. If this same runner finds a fantastic running technique coach who shares new, efficient running techniques, the runner can, with focus and intentionality, become faster, enjoy running more, and perhaps be able to run later in life, while potentially saving herself from future injury and costly rehabilitation.

So it is with the whole of life.

Practice builds permanence in thought, spiritual development, choice, habit, connection, relationships, career, success, beliefs, emotions, and everything in between.

What you have become, what you will be in the future, what you think, what you feel, what you expect, how you communicate, what you do or achieve, AND how or IF you *suffer*, are all products of past, current, and future practices (conscious and intentional or unconscious and haphazard).

Practice of any and every kind makes it permanent.

Think about what you have practiced thus far today—what thoughts and emotions did you begin your day with?

Did you open your eyes and sing praises of gratitude for actually waking up to greet another day, for being healthy, for the people in your life to love, and who love you?

Or did you open your eyes and practice thoughts and emotions of gloom, doom, and drudgery, lamenting all that "must" be done, irritated that you have to get up so early, annoyed thinking about the mess your spouse or kids made last evening or dreading the impeding traffic and annoying drivers?

The powerful question to ask yourself is this: "How do you prefer to feel on a consistent basis?"

When you make choices from the heart space of increasing intentionality, you can begin to reverse engineer all the pieces of your life—all that you do and practice. To practice life, career, and love in deep, value-driven ways, you must view all moments as if you are practicing for the Olympics, with sheer dedication and devotion to intentionality.

Take Loving Action!

This chapter contains three "Take Loving Action" sections. Take your time, and know you do not have to use them all at once. Let this be a reminder that we are not striving for perfection, we are working for progress. This is the first of the three actions.

Continue to consider the concept of practice makes permanent not only as you read this book but as often as you are willing to *practice* thinking or talking about this idea for the next seven days as an experiment to see what transpires in your life, career, and relationships.

Keep your journal handy to jot down things you want to give up practicing and what specifically you will put in its place or what you would like to begin practicing. Take it slow. Choose one thing at a time to practice and to stop practicing, otherwise, you'll be inclined to get overwhelmed and stop your efforts.

Consider what you are currently practicing in each realm of life. Where are you gaining permanence in life, business, romance, family, self-care, and emotional, physical, and mental well-being in ways that honor *and* dishonor you?

Continue to be mindful of the fact that all we have, all we have become, all we perceive or think about, and all we experience in every situation, interaction, outcome, thought, feeling, or *season* of life is a culmination of what we have chosen (consciously or unconsciously) to practice to proficiency.

Stop Trading High-Value For Low-Value Living

Living for love is about grabbing courage by its precious hand and going for it—I mean literally creating your most joyful life. You CAN create anything! It is about intentional design, creation, and execution. So many people have traded family dinners for fast food; leisure time for online shopping; restful reading for taxiing children to various activities; travel for extra work to pay for the new kitchen; play and joy for upset, irritation, and resentment; courageous, heart-centered action for blaming; time with family for guilt and shame associated with "getting stuff done"; and genuine connection for the often elusive efforts forged by social media, texting, gaming, and other technology-based correspondence.

I mean, really, who has the time or energy for self-care, afternoon love-making, or relaxing in the hammock when there is perpetually "so *much to do?*"

Practicing values of distraction or escape mechanisms has taken precedence over values of play, service, adventure, and connection.

Not everything is doom and gloom! Quite the contrary, most everything is extraordinary—yet, how people practice thinking, perceiving, and experiencing often paints a picture of doom and gloom.

There is a ton of good and great stuff going on in everyone's life at all times, whether acknowledged or not! But the heavy mental-emotional distractions, and therefore exhaustion, often seem bigger or more urgent and tend to take over and even color the rest of life, work, and love. We can get so stuck in the mind and toiling thoughts that even when the great stuff is available, we are tuned into another channel.

Is life really so serious? Are things like other people, jobs, upset, frustration, errands, and social media really so important that time cannot be taken to rest, connect, play, and create?

I seriously doubt it! Sadly, the lives people build—more often than not—reflect the contrary.

People seem to *practice* life as if everything is in dire straits as if there are a thousand WILDLY important, SERIOUSLY valuable, or AMAZINGLY high-priority items.

Are you picking up on the exaggerated tone here?

The thing is, if you have twenty "high" priorities, then you have zero high priorities (in love, life, family, or business).

Thoughts and ideas often begin with ideas like these:

- "I must do...."
- "I don't have time to...."
- "I'm too stressed to...."
- "I have to go to...."
- "I should / shouldn't...."
- "I'll never...."
- "I always..."
- "I try so hard to...."

All of these phrases, whether you realize it or not, imply that you are practicing a mindset of doom and gloom, victimhood, and overwhelm, and it demonstrates a serious lack of intentional guiding values and loving practices and rituals.

What gives?

What is standing in the way of slowing down, feeling free, taking naps, connecting deeply, drinking in this gorgeous life, being filled with inspiration, having boundless energy and creativity, and playing like children (or with children)?

Why are most people not focusing their entire human experience strictly upon that which makes life, work, and love exquisite, inspiring, and magical?

Honestly, people simply get caught up in limiting beliefs, desires, and cravings and have been conditioned toward following their elders and the masses.

People think success means having a big house, fancy cars, lots of money, an overwhelming amount of stress, looking twenty-five for eternity, and so on. Of course, there is nothing intrinsically wrong with any of the above—except for the fact that most people who are stuck in striving practices (of any variety) practice striving because they believe that what they are striving for WILL bring about happiness and elicit feelings of worthiness, lovability, and deservingness.

This is perhaps life's biggest illusion.

There is no happiness outside of inner sacred lovingness.

My favorite author, Dr. David R. Hawkins, characterizes this as "living life as a prayer."

Spiritual devotion is a practice that results in true happiness. Anything else simply provides a short burst of pleasure, which is fun, of course, and sometimes meaningful or playful. But true, sustainable, moment-to-moment happiness and joy come ONLY from within. This is the most valuable component of the concept of practice makes permanent.

All moments have consequences. And all learned consequences add permanence to a particular "skill." You can look at everything you do, say, think, and experience as a skill.

Looking at everything as "skill development" makes choosing change seem more simple and more achievable. What you do, say, think, and feel is, in truth, impersonal in most cases since it is all a consequence of innocent programming and conditioning. Yet it is tempting to personalize essentially *everything*, especially that which is perceived as bad, wrong, mean, or a mistake or failure.

While building new practices is simple, it is not always easy to remember or practice when you are already emotionally triggered by negativity and thus practice negativity and all of its consequences as permanent skills and values.

You can have a very strong *desire* to change habits, skills, or values that no longer serve you. However, desire does not always equate to action. It can be challenging to change what we practice. Our brains prefer and are, in a sense, attached to the status quo of current habits.

True inner happiness requires practices that cultivate happiness from within.

To cultivate inner happiness, you must practice living for love (the love of self and others), willingness to be still and joyful (regardless of external circumstances), courage and acceptance (even when you do not want to), and relinquishing inner ick, like judgment, gossip, pridefulness, anger, and criticism, and the inevitable (even if unconscious) guilt, fear, grief, and shame that accompany such practices.

Take Loving Action!

It is vital to take stock of all your practices, habits, and rituals (in thought, action, or deed). Create three categories to begin with:

1) Practices, habits, and rituals that you adore and serve your highest good.

2) Practices, habits, and rituals that are okay, not awesome, but that are not harming you or others in any way.

3) Practices, habits, and rituals that you want to change, eliminate, replace, or that need a better flow or system.

Next, select one or two practices, habits, or rituals from the "adore and serve your highest good" category to capitalize on. How can you leverage these practices to become even more supportive of your life, love, and/or business?

For example, perhaps you practice doing yoga twice per week. And you recognize that yoga relaxes you, reduces stress, encourages prayer or meditation, and just plain feels good.

In this case, you might want to make yoga practice a daily priority or at least increase the number of days you practice.

Next, select one or two practices, habits, or rituals from the "really want to change, eliminate, or replace" list to handle.

For example, maybe you are in the habit of losing yourself in social media for far longer than you would like, and this leaves you feeling lazy, guilty, or even ashamed that you were not spending your time in heart-centered, value-driven ways.

In this case, a great system is in order. You can first determine how much daily time is appropriate for you to spend on social media. Say, fifteen minutes per day. Then, you choose the time in which you spend these fifteen minutes on social media—perhaps the fifteen minutes just before you eat lunch. Then, at this time, you set a timer on your phone for fifteen minutes and go social media crazy until your timer goes off. Then, you close it down before you turn off your alarm, so you are not tempted to continue! Also, doing this activity before lunch (not during) will encourage you to stop because you will be hungry and want to eat!

Make sense?

Finally, rinse and repeat! Every two to eight weeks, or sometime after your new practices, habits, and rituals are firmly established, you can choose another practice to leverage, capitalize on, and change, eliminate, replace, or systematize.

From Status Quo to Sustainable Practices:
Trigger—Practice—Payoff—Recontextualization

Ultimately, fresh, powerful, joyful, meaningful, and profound practices create a fresh, powerful, joyful, meaningful, and profound life. The culmination of a life in any moment is a consequence of what we think and, therefore, bring to fruition.

There are important mental buttons that need to be engaged as you take responsibility to change all manner of habits and patterns that support your body, mind, and spirit. All habits and patterns, positive and negative, have four common components, or *buttons to press*, that help you shift from practicing haphazard to heart-centered life navigation:

- A trigger
- A practice
- A payoff
- A recontextualization

Trigger, practice, payoff, and recontextualization work together as a team, for better or for worse.

Even when you identify a practice that no longer serves you or that you would like to discontinue or replace, you must remember that everything you do, think, and feel has a payoff that you are inevitably attached to, whether you realize it or not.

Payoffs must be taken into consideration for any desired change to take root, especially since the brain has a preference for two very strong determining factors when it comes to habit change: 1) it prefers for things to stay the same, to maintain the status quo, and 2) the brain prefers the current payoff, whatever it may be, regardless of it being positive or negative. It may make logical sense to change a specific practice, but the brain and emotional body may not be *ready*, so to speak, to let go of the juicy payoff, no matter how negative of a consequence it may bring along.

For example, an alcoholic knows logically that consuming too much alcohol can have grave effects on mood, marriage, relationship with children, work, and health. And most alcoholics genuinely want to stop drinking or stop drinking *too* much. Yet there are payoffs that the brain, body, mind, and emotions receive from overconsumption of alcohol that the brain-body connection has no interest in giving up.

These payoffs—the shift into a more pleasant or even euphoric mood, softening of anxiety, becoming the life of the party, curbing boredom, etc.—are powerful, especially when you add in the combination of trigger (having a bad day and knowing that you want to feel better) and practice (the habit of walking in the door and grabbing a drink). This is a powerful cocktail that the brain and emotional body will not easily part with.

Client Case Study: Kathy

My client Kathy was the queen of staying stuck in the status quo of haphazard values and practices due to hidden payoffs, even when they brought negative consequences she did not enjoy or want.

Kathy is an amazingly bright and gifted physical therapist. Graduated top of her class and was loved dearly by all who know her. Kathy has a huge giving heart and is precious beyond words.

And...she trends toward valuing and practicing debilitating perfectionism, self-abuse, and body image issues—all with payoffs of perceived control.

She had been developing new self-honor skills for several months when suddenly, she temporarily reverted back to old perfectionism and self-loathing practices.

What we found as part of her conditioned, practiced cycle was a very key payoff that was being overlooked. When she was negative and hard on herself and therefore feeling down (which was driven by a natural primitive propensity of the limbic system), she had a habitual practice of calling friends or family and telling them just how "awful" she was.

This habit served to her detriment in three key ways: 1) to promote playing the victim by complaining instead of taking action that will benefit her, 2) as a form of escaping and numbing out by phoning a friend, and 3) it was a super distraction that allowed for procrastination. All things that ultimately help us to feel like complete shit!

During these calls, her family and friends naturally proceeded to build her up by telling her how great she was, how smart she was, how lovable she was, and so on.

While it might seem like a common and healthy behavior to reach out for support, in reality, she was not asking for support at all. She depended upon others to be her confidence instead of cultivating it internally in her mind, heart, and spirit. This habit served as a way to abdicate self-responsibility rather than engage it. This behavior was diabolically different from asking for specific help or support.

In essence, she was in a haphazard trigger-practice-payoff pattern.

- She becomes TRIGGERED by a comment from a co-worker or her husband that is perceived as negative, hurtful, or critical.
- She then PRACTICES all the negativity, powerlessness, shame, self-loathing, and terrible feelings that cascade from the trigger and the accompanying limiting belief (or internal message) that says, "I am never good enough (perfect enough, wife enough, mom enough, skinny enough, or productive enough)."
- She then dives into the PAYOFF of feeling like a victim and into a pint of her favorite ice cream, which she inevitably regrets and feels even more shame and self-loathing. These payoffs serve as a short-term Band-Aid in hopes of feeling even a little bit better. An additional PAYOFF comes when she phones a friend or family member to tell them the tales of her crappy day, and her loved ones jump on the bandwagon and take her side, which feels like she is receiving the love, care, and protection that she was unwilling to give herself in the first place.

  Payoffs are very sneaky and usually unconscious!
- She also feels shameful and guilty for this entire cycle, which then unconsciously acts as the next TRIGGER and brings about more self-sabotage and stuckness.

And so the cycle repeats...

To truly pull the root out of this weed, she needed to address the payoff directly and recontextualize the entire situation.

When Kathy would dive into victimhood and powerlessness, her friends and family unknowingly gave her an emotional "paycheck."

101

Just by diving in and trying to convince her of a value (which can only be realized by one's self), they "pay" her for negative behavior, thus promoting it and encouraging more of it. This habit allows people to temporarily feel good about being either the "rescuer" or "rescu-ee." But in the end, to be genuinely, sustainably happy, one must learn to rescue herself!

This is a cycle that most people are accustomed to practicing. All humans enact this cycle to one degree or another.

Not to worry, it is just a practice, and a new one can be put in its place.

So, what did Kathy do?

Kathy practiced three strategies that worked well for her:

1. **Prompt others with a new trigger to elicit a new payoff.**

   Her task was to simply ask friends and family to support her differently and be prepared to ask her one simple question when she called feeling down in the dumps: "How can I support you, Kathy?" This was powerful because it took away the incentive to practice playing the "poor me" victim and indulging in self-pity. She explained to them the cycle she was practicing, and they were all too happy to help. One friend even recognized a similar pattern in herself and asked the same favor from Kathy—a super win-win!

   This shift set Kathy up to practice communicating in empowered new ways. It removed the payoff for the practice of sharing drama, self-loathing, self-pity, and victim drama while, at the same time, encouraging her to get clear about the kind of support and positive payoff that would be helpful in her journey to live for love!

2. Letting Go Technique

The second practice is very simple for anyone but can seem too easy to be useful at the beginning. This simple practice is to breathe and let it go. We can learn over time to skip the emotional drama story altogether! I love this practice and have been practicing it for twenty years now; it has become the practice of choice for essentially any and every perceived negative emotion or experience in our home.

Once you become practiced in this skill (which will be expanded in detail in a later chapter), it becomes extremely efficient in bringing you back to center, eliminating negative emotions (NOT just managing them), and allowing calm and peace to come into your world in mere moments. Again, that is with consistent, disciplined practice. You will find that, at first, you are VERY drawn toward sharing the drama story happening within you, which is part of the payoff.

Negativity and drama are a way that people are programmed to socialize and bond, which is a significant emotional and inner payoff that provides a sense of belonging. So, be gentle and patient with yourself and remind yourself a thousand times that practice is key because payoffs are powerful. And while breathing and letting go is your birthright and essential nature, it will take on the illusion of feeling difficult at first. But, as you practice breathing and letting go, you loosen your emotional attachment to the dramatic, overly emotional, and negative payoff.

3. Recontextualization

The third practice that Kathy played with is a self-practice called recontextualization. I learned this skill from the many Dr. David R. Hawkins books I have read. He was a master of the art of living life in an unconditionally loving and joyful state. Recontextualizing is a total game-changer! In essence, recontextualization means telling yourself a story that feels good instead of a story that feels yucky.

All the thoughts in your mind are stories. *Yes, all of them.* And your stories are based on programming, practice, experiences, memories, opinions, triggers, feelings, and so on. The bottom line of storytelling is this: if you are going to tell yourself a story, make it a good one! When we recontextualize, we naturally transcend the negative payoff and begin leaning into positive and rewarding payoffs in increasingly healthy and loving ways.

This is the key. Payoffs are tricky and can be easily justified, defended, ignored, or denied.

Putting Trigger — Practice — Payoff — Recontextualization In Action

To put trigger – practice – payoff – recontextualization into action, choose a goal, habit, or pattern you wish to change, shift, or delete and follow these steps:

1) **Identify the trigger**

   Become aware of your usual triggers and make a list so you can more easily catch yourself in the act. In Kathy's case, the trigger was receiving a negative comment—it was what drove her to phone a friend or family member.

2) **Identify new powerful practices**

   Identify the new practices in which you would like to develop and add permanence. Be very specific here; vague generalities are not helpful and will only serve to keep you stuck. For example, if you want to stop drinking, you may decide to join AA and attend ninety meetings in ninety days (this is a very specific action). Even if you have not yet stopped drinking, who cares—this is an outstanding support system practice!

3) Identify old and new desired payoffs

Look at your current negative payoffs and make a list of your go-to's. You can think of negative payoffs as high-octane fuel for perpetuating feeling like crap! Sounds silly, but it is true nonetheless. Payoffs can be anything from getting your way, being right, winning a conflict, self-pity, playing the victim, self-abuse, self-loathing, getting attention or protection from others, or any negative emotion like anger, guilt, or shame.

Then, identify new payoffs (e.g., feeling energized, sustainable inner joy and happiness, feeling loved and loving no matter what, feeling joyful, and so on).

4) Recontextualize

Tell a new story that aligns with a heart-centered value and that will allow you to increasingly add permanence to new, desired, and supportive habits, practices, patterns, and experiences.

Here are some examples that may resonate:

Example: Old Practice Cycle

Goal: Lose weight.

Negative Triggers: Trying on clothing, getting on the scale, seeing *perfect* women on social media

Negative Stories: "I am such a loser. I will never be skinny." "I might as well eat with the other pigs at the trough." "No one will ever love me like this." "I am a complete failure."

Negative Payoffs: Self-loathing, self-pity, practicing helplessness, binge eating, living small, anger, resentment, self-abuse.

Result: Stay stuck in the same pattern, adding permanence to this entire exhausting and sad cycle while either losing weight for short periods but not keeping it off or not losing weight at all.

Example: New Practice Cycle

Clear and Specific Goal: Lose 15 pounds by _____ date.

Negative Triggers: (For a while, you will not get out of experiencing the negative triggers—it is what you DO on the heels of these triggers that makes the difference!) Trying on clothing, getting on the scale, seeing *perfect* women on social media

Clear Value: You may have chosen the value "unconditional self-honor," which could easily translate to, "Take loving, compassionate care of my body, EVEN when I am triggered."

Once you experience a trigger, you remind yourself of the value you selected when you were inspired, or "in-spirit," or living for love. You then draw upon this value to guide your new way of navigating the treatment of your body and the stories you allow into your head. Self-honor includes NO habits of self-cruelty, but instead, showering oneself with unbridled love and compassion! This is the stuff of complete life transformation.

New Practices: 1) Having a website page like www.ohsheglows.com bookmarked where you readily see images and recipes of beautiful, nutritious foods when you are tempted to dive headfirst into a pint of ice cream or bag of chips. Seeing the website can help develop a new self-honoring trigger that makes your mouth water and encourages healthy meal preparation and cooking practices. 2) Start the day with a gallon of water that you finish before bed. 3) Throw away your damn scale, so the trigger of shame and fear is eliminated. Use your intuition to guide you. After all, you are no more or less valuable at one hundred twenty pounds or two hundred and twenty pounds. 4) Practice showering yourself with love and gratitude for the body you were given, how well it works, how perfect it IS for you, and loving it UNCONDITIONALLY.

Positive Payoffs: Rising energy, far less stress, greater confidence, fewer negative physical symptoms like stomach aches and lethargy, or hormone issues (related to stress and low-nutrition foods), having more youthful or clear skin, feeling good in clothing, feeling proud of and confident in yourself, self-love, raising perceived worthiness, feeling unconditionally loved by YOURSELF!

AND... when we lose weight from a strong position of love and compassion, it might come off slower for some, but it will stay off!

Recontextualize: When you feel triggered into feeling bad about your body, take the opportunity to tell yourself a different and joyful story. For example, "I am so thankful for the body I have. It does all the essential things I need. This body is NOT me or my essence or who I am—it is a lovely vehicle that carries my spirit for this life."

Take Loving Action!

Okay, now it's your turn!

Grab your journal or notebook and follow these steps to reveal opportunities for fresh, deliberate practice.

1. **Identify your most common triggers.**

   What are the things people say or do that send you into a tailspin? What events trigger feelings of failure, not being

107

good enough, lovable, or worthy? What experiences elicit pain, suffering, anxiety, depression, anger, and the like?

2. **Write out the current undesirable Trigger – Practice – Payoff associated with each undesirable scenario.**

3. **Now, write a new and helpful Trigger – Practice – Payoff – Recontextualization that will allow you to shift toward your desired, heart-centered goals.**

   Use the weight loss example above as a specific guide.

4. **Set yourself up with baby steps.**

   You might decide that the only thing you will try this month is becoming aware of your biggest triggers, and then take thirty days and write each one in your journal and consider how each is impacting your life.

   Then, during month two, you might choose to begin identifying the payoffs. For month three, you can then work to put it all together with new practices and recontextualizing.

   The pace you do this work does not matter as long as it honors and serves you. Making small bits of progress is far superior to a *perfect* plan that is never executed.

5. **Observe what unfolds for you in the days or weeks that follow your new commitments.**

   When I decided I wanted to change the narrative around my intelligence and the belief I had very little of it, I initially committed to practice by studying and reading for just ten minutes each day. Because I loved learning and because the consequences of inspiration and joy were so profound, I wound up naturally leaning into the practice of reading for one to two hours each day. I share this to illustrate that practices need to be fluid and allow freedom and flexibility to expand and shift when needed.

What will you begin to practice right now that will clean up some of the gunk in your life, career, love life, and family? What will change as a result of your new practice?

From Daily Practice to Unimaginable Payoff

You see, any change you want to make will very likely require:

- A specific and focused goal or vision
- Clear values
- A basic understanding of your triggers
- New and specific practices you want to implement
- A clear understanding of the negative payoffs that keep you stuck
- The new payoffs you want to experience so that you can receive beautiful, sustainable results
- The ability to mentally recontextualize any experience to navigate life with increased happiness and fulfillment.

Pretty cool system, eh?

As I shared before, "dedicated education time" became a daily ritual for me.

Waking up became the trigger I used to initiate this new practice. Previously, I would wake up and be triggered by thoughts of overwhelm about the day ahead, but as I practiced recontextualizing the morning stories, the act of waking up became a joyful trigger and an inspiration to hop up and read! Reading first thing in the morning (which began inconsistently at first and gained momentum over time) was the practice, while growing in confidence, education, and wisdom were the juicy new payoffs.

Previous negative payoffs were the unconscious ego gratification of victimhood, martyrdom, and helplessness in practicing the haphazard value of "believing I was not smart."

This practice, which has sustained for twenty years (and has expanded into a two-to-four-hour ritual of a combination of body movement, reading, surrender meditation, contemplation, and amazing conversation with Chris regarding what we are currently reading), has served to facilitate the clearing out of a lifetime of insecurity, self-doubt, trauma, fear, worry, anxiety, negative thinking, self-loathing, hurt, sadness, suffering, and depression. Life now feels truly miraculous every single day.

At the same time, this one great new practice spawned other practices and unexpected positive payoffs. An ironclad commitment to spiritual development emerged, along with increasing self-awareness and learning the tools to create a conflict-free home. This is now a skill set that I joyfully get to teach to clients.

It served to catapult my career, led to financial abundance, and gave me the confidence to sever negative relationships that were not favorable for my heart, health, or spirit.

During the process of daily education and all that accompanied it, I also came to believe that I had the power to do anything, be anything, or solve anything—a very favorable paradigm.

Being focused on setting myself up for success in the daily process of practicing new values and the recontextualization system brought a way grander vision than I originally set out to achieve.

Wowzah! I could attribute the kickoff of my life's happiness and success to the creation of this one fateful practice! And so can you...

This is what it looks like to choose *wisely and intentionally*.

Making an intentional decision based on wisdom and inspiration regarding what you will and will not practice is paramount to crafting a liberated life.

Of course, this single practice did not solve every single problem, pain, limiting belief, wound, or unwanted result or experience for me. But because it was such a profound and impacting practice, it made a heroic impact on my life and continues to affect it positively, profoundly, and blissfully each day.

You, too, can choose practices that have a big bang for the buck!

Key Takeaways

- All that you experience currently is a culmination of all that you have consciously or unconsciously practiced.

- You have innocently adopted and absorbed what you are today, which opens a gorgeous opportunity for you to truly love, trust, and share compassion with yourself for all that you are and all that you have become up until this very moment.

- You must take responsibility to stop practicing things that no longer serve your higher self, your excellence, your contribution, and your inner power. Dedicate yourself to practicing things that DO serve you.

- The truth is practice does not inherently make perfect. Practice makes permanent.

- Literally, any habit, any emotion, and any experience can be whittled down or built up with intentional practice.

- What you think from moment to moment is the most important practice with which to be intentional.

- Any change you want to make will very likely require a focused goal or vision, clear values, a basic understanding of your triggers, new and specific practices you want to implement, and a clear understanding of the negative payoffs that keep you stuck.

- Making an intentional decision based on wisdom and inspiration regarding what you will and will not practice is paramount to crafting a liberated life.

CHAPTER 4

Radical Self-Responsibility

Radical self-responsibility means that you and only you are **one hundred percent responsible** for your experience of life. It is to know and understand that whatever the situation, you can consciously choose how to frame it and, therefore, how to feel about it or not feel about it. Radical self-responsibility is a gateway to living for love and to being incredibly happy and emotionally free. In place of radical self-responsibility is victimhood, complaining, depression, and constant blaming of others for your experience of life. Playing the victim means that you think that the world happens to you instead of being a willing participant and knowing that everything is a co-creation and an opportunity to align with love and truth. Victimhood is a sad inner existence and promotes a sense of powerlessness that can, at any time, be replaced by the inner freedom of embracing radical self-responsibility.

Like all of the practices in this book, this concept takes commitment, discipline, determination, and of course, time to practice and master. Learning radical self-responsibility is well worth the effort, as few tools support the kind of inner freedom you can experience with this one.

When you claim radical self-responsibility, you also claim ownership and leadership of your life. You instantly claim the truth that neither others nor experiences can force you to do anything or feel anything. For the vast majority of people, life's experiences are their puppeteers, and they are the marionette—they have given away their power. But you are here, learning a different way of being in the world. You can choose emotional freedom as you practice radical self-responsibility. As with all expansion skills, you will begin clumsily, staggering around in the fog for a bit, and eventually persevere through to the unmovable, undeniable, unshakable sunshine of life that becomes continuous happiness and joy. When you do not step into radical self-responsibility, you make the choice that you are at the mercy of your surroundings instead of being the creator of your life.

Client Case Study: Melinda

Here is an example of radical self-responsibility in progress. As my client Melinda and I began one of our coaching sessions, she shared that she was seriously struggling with an emotional *sandbag* (which is what I call the years of negative conditioning and programming that accumulate over time—more about this in a later chapter) of resentment and one seemingly filled to the brim with shame related to her husband "leaving his beard clippings all over the sink and floor after man-scaping that morning!"

That day, her neighbor had popped over for a fun, surprise visit. After the neighbor left, Melinda realized that she had used the bathroom...not a big deal, of course, except for the fact that Melinda had not been in the bathroom after her hubby had gotten ready and left for work. To her horror, the countertop, sink, and floor were littered with beard clippings. Melinda felt humiliated and mortified, followed by resentment and anger toward her husband.

Now, Melinda had been a client for some time by this point and was working hard to practice applying radical self-responsibility and used the trigger-practice-payoff-recontextualize toolset to bring about more understanding, acceptance, and peace in her life. A wonderful representation of radical self-responsibility.

Melinda immediately jumped into a story, telling herself (and me) that her husband did not care at all about her or their house because he repeatedly neglected to clean up his beard clippings! Having practiced recognizing these triggers for quite some time, she eventually saw that she did not want to feel so bad nor get triggered into so much emotional turmoil each time she perceived (told a story) that her husband did not care about her. As we spoke, she thought perhaps there was another way to look at the situation.

She took a long, deep breath and began laughing at herself and at how silly her story was. Melinda knew that her husband did indeed adore her and that forgotten beard clippings were nothing but an old habit he had collected from high school and college.

So, she decided to recontextualize the story into a loving one.

She said, "I'm blaming him when really I have a sandbag of shame. I worry too much about what neighbors might think about forgotten beard clippings. Perhaps he was in a rush because he was distracted by the dog who was crying in the next room, and he forgot to clean up the beard clippings." Instantly, Melinda felt more relaxed and calm and was lovingly excited and willing to take care of the beard clippings herself, grateful that her husband was such a great dog dad!

In Melinda's case, rather than blame her husband for HER emotions and drag all that heaviness around all day, she took radical self-responsibility for the emotional experiences she was carrying and realized the root of her emotional upset was nowhere but her own mind. Like with Melinda, it is crucial you begin to understand that you and only you are responsible for YOUR *experience* of life and for your perception of the events in your life.

The practice of radical self-responsibility is paramount to sustaining happiness.

Radical Self-Responsibility In Action!

Like *my* old self, the clients I work with had (or are working through) habits that indicate a high level of mastery and permanence in the art of blame and abdicating responsibility, blaming themselves or others for their feelings, behaviors, habits, results, outcomes, and even their thoughts. Unfortunately, blame is never fruitful or useful—it is merely a way to avoid responsibility and play the role of powerless victim (something to remember every time you start a sentence with "You...")!

In other words, like Melinda, it is up to you to decide the manner in which you want to perceive the world. Do you want to see the world as good and loving, or do you find it to be a world of hate? Do you believe people generally do their best with the tools they have at any given moment, or do you think people are idiots, mean, bad, lazy, and so on? Do you experience strangers, family, friends, co-workers, and even your lover as good and trying *their* best (not the best you think they should be doing) to be loving and helpful, or do you find them as being "out to get you," or to harm, offend, or otherwise upset you purposefully?

With each life experience, it is up to you to be radically self-responsible with how you choose to perceive or recontextualize the experience. Of course, this is not easy, especially at the beginning of a new practice. I have been practicing the tools found in this book in some capacity for more than twenty years, and while most of the big issues are well handled, there are still things that pop up when old programming encourages me to blame and dive into a drama story so I can be painted as a betrayed victim!

Alas, I have not indulged in the victim payoff *as a lifestyle* for quite some time because radical self-responsibility is now my dominant lifestyle. This way of life is a discipline. A devotion. And it requires courage and strength of will. The art of radical self-responsibility requires great repetition and practice to take complete ownership of your life and your experience of all that you perceive in your life. With this practice, you will begin to navigate the difference between how life's external experiences are perceived and how you let them impact you, and the degree of impact you allow.

As with all conditioning and programming, people are strictly taught to blame others when they feel bad. A scant number of people are taught that negative emotions are theirs to own, keep, or eliminate. But when a person is intentional and positive with their chosen interpretations of the world and other people, we indeed experience a diabolically different world than our negative counterparts.

The truest application of radical self-responsibility is to claim one hundred percent ownership of your *experience* of life. This understanding, and then increasing practice, is a monumentally abundant gift.

Remember first-grade Shawn, who had accepted that she was stupid?

I first began applying this fresh idea by recognizing how often my own wretched inner voice of self-loathing had become second nature.

Shawn, you are stupid (dumb, idiot, worthless, lazy, fat, ugly, etc.).

I believed and built permanence to this well-practiced, accidental voice with great conviction all the way into my late twenties when it slowly began to dissolve, then gained great traction over the next twenty years.

Serendipitously, I began to discover the idea that practice makes *permanent* right around the time I learned that perhaps I had a different dominant learning style and *type* of intelligence than others.

I learned to recontextualize this haphazard practice by adopting a new practice, which is the epitome of radical self-responsibility. This enabled me to start reclaiming my personal divine inner power! In this, I found the courage to seek actual truth and trade old ingrained thought patterns of victimhood and powerlessness (dumb, idiot, worthless, lazy, fat, ugly, etc.) for empowerment. The truth was (and is) that I am most naturally a kinesthetic and auditory learner, whereas, during my grade-school years, most schools taught predominantly to visual learning styles.

I had been unconsciously and innocently conditioned, but, rather than continue to blame and play the victim, I chose to take radical self-responsibility for that programming and make an empowered change, which led to dozens of powerful changes.

This is what it means to take radical self-responsibility.

How you practice perceiving the world is an available choice in each and every moment. This is where your intentional or accidental practice comes into play.

How you practice life and how you respond, perceive, react, interact, and behave are all choices (though they may not feel like it when first working to make different choices).

You can choose to recognize any trigger, take responsibility for negative emotions, adjust the "practice, payoff, and recontextualization" to serve you (or the greater good), and promote a loving environment and emotional balance. You can choose any story or thought, one that births compassion and kindness and leads with self-honor.

For example, you could notice yourself becoming "triggered into upset" by a driver who accidentally cuts you off and then chooses to take one of two mental and emotional paths: 1) "That person is a reckless maniac—he is trying to kill me." Or 2) "This driver must be very distracted—perhaps a loved one is in the hospital, and they are in a hurry to get there, or perhaps they were fired from their job and are distraught."

The latter will encourage you to extend compassion and lead to loving thoughts toward yourself: "I remember last week when I did not see a person in my blind spot and nearly got into an accident. It was a scary mistake, but I am not an idiot, and neither is this person."

Is radical self-responsibility starting to make sense? And can you see how radical self-responsibility connects with the lessons you have learned from previous chapters?

In an instant, resentment, loneliness, or aggression can swiftly turn into compassion, care, or patience when radical self-responsibility is applied.

Like Melinda's example, many couples build resentment just by being haphazard, careless, or negative in their perceptions and allowing devastating, even false, stories to run rampant once a negative emotion has sprung into action. When negative emotions and stories are permitted to emerge, like bandits in the night, the sacred space couples (or any relationship, even the one with yourself) so deeply desire is stolen in an instant. Sadly, what is stolen can take hours, days, or even weeks or months to reclaim, and over time it becomes increasingly difficult to reclaim.

Are you catching on to this delicious way of shifting from looking for reasons to be offended and blame others and feel rotten into a more loving and peaceful practice? You can remove blame and other issues that accidentally attack the sacredness of your relationships. Recontextualizing a story that is harmful to one that is loving, or even benign, can easily be the difference between a relationship that heals and grows and one that comes to a close. After all, relationships rarely dissolve because of a lack of love but more commonly from a lack of taking radical self-responsibility for one's own emotions and perceptions. Negative perceptions are the fast track to not only the end of a given relationship but also ongoing unhappiness and discontent.

In the examples above about drivers and relationships (or any common upsetting situation), you get to choose your reality. You get to choose a story that allows for feeling good, transcending the negative, and living in peace and love.

Your emotions heavily influence the ways in which you perceive your current *reality* in all facets of life. For example, if you are a person who is easily aggravated by others' perceived mistakes, impatience and anger were likely modeled in your home, and you, too, learned to practice impatience and anger. You learned to judge others for making mistakes instead of viewing mistakes as benign errors that need compassion or correction and are nothing but experiences to learn from in order to support a more joyful future. Most errors need to have no real impact on you or your emotional wellbeing—they can simply be viewed as errors. Sprinkle on some self-love and compassion, grab the needed lesson, and move on with little or no upset at all.

Having this kind of impatience and judgment modeled often leads to other internal battles like perfectionism or self-criticism. Or even extreme self-loathing, as well as disbelief in one's self and others' worthiness and lovability. Be mindful that this does not give you permission to throw your parents or other loved ones under the bus for modeling unwanted or negative habits. ALL people do their best. ALL people get programmed. **ALL people are responsible for their own divine healing journey.**

Here's the thing about every single human's journey: it is perfect for what we each need to learn in order to become an increasingly healed and loving version of ourselves. Personally, I would not change a single moment in my life, even the super grueling shit. Each moment (including perceived past abuse and trauma) has shaped the woman I have become, and I am proud of her—I love her deeply, and I invite you to adopt the same ideology. It is a loving, peaceful space that illuminates what it means to live for love.

In a nutshell, no one has the ability to *make you* feel anything. There must be a pre-existing negative experience, thought, or emotion in order for you to feel bad. Instead of people *making you feel*, you actually agree to feel negatively based on pre-existing situations and limiting beliefs and drama stories that have been programmed, conditioned, and practiced.

Remember how I used to believe I was stupid? Because of this belief, I had the ability to turn just about any situation into a perceived attack on how I already viewed my intelligence, which was never the truth about my actual intelligence or potential. Take, for example, "man-splaining." If a dude was explaining something in his natural way, I would make up some version of a story that assumed he thought I was "too dumb to comprehend." This was my story, coupled with his unique way of describing something, which coincidentally is how my darling husband naturally explains things. Do you see how easy it was for me to become triggered in situations like this? Before I understood this concept, Chris and I used to have many arguments. I was very skilled at manufacturing interpretations to align with my limiting belief. Of course, once this piece was recontextualized and I learned to embrace my beautiful brain, I could simply accept the natural way Chris communicated, and the arguments completely stopped.

Over time, I learned to take radical self-responsibility and recontextualize the words in my head and the feelings in my heart. I created new beliefs and perceptions, ones that supported mental, emotional, and spiritual well-being, the life I wanted to create, and the delicious relationships I wanted to experience.

Remember, all thoughts are merely stories that are derived from memories, conditioning, socialization, past programming, manufactured interpretations, perceptions, opinions, gossip, and judgments. So, if you are going to make up a story or fabricate an

interpretation or perception, it might as well be one that feels oh-so-good!

Can you see how recontextualizing thoughts and stories and taking radical self-responsibility shifts an experience from a negative and potentially painful experience to a positive and productive one?

Over time, people learn to experience negative emotions and pack them into bags to lug around instead of letting them go or recontextualizing a given situation to view it as GOOD or at least neutral.

Because each individual has numerous emotional sandbags and therefore limiting beliefs and practiced ways of filtering and reacting to information, we are, at all times, locked and loaded, ready to dive head first into a given negative, painful experience. I had a client who perceived essentially everyone as "looking at her with a scowl or judgment." When she learned to recontextualize, she changed the narrative to "People look at me because my energy is kind and it feels magnetic and because I am pretty!" This is powerful stuff!

Here is one more example.

If I spent enough time with you, I could locate a source of pain, fear, or insecurity that currently resides inside your heart, thinking, and emotional body. I might say, "Ohh, gross. Your green hair is ugly." And if you have blonde hair, you might just think I am color blind or strange, but you would not likely become offended or hurt. If I said, "Whoa, you have a big ole' booty," and you have tiny little buns, you might think I have a skewed perception of rear ends. But what if you are self-conscious of your rear end, regardless of its size? Then how might you perceive that statement? Or, what if you have a gorgeous, luscious booty, but you always wanted a small one? Then, might you become upset, angry, or hurt and want to lash out or shut down?

The truth for me is that I love luscious booties. I see them as fabulous and sexy. So if I had said, "Whoa, you have a big ole' booty," while crass perhaps, it would indeed be a high compliment. Based on *your* personal self-beliefs and interpretation, your story could be quite a different story, right?

If you were to engage in radical self-responsibility, you would feel the initial triggered feelings and then choose to love and support yourself no matter what others do or say. Or, you might have compassion for a person who says crass things and just does not seem to get social graces. Or, you might say, "Thanks, I do have a great booty, don't I!" You get the idea!

Each person can be triggered at the drop of a hat. Regardless of others' intentions or even their words, for that matter, the negative sandbags we carry are ready to be unleashed, even if we have to manufacture an interpretation to justify the lashing out.

A great way to become happier in life, love, and career is to dig deep into radical self-responsibility and own your limiting beliefs and insecurities. Then, you can recontextualize the messages that come into your ears or the thoughts in your own mind and set them to that which creates inner joy.

To reiterate this super important point, thoughts and perceptions are mostly made up of untrue stories anyway, all rooted in emotional sandbags we carry. So if we are going to make up a story, it might as well be fun, playful, loving, supportive, or helpful!

"But, What About People Who Are Intentionally 'Mean' Shawn?"

You might be wondering about those who *seem* to bend toward intentional meanness or cruelty. Do you need to be loving and recontextualize your perceptions of those who appear intentionally mean, nasty, or cruel? You may be thinking, "Shawn, surely being angry or upset at *these* people is appropriate or justified, right?"

Is it, though?

Or have you just been conditioned to believe and act according to this belief system? Perhaps you have packed a sandbag that carries the belief that "it's justified to be angry, and therefore it's okay in this situation." As a result, you have become practiced at viewing certain things in certain ways, simultaneously justifying your own negative behavior in some cases.

Is it right to behave nastily to those who act mean or lash out first? After all, didn't your mother teach you "not to fight fire with fire" or that "you draw more bees with honey" or "the Golden Rule is to treat others how you would like to be treated?"

And, is it not true that those who seem hardest to love likely need the most of it?

Just because you have practiced something your whole life or just because you learned an idea, belief, or way of being in the world from a loved one, this does not mean that it serves you now. It just means "it" is a practice that was programmed at some point in the past, and you can give it up or trade it in anytime!

Why would you want to choose the experience of acting and feeling nasty, icky, or mean simply because another person did it first? It is not even logical—you are the one who has to experience your own icky behavior. You are always free to opt-out of a relationship that is abusive or harmful—this IS a self-loving choice for sure. But, until you make that decision, you get to practice taking radical self-responsibility.

A truly great thing to remember that has served me all of my life is something my mother taught me when I was a little girl. I came home from school one day, telling her how a boy pushed me off of a really big snow pile. I was hopping mad, I had my feelings hurt, I was embarrassed, and I had a skinned-up hand. And Mom replied with the most masterful response. She said, "Sweetie, I'm so sorry that happened to you. And that was not right or kind. But it might be helpful to remember this: You never know what a child has endured in their life, and everyone deserves love. You don't have to be friends, but I hope you can find some love for this boy."

How powerful is that?

And while I did not heed my mother's beautiful wisdom until much later in life, these are words to live by. My mother has always understood living for love. She is the embodiment of this lesson.

You never know what a person has endured that has brought them to where they are today. And it is true that "those who are hardest to love need the most of it." This quote is from the book *Peaceful Warrior* by Dan Millman.

Everyone has deep-rooted hurt, insecurity, and pain—EVERYONE. Some people figure out a path to healing, while others do not. Still, *everyone* is doing their very best in each moment with the tools, awareness, and wisdom they have in each moment.

Serial killers, for example, have a dominant history of not being held, nurtured, or loved as an infant. This lack of bonding is thought to drastically and negatively change how an infant's brain develops. This is the mark of a sociopath. What might have been a wonderful person under different conditions turned out to be a murderer through no "fault" of his own.

The argument could be made that *he* should know better now.

Obviously not. When people know better, they actually do better. When one heals, their approach to life transforms, and one begins to do better for others.

So when we back out of situations as extreme as, say, a serial killer and consider almost any other situation, we can successfully recontextualize and add understanding, acceptance, or wisdom to a situation so we can more easily soften and practice radical self-responsibility in virtually every experience.

Of course, I am not suggesting that people should not face consequences—in fact, consequences are imperative, natural, and necessary for making forward movement. The point is you have the power and choice to view anything in any way at any time. This is an empowerment skill to practice.

If there are people in your life whom you genuinely believe act in ways that are intentionally hurtful (barring abuse of any kind, which is never okay and is grounds for terminating a relationship immediately), and you have sound evidence (not simply negative emotions or skewed perceptions), you might try one or both of the following paths.

First, begin to practice recontextualizing or reframing information, words, or experiences related to interacting with these persons. This way, you can become less and less personally affected by their words or actions. This is a gift in and of itself. In other words, give people a break. Give your fellow humans the benefit of the doubt.

Secondly, you might want to deeply consider why you spend time with a person you truly believe is intentionally trying to harm, hurt, or offend you or others. You can set boundaries—boundaries are loving and often necessary. If you are not setting boundaries, you might want to ask why not? Do you not feel deserving of unconditionally loving or protecting yourself? Do you believe you deserve to receive hurt or harm? Do you believe you are not lovable and therefore seek out unloving situations? These are valuable ideas to consider.

We'll talk more about boundaries and other self-loving skills in a later chapter, but for now, maybe a bit of journaling could be helpful. It is a great choice to love everyone, yet, spending time with others is also a choice and a lesson in self-honor. Love does not mean you put yourself in situations that do not feel good or self-honoring. You are beautifully free to set any boundaries that support and honor your beautiful spirit, including terminating a relationship or job.

Take Loving Action!

Let us look at a few questions as you begin to navigate a path toward radical self-responsibility and continue shrinking negative emotional experiences with new practices.

1) Which negative emotions seem to be your largest and most prevalent (anger, grief, pride, apathy, guilt, worry, resentment, sadness)?

2) What is one area where you seem to consistently become triggered into upset and/or lashing out? Something that really gets you going every time?

3) What do you do when this situation arises?

4) What would it mean to be radically self-responsible in this situation?

5) How can you recontextualize this scenario to create a positive outlook so you can practice a new feeling, thought, and outcome?

6) What are two areas where you already take responsibility and ownership in your life?

In a pinch, a shortcut can simply be shifting out of blame. Anytime you are upset about anything, there IS blame. When you remove blame, your life will diabolically change. This is one of the main strategies (shifting blame to radical self-responsibility) that has allowed Chris and me to have experienced four-plus years of zero conflict in our marriage. Because without blame, it is impossible to fight!

Great job! As you eliminate one negative experience by taking radical self-responsibility and recontextualizing how you experience this situation, feel free to go back to these questions and systematically eliminate as many triggers as you like—this is a great pathway to living in unimaginable joy and peace. While taking radical self-responsibility is simple, it is not easy when you first begin practicing, so give yourself a high five and lots of compassion and grace for messing up as you make your way toward mastery.

Key Takeaways

-   Radical self-responsibility means that you and only you are one hundred percent responsible for your experience of life.
-   You can choose emotional freedom as you practice radical self-responsibility.
-   The art of radical self-responsibility requires great repetition and practice to take complete ownership of your life and your experience of all that you perceive in your life.
-   How you practice perceiving the world is an available choice in each and every moment. How you practice life and how you respond, perceive, react, interact, and behave are all choices.
-   Your emotions heavily influence the ways in which you perceive your current *reality* in all facets of life.
-   No one has the ability to make you feel anything. Instead of people *making you feel*, you actually agree to feel negatively based on pre-existing situations and limiting beliefs and drama stories that have been programmed, conditioned, and practiced.
-   All thoughts are merely stories that are derived from memories, conditioning, socialization, past programming, manufactured interpretations, perceptions, opinions, gossip, and judgments.
-   Everyone is doing their very best in each moment with the tools, awareness, and wisdom they have in each moment.

CHAPTER 5

Selling Yourself Out

"Oh, perfectionism!
How do you taunt thee?
Let me count the ways...."

This is a playful yet serious quote from one of my 2001 journals.

Self-sellout occurs when you choose anything over self-honor practices as well as honoring others. Self-sellout is the opposite of living for love. Gossip, for example, is a tool that young girls are conditioned to use to cultivate a sense of belonging, yet it is only a practice of selling out yourself and others.

Learning to sell out oneself is all too common for women. Young women are socialized to cater to the needs of others and to be pretty, thin, and compliant. But rarely are young women socialized to be authentically self-supportive or self-honoring. Women are taught to serve but not to speak their minds in loving ways, to set boundaries, or to ask boldly and confidently to have their needs and wants met. In the absence of self-honor, self-sellout strategies take root instead.

I vividly remember my grandfather saying, "Young ladies are to be seen, not heard," and even as a very young girl, maybe six or seven, this statement used to fill me with rage! Alas, this is when selling ourselves out begins. We learn to play small, to make ourselves small, and to shrink and cower instead of being our whole, divine, and authentic selves.

Of course, these are not the only things that little girls are taught. In some ways and in some homes, we are also taught to be tough and not to take crap from anyone. But in the end, these contradictory messages are confusing and leave women too often behaving and thinking in strict polarities of good or bad, right or wrong, success or failure, perfect or unworthy. For example, selfless service through love (not as an obligation) is a complement to strength and boldness, not its absence.

This confusion can lead to being overly boisterous and controlling in some situations and too meek, quiet, and avoidant in other situations. Balance can become non-existent in all facets of life.

In the end, this dichotomy of self-sellout is a soul-sucking way to exist and is a breeding ground for anxiety, fear, chronic worry, hurry sickness, stress, exhaustion, manic thinking, and generally feeling like a heap of flaming poo!

The Problem: Perfectionism

Before you can understand what it means to trade self-sellout habits for self-honor, so you can learn to focus, be wildly productive, let go of frustration and seething resentment, and feel truly free, content, and happy, you must first comprehend the role that perfectionism plays in your life and how you want to handle perfectionism moving forward.

Why?

Because people believe that perfectionism is helpful and useful and wear it as a badge of honor. When in reality, perfectionism is the jewel of self-sellout—which makes it the first and most harmful self-sellout strategy we're going to discuss. We will address how to weed out perfectionism and uplevel to skills that truly make your life and heart soar.

Perfectionism is an interesting and alluring concept to most, but it is too often chased, promoted, and glorified. It is accompanied by its full-time party buddies— pride, anger, resentment, and frustration. Most notably and most damaging, it is accompanied by shame. Where perfectionism lies, shame stands firmly as its mate. Be sure to understand this piece: perfectionism and shame are a mated pair. They are inseparable. So the next time you give a giggle and say something that begins with, "I'm just a perfectionist...." I know that you are also saying, "I feel ashamed because I believe I am not enough and may never be."

Make no mistake. Perfectionism will use you up like a tattered rag until you are exhausted, sick, depressed, depleted, and waking up every morning with a sickly pit of anxiety in your stomach. Yet, even when you are completely and utterly exhausted, sick, anxious, and depleted, you try and try again to be, do, get, have, and force perfection and the illusion of productivity to which you so tightly tie your perceived value and worthiness.

First and foremost, perfectionism is a maladaptive coping strategy, which is just a fancy way of explaining that it is a learned way to cope with experiences from childhood that one does not know how to navigate in a healthy way. To be clear, perfectionism is NEVER healthy. It is no different than substance abuse, chronic rumination, binge eating, anxious avoidance, overworking, blame, emotional numbing, or paralyzing procrastination.

In fact, Brené Brown punctuates this point beautifully when she states in *The Gifts of Imperfection* that "understanding the difference between healthy striving and perfectionism is critical to laying down the shield and picking up your life. Perfectionism hampers success. It's often a path to depression, anxiety, addiction, and life paralysis."

Yes, perfectionism does show up as addictive. It hosts distinct obsessive qualities as well. It is like perfectionism comes with its own engine, driving you forward, no matter what the emotional, mental, physical, or spiritual cost is to you or the people in your life. Yet, it is true that the emotional fallout associated with perfectionism is extensive and intense. Along with an overarching effort to mitigate experiencing shame, blame, and judgment, perfectionists are easily triggered because they live on the edge of exhaustion and frustration—essentially, any little thing can serve to nudge you right off the emotional cliff and into the pits of despair, anxiety, loneliness, anger, depression, or a manic state of trying to do and accomplish more to make up for a perceived failure.

Yet, when it comes to perfectionism, people are inclined to boast and wave their perfectionism flag like it is a positive thing like I used to do. However, if you were an addict, you would be doing everything you could to stop (or at least hide it). Perfectionism is incredibly detrimental.

The downfall of perfectionism is twofold. First, perfectionism embodies impossible standards and expectations that taunt the recipient almost constantly, which makes it impossible to live without its other partner in crime: constant and often covert anger. The anger might not be felt or acted on in every moment and oftentimes is denied altogether. But it is ready to be triggered or unleashed at any moment. This unleashing can be displayed in nearly any form: impatience, frustration, yelling, door slamming, shaming, criticizing, irritation, pet peeves, and more. And the denial of the anger that stems from perfectionism looks like hovering, micro-managing, criticism masquerading as "helpful feedback," binge eating or other escapes, self-deprecation, and the like.

This brings us to the second downfall of perfectionism: a person can never feel whole or peaceful, or joyful under the rule of perfectionism. Please absorb and feel the full weight of that statement. As long as you are practicing perfectionism, you can never feel whole or at peace. Yikes, right?! Pleasure is sometimes available, but genuine inner joy and happiness are not.

Striving for strict perfection goes hand in hand with pressure, shame, and a myriad of "shoulds," making peaceful day-to-day living impossible. It steals the inner peace that is your birthright. While perfectionism might just get you some *socially acceptable* success, it robs you of emotional and relationship success.

Why? Because perfectionism is a constantly demanding tyrant, echoing sharply "more," "better," "faster," and worst of all, "You're never enough." This tyrannical voice is constantly lurking in the halls of the mind, ready to pop out from any and every corner to remind you just how small you are. Alongside this message is an underpinning voice that says, "You will be worthless until you are perfect."

What is soul-crushing about the perfection quest is that it is a completely empty and depleting endeavor. Even if you believe perfectionism has helped you succeed or accomplish wonderful things in the past, it has harmed you far more because it promotes a complete intolerance of simply being human, which encourages harsh and cruel criticism and judgment of yourself, loved ones, and even strangers.

In truth, you cannot prove your worth. You simply are worthy.

The quest for perfection is filled to the brim with loneliness, fear, worry, anger, and strife from business to the bedroom. Perfectionism keeps your guard up and your armor on, making vulnerability impossible. This often means that you never really let your guard down, let others in, let others help and support you (no matter how much you complain about wanting support), nor does the perfectionist let herself need or depend on anyone fully. Not letting others in is justified by the voice that claims, "No one will do it the way I do," "No one is competent," or "Other people are idiots."

Yet, perfectionism, due to chronic impatience, rarely takes the time to kindly and lovingly ask or train others to do what needs to be done, or make space for others to do things, god-forbid, another way other than yours! Perfectionists just become angry and lament how they "have to do everything themselves," all the while making zero space for others to help or support them in ways that feel good to them. "My way or the highway" is the dictum of the perfectionist and acts as a significant source for others in the perfectionist's life to also feel like they are not good enough or can never measure up.

Perfectionism is defeating and self-destructive simply because one is striving for something that already exists in all things and all people at all times. The rest is a dedicated quest for the fictitious Loch Ness monster! So, what is being chased is, in every possible way, an illusion, thus setting yourself up for a continuous cascade of disappointment, drama, and upset.

An example is wanting to have a "perfect" body. But what does that mean? Why isn't your body perfect now? How are you defining a perfect body? And is your idealized version of a perfect body even remotely attainable? Starting in my young teens, into my thirties, and even a bit into my forties, I, too, wanted a perfect body. However, my idealized "perfect body" was a long, lanky yogi-type body. Um, news flash, I am five foot three inches tall! I am an ex-gymnast. This is apples and oranges. I was never going to be long and lanky! I had set up a vision that could only bring me heartache and an ongoing sense of failure. And so it goes with perfectionism—a consistent set-up-to-fail dynamic in one way or another. Most of the time, wanting a perfect body in and of itself leads to chronic dieting, binging, self-reproach, and boatload after boatload of shame, guilt, fear, and frustration.

Let us take a pulse on where you currently land on your beliefs about perfectionism. Do you currently believe that perfectionism is a blessing or a curse? A help or a hindrance? Deeply self-honoring or self-sabotaging?

A Recovering Perfectionist

I grew up with a tribe of strong, perfectionistic warrior women—my dear mother, fiery red-headed grandmother, and two amazing aunts—who all had powerful influences on me, especially as the only girl in my generation! Learning all facets of perfectionism was certainly a trained skill.

In addition to being total rockstars, these warrior women were fiercely independent (i.e., perfectionists). For example, "I don't need a man for anything" was a sentiment I would hear quite frequently.

As a result, I also learned to be fiercely independent. I bought the story that I should not need ANYONE, not even my husband.

As I've shared previously, I was an adorable little gymnast from six to nineteen. If you do not know much about gymnastics, it is one of the top five sports created, seemingly specifically, for temperaments who are drawn to all things requiring extreme "perfection."

Ahhh, I did love this about gymnastics.

I loved every juicy detail—the precision of each movement, the power and strength that my little body could generate, and the fact that there were multiple things to correct in a single arm movement. From my fingertips to the tips of my toes and every bit in between, I was provided dozens of opportunities to be "just perfect." And then, of course, there are the literal hundreds of moments in a single day to judge, criticize, abuse, and condemn each and every little bit that was "imperfect."

Yet, even with all the abuse, gymnastics was my one safe haven in many ways. And the gym was my sanctuary. It was also a palace of pain and suffering. I thrived on those intricate details, and because I am naturally attuned to small nuances and tiny details, I was very good at nitpicking, a gift on a few occasions but mostly a curse.

The majority of the time I spent as a gymnast was spent horrifically abusing myself mentally, emotionally, spiritually, and physically because "it" (or I) was rarely *perfect* enough. But what was enough? What would have been enough? Of course, I had no idea. I didn't have a measuring stick by which to accurately measure the level of perfection (or not)—I just lived in a constant mental state that echoed "not good enough" or "*never enough.*"

A soul-sickening way to live...never...enough...

In the early years with Chris and me, perfectionism got in the way of my ability to be vulnerable, allow myself to need my husband, and stay connected. This took a great toll on our marriage. It took quite some time to figure out the actual role perfectionism played. There were numerous versions of the "I have to be perfect" story, but the basic scenario went something like this: I would be working on something on my computer, say learning to use new software or changing things on the website. All of a sudden, I would get stuck and not know how to move forward. I would ask Chris in a very angry tone for help, and because he has always been unconditionally loving, he would stop what he was doing (if he could) and help me figure out a solution. Though sometimes, all I had to do was huff and puff a few frustrated grunts, and Chris would "magically" pop over to see if I needed help (or rescue me?!). One old payoff from the anger that stemmed from the frustration of perfectionism (and the voice that said, "You worthless idiot, why can't you just figure this out on your own?") was control and getting what I wanted without ever having to be brave or vulnerable and ask for it with grace, patience, and love. Yes, the inner workings of the mind and ego are snazzy little manipulators.

Instead of being vulnerable (which I had no concept of at the time) and allowing myself to need people, I simply recycled the defense mechanisms and emotional weapons I had seen play out during my childhood.

Chris is extremely skilled and natural in all things technology, which is a gift that highlights our unique blend of gifts and has strengthened both of our businesses! But in those days, because I was not perfectly skilled in the ways he was, I felt inferior, not enough, and—a bummer of bummers—envy, which breeds additional anger, resentment, and not-enoughness. When the anger and frustration would swell up, I would ask him for help, but simultaneously be mad at him for being "better" than me and use these situations as excuses to pick fights, pout, and punish (which was a self-punishment for not being, yep, you guessed, perfect enough!). Once a flare-up happened, I would dish out the silent treatment for a bit, and then in an hour (or several), we would "move on."

This vein of perfectionism made sure there were always flare-ups between Chris and me and that consistent emotional safety, vulnerability, and connection were impossible.

Outside of my gymnast days and my relationship with Chris, I was a practiced superstar in perfectionism—I carried it into every other facet of my life as I grew up and into adulthood. So much so that if I did not think I would shine brightly at something, I would not even try. On top of that, I had an intensely low tolerance for mistakes and frustration before I fell off the proverbial ledge into either extreme anger and self-hate or depression.

I used to constantly strive to have the perfect figure, perfect personality, perfect humor, be the perfect wife, have the perfect career, be the perfect amount of intelligence, and anything else I could conceive of needing to be perfect in or with.

Chasing this particular mythical unicorn enveloped my life for way too many lonely, exhausting, frustrating, and self-honor-free years. In my efforts to be perfect, I accumulated a lot of habits and strategies for attempting to live up to my unrealistic expectations and win the approval of others.

The truth is perfectionism IS a curse. An illusion. A mythical Pegasus hunted with extreme, all-consuming, and exhausting discipline that dangles a "happiness just ahead" sign but is, in fact, a destination that never actually materializes. It is a waterless desert, a barren pear tree, and an emptying of the spirit.

Am I painting a vivid enough picture?

I am now a *recovering perfectionist.* I hope you will be soon as well. Laying down perfectionism is not easy. The retired perfection tyrant inside sometimes still hops up off the bench to challenge my resolve, and tell me I am not good enough, productive enough, successful enough, loving enough, meditating enough, spiritual enough, kind enough, doing enough, and worst, loving enough—or any other "enough" insecurity the mind can dig up to prey upon. Most of the time, I see through the ego's feeble facade and give her a giggle, sprinkle on a little self-love, and a "thank you, but no thank you" to this demeaning voice. Once "she" (the voice of demanding perfectionism) finds that her efforts are futile, she quickly scurries back to the bench.

As she soon will for you too.

Again, you are already perfect. You have absolutely nothing to prove.

The Solution: From Perfectionism to Excellence

Perfectionism can seem a bit tricky to release. Unlike substance abuse (to use or not to use), recovering from perfectionism seems less black and white. If you are an alcoholic, you understand that you need to stop drinking altogether to recover. But with perfectionism, it is not as simple as never thinking again, although that might be a wonderful mental and emotional vacation! So how does one begin letting go of perfectionism? Like everything else, you begin by defining practices you want to stop and others you are ready to adopt.

To truly break up with perfectionism, you will need to trade it for excellence. In a nutshell, the woman who adopts excellence learns to become fiercely courageous, loving and inviting, nimble and resilient, boldly vulnerable, and can and will achieve far more than the perfectionist could ever dream.

As we look at shifting from perfectionism to excellence, let's begin by supporting you in getting clear and aware of your perfectionism triggers. Here is a list of signs you can keep an eye out for to help you recognize perfectionism, as it wears many guises. Perfectionists usually recognize the following as common practices:

- In a constant battle to succeed, for fear of being "just average"
- A disdain for achieving average results
- Near hatred for needing or asking for help
- Feeling like "I can do it better (faster) myself, so what's the point of asking"
- Easily irritated by or judgmental of people who appear lazy or slow
- People rarely measure up to your "impossible" standards or expectations

- Often feel disappointed by people, including family, friends, children, employees, or workmates
- A preference for doing projects on your own, for fear of others doing them wrong, slowly, or not your way
- A strong fear of looking incompetent and/or disappointing others
- A "never quite good enough" feeling looms like a dark cloud
- A lot of unnecessary time is spent (wasted) on projects so that everything is beyond perfect
- Your home has to be perfect for the company, and you exhaust yourself trying to make it perfect
- Scared for your kids to not be successful, for fear of being labeled a bad parent, thus constant pressure for kids to be perfect as well
- A difficult time starting or finishing projects for fear of it not being perfect or good enough
- A habit of pointing out others' mistakes or imperfections (projection of own insecurities)
- Frequently either late or very early
- Depressed over perceived failures, which can take quite a while to bounce back from, but are always in the back of your mind
- Consistent anxiety or overwhelm at "all there is to accomplish"

Are any of these or similar ideas hitting home with you? At first glance, how might you shift or flip each bullet from perfectionism to excellence?

For example:

- "I loathe the idea of being average," turns into, "I am always doing my best, even when I have doubts."

- "People rarely measure up to my 'impossible' standards and expectations," which turns into, "I practice giving grace to all people, and it's okay for others to work at their pace and in their unique ways."

Are you getting the hang of how to flip the script from perfectionism to excellence and also how this is a beautiful, fresh way to live for love?

Perfectionism is a time-consuming, exhausting, and frustrating plight. Practicing perfectionism can easily add ten, fifteen, or more hours of unnecessary time and mental and emotional distraction to all types of projects while creating opportunities for endless (and typically unnecessary) to-dos.

And lemme guess—you probably wish you had more time and energy, right?

Well, trading perfectionism for excellence is more than a fair trade. There are only rewards and no negative consequences.

Excellence provides space for you to break up with a lot of life's drama. It provides space for deep authenticity, humility, and increasing levels of integrity, vulnerability, and self-honor habits. Excellence breeds calm and freedom, whereas perfectionism is aligned with high stress, chronic busyness, overwhelm, and frustration. Emotionally, releasing perfectionism feels like releasing a boat anchor!

Excellence means focusing at a high level, in the moment, on value-driven initiatives and doing so without fear. Excellence is about living without being haunted by the past or fearing the future. Excellence includes making concrete, tangible goals that define "enough-ness" while simultaneously surrendering goals and aspirations that are not aligned with purpose and deep fulfillment. And knowing you ARE worthy and innately *perfect* whether you meet goals or not. Excellence is devoid of comparison and competition. It embraces teamwork, collaboration, unity, and harmony without using emotional weapons or other methods of control or negative manipulation to reach any objective, be it anything from business to the bedroom.

For so many, practicing anything but perfectionism seems like a terrible failure. Women believe that without it, they would become total slackers. Likewise, most of the high-level, rockstar female entrepreneurs, executives, and professionals I work with have one common fear: "What if I become lazy and lose my edge?"

Seriously, gang, this is impossible for you—have you met yourself?!

Your personality could not be "lazy" if your life depended upon it!

And anyway, who cares? It is your life. You get one spin around this planet, and if it is not a grand party of joy, connection, contribution, love, and fulfillment, then what is the point? No one lays on their deathbed wishing they had spent more time folding the towels exactly perfectly or shaming their husband or kids for not folding the towels exactly perfectly, right? But you might get to your deathbed wishing you had spent less time on these frivolous details and MORE time just loving and playing with the people in your life.

So, here is the real question: if you can get more accomplished, at a higher level and in less time, without the grueling impact of perfectionism, would you do it? Would you be willing to part with tyrannical perfectionism? And to the earlier point about fearing being lazy, less successful, or losing your edge, would it matter if you slowed down a few times a week if you are getting better results? Would it be worth it?

"Lazy" and "relaxation" are often swear words to a perfectionist. But you win no trophies for being the most stressed or being so tapped out that you have no energy to play (actually play, not just watch) with your children, nor is there a prize for having a heart attack by age fifty. Here's the thing. You may think these are bad words, but I would be willing to bet some of your goals in life ARE to slow down, have more peace and quiet, lay in a hammock and read a book without feeling like you should be doing something else, and to enjoy life more, right?

Shedding perfectionism and embracing excellence is your new Yoda.

At one point along my evolution of releasing perfectionism and adopting excellence as a way of life, I began sharing vulnerability with Chris and would say, "Honey, I'm getting close to the edge of the emotional cliff." This became a new and positive trigger for stopping everything and resetting in some way, like going for a walk, snuggling one of our pups, asking for a hug, repeating a mantra or affirmation, sitting in a surrender meditation, or whatever I needed in the moment to let go of the perfection drive and allow myself to recontextualize and recalibrate. This was not only an excellence-driven practice, but it helped in raising vulnerability and connection between Chris and myself. Instead of picking a fight, projecting something onto Chris, or finding a way to blame him, I leaned into radical courage and simply shared my heart.

Setting up goals and habits that lead you toward excellence may require a change in the way you say things. For instance, instead of saying, "I want a perfect body," you might say statements like, "I love this body no matter what its shape," "I would like to weigh one hundred and thirty pounds and will create SMART goals to get there," "I feel great when I have at least one salad each day, so I will make that a habit for breakfast," or, "It feels so great to dance, so I will create the habit of turning on my favorite music around three o'clock each day for a fifteen-minute dance party! That will recharge my battery and be a ton of fun!"

Do you see how excellence begins to unfold in VERY tangible but emotional, physical, spiritual, and time-freeing ways? Eating a salad each day and dancing for fifteen minutes because it is joyful and nurturing feels truly great and not at all like the emotional prison perfectionism mandates. The perfectionist says, "If I don't work out for at least an hour, it's just a waste of time. I'll never burn enough calories, so what's the point?" Excellence practices expand and grow as you expand and grow. In six months, you can add five to ten minutes to your dance party or add a leisurely walk to the end of the day. And since you will be reclaiming a ton of energy as you trade perfectionism for excellence, you might just feel like running a marathon!

Client Case Study: Rachael

Rachael is a partner in and helped build a wildly successful law firm.

She used to brag about being the first to arrive and the last to leave. She spent dinners with her family on the phone, answering emails, and feigning listening to her daughter and husband's day. There were just so many things that "had to be done."

Rachael was driven by the engine of perfection. More, bigger, better, faster was the name of her life's game.

That was, however, until she was diagnosed with breast cancer at the sweet young age of thirty-seven. As she stated, "I was in the prime of my life, and the world was my oyster!"

This was a wake-up call of epic proportions. She hired me the day after she began treatment.

During our first call, she expressed panic in every direction—it was like she was about to explode. Her brain and heart were melting. She knew that with chemotherapy, she would have to slow down (even though a part of her believed she'd be the first to simply work right through cancer treatment like a champion, without ever missing a beat, a true perfectionist!).

She began our first conversation with, "Shawn, I have so many responsibilities, I can't slow down. What about my clients, what about my forty-eight staff members, what about the business, and sales, and marketing?"

Then her voice trailed off, and tears began to flow. "What if I die, and all my family remembers me for is how much I worked and ignored them? Shawn, I don't want to die with that legacy hanging over my head."

Yep, a lump in my throat formed right along with her out of pure love and compassion. Yet, an overwhelming joy took over me just as quickly. Why? Because I knew this was her rock bottom. I knew she had just hopped on the train to ditch perfectionism and embrace the grace and power of excellence.

Letting Go of Not-Enough-Ness

We have discussed "not-enough-ness" several times now. Obviously a term I made up! I started using it with clients many years ago, and it just kind of stuck. Not-enough-ness is a tried and true companion of perfectionism and the instigator of deep emotional turmoil. It can easily and consistently elicit guilt, shame, anger, and fear, often in succession or simultaneously. Perfectionism is not the only instigator of these painful emotions, but it is a serious repeat offender! Perfectionism is a collection of practices and a belief system that propagates negative emotions and negative experiences with wild consistency. Until you start removing perfectionism, embrace balance, growth, and expansion, and specifically begin developing excellence, you will continue to be somewhat blind to the many consequences perfectionism has on your well-being, health, finances, and relationship with those you care for—including the relationship with yourself.

The essence of not-enoughness is sometimes easier to see or access than perfectionism itself. It can also be more emotionally accessible in your desire to eliminate it.

For example, you might not be ready to relinquish perfectionism and its many payoffs, especially the payoffs that seem fruitful, but if you think about the idea of wanting to remove the feelings of not-enough-ness, anger, shame, guilt, and fear, you are likely to buy in quicker and get faster traction. So, if removing perfectionism seems difficult, you can start by letting go of all the pieces that are attached to not-enoughness.

Let us look at this idea in action!

I speak with both stay-at-home moms and working-outside-the-home moms who seldom feel "good enough" as a mom. They feel like they are NOT present enough, patient enough, engaged enough, strict enough, feeding the kids healthfully enough, showing up enough, connecting enough, and so on. The false *excuses* women come up with to *view* themselves as "not enough" are prolific. Instead, a more joyful and excellence-driven way to experience motherhood is to begin by seeing yourself in the light of the truth–you are pure perfection AND a gorgeous slice of divine artwork that is in progress for a lifetime. Women have a tendency to look at what is wrong and problematic when the joy is actually in looking for what is wonderful. This is where we can choose to fix our sights and practice seeing the goodness. Can you see the not-enoughness that is always tied to perfectionism? Perfectionism says, "If I were a perfect mom, I would do better, get things done faster, cook healthier, feel more energetic, and connect with my kids with more love and patience."

But the truth is when perfectionism is given up, mommies (or business owners, executives, or anyone in between) have a huge amount of extra time and energy that they can joyfully share with loved ones. Again, this is the power of excellence over perfectionism. In fact, one of the first things I do with new clients is to spend the first thirty days teaching them to, fairly effortlessly, reclaim an amazing twenty hours per week! Feel free to reach out (drhaywood@reimaginelove.com) if you would enjoy reclaiming twenty hours every week too!

The first thing to note with the mom example above is how vague the perfectionistic striving is and how implicitly unattainable it is. If we turn our eye toward excellence and reframe any situation while adding some version of very specific and attainable SMART goals, we find it much easier to set ourselves up to feel like we are winning daily, which is a must if you want to be happy.

If you as a mom or wife (or dad/husband) want to be more available, then the necessary goals might entail things like finding ways to work a shorter workday, productivity hacks, or hiring an assistant a few hours each week to free up some time and energy. Recontextualizing with concrete planning and execution moves you quickly from chasing unicorns to pragmatic action that supports self-honor, joyful emotional well-being, business objectives, and family or love life.

Next, you might look at systems for meal prep and meal planning. What goals can you set up here? Maybe you begin by simply purchasing healthier snacks. Then, prepping one or two healthy meals on Sunday before the week begins—or even creating Taco Tuesday where dad and the kids make the same darn thing every single Tuesday. This will take two to three weekly dinners off your plate instantly! Again, this is what it means to be excellence-driven, to ask for support, and to put great systems in place to support your entire life.

Client Case Study: Penny

Penny is a truly extraordinary businesswoman. She can build and sell companies with the best of them. From software to advertising, Penny is a business wizard!

The most interesting thing about Penny's brand of perfectionism was how successful she is but how utterly chaotic her life was when she and I first began coaching together. I mean, she was building and selling off many multi-million dollar companies without ever creating the first strategic plan! Wow, right!? What an amazing brain she has.

Are you waiting for the but?

But her lack of planning and systems and a strong propensity for super perfectionism set her up to work an average of ninety to one hundred hours per week—every week!

What in the actual hell!?

Thankfully, Penny had a very patient husband. He wanted her to live her dream. But they frequently fought about the lack of intimacy, connection, and time together.

Penny, in her perfectionism practices, liked to "keep everything in her head," do things on her own, and would become very frustrated when she did need help because no one did it like her.

Over the years of becoming a business building and selling maven, Penny began to experience failing health. She was stressed and exhausted most of the time. And then she found out that she had Crohn's disease (a fairly common and treatable autoimmune disease). This was the nail in the coffin—Penny was finally ready to slow down and enjoy some of the success she had experienced and accumulated financially.

So, we got to work! A simple but very specific strategic plan that guided each month, week, and day of the next twelve-month cycle was our jumping-off point. Next, a thirty-day sprint was dedicated to creating systems, eliminating non-essentials, and delegation! Penny got to learn the joyous gift that, no, in fact, no one does things like her (or like any owner), but when you give people a chance and hire the right people, they often do it better! Soon, she reclaimed her first twenty hours per week. And if you can believe it, within six months, Penny was working just six hours a day. From hundred-hour weeks to just twenty-four. AND her company had become even more profitable. Penny was capable of anything (just like you).

Of course, her darling husband was thrilled beyond belief and thought a miracle had occurred, which of course, it had: the miracle of transforming one's inner self—and the journey from releasing perfectionism and engaging an excellence-driven, heart-centered, living for love kinda life. Penny and her husband felt like newlyweds: playing, laughing, dating, going on weekend adventures on a whim, and spending long afternoons reading or making love or just snuggling in the bed for hours watching movies—things that Penny had never allowed herself to do previously because that was "what lazy slackers did."

What a powerful example of loosening the reins on perfectionism, giving up old limiting beliefs, and realizing that you ARE more than good enough, no matter how many hours you work!

Other Self-Sellout Strategies

Self-sellout strategies are ways people dishonor themselves and inevitably end up feeling resentful, angry, and bitter. Every time you engage in self-sellout, you go against the nature of your heart and begin to resent yourself due to your own self-abandonment. Self-sellout is often rooted in perfectionism because in striving for the "perfect" self, you reject and say "no" to your true self again and again. It is important to look at self-sellout strategies so we can identify them and replace them with acts of self-honor. Think of the following self-sellout strategies as leaves on the perfectionism tree!

- Procrastination
- Pleasing, Performing, and Proving
- Competition and Comparison
- Let's look at each of these strategies one at a time.

Procrastination

Procrastination is the art of delaying or postponing something you need or want to do. And sometimes, we become masterful at this craft. But, before you roll your eyes at yourself while lamenting all the things you have procrastinated with recently and shame yourself for all that you "should" be doing, let's take a look at procrastination from a fresh perspective.

Procrastination serves as a gorgeous excuse people use to browbeat themselves into a complete puddle of guilt and shame, which they somehow think will "motivate" them to do more, better, faster, bigger (remember this from the life of the perfectionist?). Yet, procrastination is just another way to sell yourself out (i.e., withhold self-honor). Interestingly, people procrastinate for *good* and specific reasons. The three main reasons are the following:

1) The task ahead seems overwhelming. This usually means that the task or project at hand includes numerous steps, stages, or moving parts, and you have not yet defined what the first thing is to accomplish. But once you begin defining very clearly just three simple steps or actions of the project at a time, the overwhelm and procrastination will fade bit by bit.

2) The task ahead is unfun. Well, let's be frank, no one wants to do things that are not fun! We are humans and literally built for curiosity, creativity, and PLAY!!! Therefore, motivation is

naturally low or even nonexistent when a task is not fun. Some struggle with this more than others. The solution? Find or make fun in any task. Or, if a task is really unfun but needs to be completed, make it the very first thing you do in a day. This way, you get it done when your reserves for motivation and stick-to-it-ness are fully intact.

3) The task ahead is shrouded in fear or uncertainty. If a task, project, or experience feels frightening, uncomfortable, or uncertain, our limbic system says, "No, run away. This is unsafe." And so we do. For example, if you are new at doing sales calls and feel apprehensive about it, you might try everything else possible to procrastinate or even avoid doing sales calls. But when you reassure yourself that you are safe and capable, you will begin to calm your fight, flight, freeze system and find it easier to show up for the things you want to accomplish in spite of the task feeling scary or uncertain. This is where your beautiful self-honor skills come in handy.

Sometimes all three of these procrastination spaces fold into one. That is okay! Simply focus on the strategy that is most supportive for you.

At times, these procrastination barriers might seem too high to climb over, even by using the strategies listed above.

Two great ways to lower the barrier are by practicing surrender and the "one next thing" idea.

Client Case Study: Remi

Just yesterday, I was on the phone with a client, Remi, an owner of a fantastic multiple-location massage center specializing in pre- and post-maternity care. She and I are going through the process of setting up several additional layers of business development and systems so the company can grow more effectively, efficiently, and profitably (creating a strategy, planning execution in simple and achievable ways, and eliminating the emotional barriers to the success of said plans).

On yesterday's call, we started laying the foundation for a new marketing plan. Remi began feeling overwhelmed and shared this was a trigger for procrastination—she did not trust herself to get her checklist accomplished before our next coaching session. She said she felt she needed a four-hour chunk of time to be able to act on and execute this plan. I knew right away this was the voice of the perfectionist, echoing that "the right way to be a competent business owner is to schedule large chunks of planning time to accomplish GREAT things in one fell swoop!" And while I always encourage my business clients to schedule several planning days throughout the year, executing this project did not require such a time slot. This served as a wonderful flashing red light moment to dive in and address the procrastination that was running in tandem with perfectionism.

We came up with two very helpful systems to turn procrastination into powerful action.

The first was to begin to practice the art of letting go and surrendering the emotional sensations associated with overwhelm so she could reclaim peace and inspiration anytime, anywhere. In fact, letting go has become my number one most valuable, nurturing, and healing skill for all negative emotions or experiences. Letting go is a natural part of spiritual and emotional evolution and liberation. It is an evolving skill that tends to grow with you. I learned this skill set from Dr. David R. Hawkins in his book *Letting Go, The Pathway To Surrender*. It is pure magic, and I highly recommend it (and all of his books, for that matter). You will learn exactly how to practice surrender and the letting go technique in a later chapter, so stay tuned.

Secondly, Remi began to apply the "one next thing" concept to mitigate overwhelm. Overwhelm says, "There is too much to do, and

I am either not equipped or cannot possibly find or make the time to do *this*," or, "*This* task is too difficult, and I just can't do it." But when you lean into the truth that there is, in fact, only "one next thing" that you can do now, you will feel instant calm. The "one next thing" technique is a super effective way to approach procrastination because, with any project or task, there is literally only one next thing you can do. For example, if you are going to put a piece of mail in the mailbox, *the one next* thing might be to get a stamp for the envelope. Then there is just one next thing, which might be placing the stamp on the envelope. Then putting your shoes on. Then picking up the envelope. Then walking to the door, and so on.

I have intentionally oversimplified this example to illustrate the power of literally ONE next thing. And when you focus solely on the small one next thing, it is impossible to fret, stress, or worry about the whole of any project or task. We can only do one thing at a time anyway, and there is only ever ONE thing to be accomplished next— and multitasking is for suckers (or perfectionists!) who like to waste time, split their attention, and pretend to do multiple things at once, which is impossible.

For Remi, the piece of her marketing plan we were working to execute was to resurrect her newsletter list, which had been cold for nearly eight years but had more than ten thousand past clients to connect with and nurture moving forward. This was a huge untapped resource that could serve as "low-hanging fruit" marketing, especially since a new location was set to open in just a couple of months.

Even though her assistant was going to be in charge of this task, she was feeling very overwhelmed simply because she did not know how to leverage the newsletter platform well enough to even explain to her assistant what to do and how to execute it!

Remi got stuck thinking about the desired results and the many steps necessary to get there: creating the template, writing new messaging that effectively reconnected with her newsletter list, worrying about people being upset that she had not been reaching out or being upset that she's reaching out now! She felt overwhelmed by not knowing exactly what to include and not to include in the newsletter, and on and on the stories went, swirling frantically around in her mind like a wild tornado!

So I asked Remi, "What is the one next thing you can do in this process?"

She gave me several responses that were tasked to do down the line, and finally, she landed on, "Schedule a meeting with my assistant to brainstorm a plan of action." We then went on to make a list of possible tasks that aligned with this project so she and her assistant could make attainable goals to execute over thirty days. As soon as Remi realized that the one and ONLY next thing she could do was to schedule a meeting, she instantly relaxed. "Oh," she said joyfully, "there is only one next thing to do. And then there will be just 'one next thing' after that." Relief took root quickly—Remi loved this mental model tool. She engaged excellence, and the all too familiar procrastination that has plagued certain areas of her life dwindled into nothing.

Overwhelm-related procrastination happens because we are running a thousand things around in the mind instead of asking the question, "What is the ONE thing I can do next?" This is a fantastically simple solution to help you navigate your day with calmness and to mitigate procrastination. Oh, and these skills work for any kind of emotional overwhelm, whether in running a business or structuring a day with your family or planning to renovate your home. This is a skill I use very frequently, as I had previously been a professional perfectionist, trying to do a thousand things at once, which always led me to overwhelm and high-stress and inevitably trickled down to being frustrated and snippy to those I loved dearly—not a winning combination!

Pleasing, Performing & Proving

Pleasing, performing, and proving are amazingly sneaky ways to sell yourself out, and the three often work in tandem. This is an area that can still trip me up at times. For example, if I am spending time with a group of people whom I feel I do not have much in common with, I might not know how to make conversation easily. Instead of joyfully leaning into silence (which greatly improved as I began surrendering the limiting belief that "silence is uncomfortable"), I might begin pleasing and performing. Why? Because the perfectionist in me wanted to prove my worthiness, to be liked and adored, and to fit in.

Yep, this is a surefire way to sell yourself out!

The truth is, I have become kind of a weirdo. Well, I have always been kind of a weirdo—just a different kind nowadays! Rather than have conversations centered on gossip and judgment, I enjoy leaning into juicy and deep conversations about spirituality. This can be a turn-off for some people.

However, in some moments, if I feel uncomfortable with silence and feel driven to "take up talking space" (ugh), I just might begin to babble on about nothing interesting or say negative things that I will in no way feel proud of later. I might slide in a judgy remark, agree with gossip, or complain about things that I seriously have no negative emotions about but know that others do, so I chime in to avoid sticking out like a sore thumb (double ugh!). Most of the time, when others are gossiping, judging, complaining, and so on, I simply reframe the situation from a place of love and acceptance, stare blankly until they feel awkward enough to discontinue the trajectory they were on, stand up and go do something else, or simply move the conversation in a different direction.

But...on occasion, and essentially only when spending time with family (a trigger that has yet to be fully surrendered and therefore eliminated), that old pleasing and performing programming sneaks up and grabs me, and I hop on the self-sellout train and go for a wild, icky ride! This inevitably leads to additional time spent in surrender meditations to eliminate the guilt and shame that surfaced as a consequence of getting on that damn train!

You see, it is just not worth selling yourself out!

Pleasing, performing, and proving are deep-rooted hurt-heart issues. We all want to feel as though we belong and fit into a community of like-minded people. For me, I spent most of my formative years feeling as though I did not fit in, so it became very easy for me to practice trying to be perfect while pleasing, performing, and attempting to prove myself worthy of fitting in, selling myself out in any way I thought might allow me to feel accepted.

Little did I know then that acceptance can only come from within. The thing is, I was never going to feel accepted until I accepted myself and committed to deep and disciplined self-honor. You must fully belong to yourself first and foremost. Nothing we want to feel exists outside of us. God is within. Therefore, so are all tools for accessing healing.

Performing rarely exists in a vacuum, and it goes hand in hand with pleasing and proving. It might look a little different at times, however. Performing usually looks like trying too hard or showing off to gain attention and acceptance. Ugh, I cringe at this one. As I think back to the Shawn of old, I think about what a complete mess I must have appeared to be! While I am naturally silly, outrageous, goofy, playful, and sassy, I used to take these natural tendencies way over the edge on a regular basis. I cannot say I never fall prey to this sellout skill now, but it is rare these days. During my formative years, I experienced several forms of abuse—sexual, physical, mental, and emotional. Abuse is the thief of innocence and serves as the root of much, if not most, mental and emotional dysfunction.

So as you might imagine, I learned to have and practice seriously low self-esteem and depleted self-worth. As such, I used to sell myself out for any kind of attention that gave the illusion of being valuable and worthy.

And while performing as a gymnast was a positive outlet, the same could not be said by my getting drunk on the weekends beginning at the age of twelve so I could be cool, act outrageous, and do my best to show off by out-drinking the dudes.

It is important to look at behaviors that feel good and have juicy payoffs in the moment but are merely an empty attempt at filling a bottomless emotional cup, which inevitably ends in more feelings of shame, guilt, and not-enoughness.

As you can see, pleasing, proving, and performing ignite the inner perfectionist, urging her on and echoing, "You will be loved, you will be worthy, you will be valuable, you will be accepted, you will finally belong if you sell yourself out by pleasing, performing, and proving yourself."

Competition & Comparison

This facet of perfectionism is like a sneaky sorcerer! After all, isn't competition healthy? And how could we live without comparison?

Competition and comparison are essentially the same, and neither usually do anyone any favors.

Competition shows up in many guises, such as the emotional weapon of "right-fighting," where you might be trying to win an argument instead of simply accepting that there are two (or more) different vantage points or perceptions. Competition in sports can lead team members and fans alike to temporarily lose their facilities and get into yelling or physical fights. Taking pride in something is not the same as selling yourself out for the sake of winning.

Comparing is still a competition, yet with a bit of a different tone. It is strictly related to not-enoughness and used to leverage superiority or inferiority.

For example, I have a traditional ex-gymnast body. Five-foot-three, broad-ish shoulders, large-ish thighs, and still pretty darn fit! Yet, for years, I would see the "traditional" yoga body—long, lean, tall, slender—and would compare myself and always come out as, you guessed it, not enough. Not tall enough, not slender enough, arms and legs too short and thick, and so on. My version of the "perfect" body was a complete impossibility. I mean, seriously, I have heard of late-onset puberty and growth spurts, but I was in my twenties and thirties at this time, so I likely was not going to grow several inches, nor was my body type going to change that drastically.

Additionally, I would feel jealous and often feel a low level of depression as a result of comparing myself in ways that were impossible to attain.

Are you seeing how selling yourself out is so darn easy?

Yikes!

It always comes back to living for love. Loving yourself, loving your body, loving your uniqueness, loving the whole of the gift that you are.

Take Loving Action!

Okay, my friends, it is time to take specific action to reclaim yourself, eliminate perfectionism, and put a stop to selling yourself out!

1) Begin by identifying your key self-sellout strategies and the negative or painful feelings that accompany them. Write this list down so it is crystal clear. Feel free to refer back to the list at the beginning of this chapter.

2) Next, what are the heart-centered, vulnerable reasons why you sell yourself out? Do you practice perfectionism because you desperately want to belong, to feel good enough, to be accepted, or to feel accomplished and successful?

Remember, there is ABSOLUTELY NOTHING external that can fill your emotional cup. This is an inside job. This is why the skills of perfectionism practice end up feeling so lonely and exhausting and then set to repeat.

3) Lastly, what are you willing to do to reclaim yourself? Are you willing to become aware of when you are procrastinating, comparing, proving, or pleasing, then give yourself some gorgeous love and compassion? Or perhaps begin catching yourself in the act of emotional overwhelm and apply the "one next thing" concept or surrender? Maybe you need better systems and a solid, step-by-step plan for execution. Or perhaps you will dedicate yourself to looking for feelings of not-enoughness and begin to uproot the perfectionism that is behind this lie.

Key Takeaways

- Self-sellout occurs when you choose anything over self-honor practices and honoring others.
- The truth is, you are perfect and in progress.
- It's easy to believe that perfectionism is helpful and useful and to want to wear it as a badge of honor. But perfectionism is the jewel of self-sellout.
- Perfectionism is NEVER healthy. It is no different than substance abuse, chronic rumination, binge eating, anxious avoidance, overworking, blame, emotional numbing, or procrastination.
- Those who adopt excellence learn to become fiercely courageous, loving and inviting, nimble and resilient, boldly vulnerable, and can and will achieve far more than the perfectionist could ever dream of.
- Excellence provides space for you to break up with a lot of life's drama. It provides space for deep authenticity, humility, and increasing levels of integrity, vulnerability, and self-honor habits. Excellence breeds calm and freedom.
- Two great ways to shift out of procrastination are by practicing surrender and the "one next thing" idea.
- Pleasing, performing, and proving are deep-rooted hurt-heart issues. We all want to feel as though we belong and fit into a community of like-minded people.

CHAPTER 6

Roots Of Negative Emotions

As I've stated previously, the roots of our emotions and mental habits begin and are shaped by the people who raise us. Children are essentially parrots with unique biological and genetic tendencies. Thus, children are essentially programmed to feel, think, and behave as their family members do.

The emotions and feelings that you experience thousands of times each day are rooted in a primitive place. The patterns and practices of how you think, feel, emote, respond, and react are, in large part, wired and determined by and during your formative years—and this is done so by the conditioning or programming you received, observed, or absorbed from family, friends, television, teachers, and any other influence that had an opportunity to impact you. Yes, of course, your brain, DNA, and karmic propensities play their roles, but for the sake of this discussion, the emphasis will be on conditioning and programming, as this is what you have the most power to change.

You learn to think, feel, and respond (or react), in large part, from your family unit, close extended family, and your friends. Essentially, the influences and voices that were viewed as valuable had the most impact on you.

Being "programmed" simply means that, consciously or unconsciously, you have adopted a belief by which to run your life, of which there are thousands. Your beliefs consist of some ideas that are true, some ideas that are false, and others that are benign. But all are operative in your life. You can examine any positive or negative result, consequence, or experience in your life and reverse engineer it to locate the belief that leads you to the thoughts and feelings that produced those results, consequences, and experiences. In this way, you can capitalize on what is going well and, therefore, desirable and begin to change the beliefs that are leading to negative circumstances.

A child or adult can be programmed anywhere, anytime, by even a single word, phrase, or sentence. Remember little Shawnie, who took on the belief that she was, in fact, "stupid" based on a single moment in time when a cruel teacher laughed at her? This is a great example of being programmed and then living for decades with a seriously limiting belief and the feelings and emotional reactions that stemmed from this programmed belief. I felt ashamed of my intelligence and devastatingly guilty for not being "smart."

This is what it means to be rooted in negative emotions that stem from past programming or conditioning.

Here's another example: think of something that you REALLY wanted to have as a kid. Where did that idea come from? From the first moment I saw the commercial for an Easy-Bake Oven, I was programmed and had to have it. I just knew it would change my life—ahem—as a six-year-old girl! I was relentless with my mom until the day it arrived as a truly great Christmas gift!

This is how the brain gets stuck on things or where desires are rooted. How would you ever know that you want a new car, or that Reese's peanut butter cups are the best candy, or that a Cabbage Patch doll was the only one worth having, or that men are supposed to open car doors for women if they are a true gentleman, or... or.... or... anything else you believe in!

Literally, every single thing you think or believe has been programmed from somewhere, which is kind of awesome because now you can begin taking stock of what you want to keep, what you want to change, and what you want to delete!

There are certainly temperamental, societal, and cultural influences on you as well, but the primary influence and predictor of emotional well-being is rooted in the years you spent with your "growing up tribe" (i.e., those who were or acted as your immediate and extended caretakers and family) because they are the ones who laid the foundation for who you have become.

In essence, the dominant feelings and emotional patterns you experience and express today were formed as a child or teen.

For many generations, my parents and extended family continued to program one another to experience, think, and react with frequent and varied levels of the following negative emotions: frustration, anger, fear, impatience, pridefulness, resentment, jealousy, depression, and anxiety. These emotions were all programmed to be presented in specific ways and situations.

I used to be excellent at unleashing, reacting, and feeling from these negative emotional roots. No doubt, you also have similar types of "family heirlooms" you have become practiced at engaging, expressing, projecting, denying, or suppressing.

For example, I used to behave in a judgmental and impatient way while standing in line to check out. I would tap my foot quickly as a signal to "hurry the hell up" and give several very audible sighs while rolling my eyes, just as my mother did.

The most unfortunate thing about all the ways in which people have been programmed is that they rarely stop to consider that they can change it. At some point, I decided that I would be unconditionally loving as I stood in line to check out. That I would smile and open my heart and even let others go ahead of me if they seemed impatient in some way. This new, self-selected, and intentional program is SO much more enjoyable!

The bottom line is, each person arrives at early adulthood and beyond with numerous beliefs, behaviors, perceptions, and habits, and they are accompanied by all things positive, negative, or benign. Each program hosts accompanying thoughts and drama stories, beliefs or limiting beliefs, judgments or opinions, defense mechanisms and emotional weapons, or vulnerability, trauma, and care. This complex collection of inner workings folds together into a myriad of true or skewed, faulty, and false perceptions that play out in every possible experience you have or create.

Emotional Sandbags

Along the way to adulthood, you were taught to fill emotional sandbags (a concept we will discuss shortly) and then *hurl* them at others, yourself, God, the world, or any situation where you feel provoked. These sandbags of learned and programmed negativity—and their accompanying stories, practices, defense mechanisms, or emotional weapons—continue to be practiced as adults, thus keeping old negative emotional roots and unpleasant experiences and patterns alive and active.

Usually, when one experiences a negative emotion like anger, anxiety, fear, or loneliness, they believe or perhaps interpret that the negative emotional experience was born from the **current experience** or situation at hand and was "caused" by something external or outside themselves.

This is untrue.

Negative emotions are directly tied to and a result of past programming, experiences, trauma, socialization, and conditioning and are not caused by a current situation. For example, if a driver accidentally cuts you off, and you become angry and mumble something like, "Look at that idiot, he's trying to kill me," you are inclined to think that you have become angry "because" of the other driver's actions. On the contrary, your angry reaction was a consequence of learning road anger from witnessing the demonstration of impatience and anger as a family norm, thus taking on this habit of "trigger–practice–payoff" when you experience situations that mimic what you saw and experienced growing up. Additionally, you have multiple belief systems regarding anger and judgment folded together with driving.

Simply put, you are not angry toward the other driver—you were simply taught to execute this dramatic pattern, just as your loved ones did and did not know you could stop. You have mistakenly believed that this pattern was actually about the "other driver" when it's really about your programming.

These ideas can be challenging new truths to get on board with initially, but you will soon accept them, and when you do, you will be far happier for it!

Here is a recap of the necessary shift in your understanding of the roots of negative emotions in order for you to more efficiently and effectively become empowered to change your experience of life pertaining to anything perceived as difficult, negative, or upsetting:

1. Negative emotions and emotional patterns are conditioned and programmed as we develop and mature.
2. Negative emotions are expressed when an experience mimics where and how the negative pattern and concurrent belief systems were first learned.
3. Each conditioned, learned, or unconsciously programmed negative experience is akin to adding sand to a proverbial

sandbag that you tote around as an adult and either learn to empty (which is ideal) or manage (less ideal).

4. Negative emotions can be triggered in an instant but are not caused by the situations at hand.

Let us visit the driving example again. A car pulls out in front of you. You get irritated or hostile, perhaps grumbling, cursing, or even flipping the bird to the unsuspecting driver. The common but limiting belief looks like this:

"That pisses me off! That jackass tried to kill us. What an idiot! He should have his driver's license revoked."

In this example, the root of the negative emotions is an anger sandbag. You learned to be angry and offended as others modeled this to you or as you overheard situations like this as a young passenger or perhaps from the television. Another programming that is expressed in this kind of situation is a sandbag of judgment (i.e., name-calling like jackass, idiot).

If you did not have these programmed responses, you might have responded from a loving place, saying something like, "Oh my goodness, I hope that person is okay. I wonder if he had an argument with his wife this morning and is so distracted that he is having trouble driving. I think I'll say a prayer for his safety."

You see, both scenarios are made-up stories—one born of old limiting beliefs and negative sandbags, the other born of love and compassion (for yourself and others). The choice of what story to align with is always up to you.

The sandbag/feeling that popped open when triggered was anger and perhaps pridefulness, resentment, and/or fear. The story was that of a personal and intentional attack. The payoff was righteous indignation. And a possible recontextualization of this situation is concern and compassion for the driver's well-being.

Manage Verses Eliminate Emotional Sandbags

It is important to note that sandbags can be either managed, which is rooted in most traditional psychotherapy modalities, or emptied, which is marked by specific spiritual teachings and coaching modalities.

It is a rare human who reaches full enlightenment and is able to cut the emotional sandbag tethers altogether. But anyone can empty them. When a sandbag is emptying and then empty, negative emotions become increasingly rare experiences and soon recede as quickly as a wave in the sea when they do arise.

When negative emotions are experienced, and you feel inclined to attribute them to current situations like a friend's tone, a partner's reaction, traffic, not having someone to spend Saturday night with, a situation with your boss, or even occurrences like binge eating, not feeling like a priority to a loved one, and the like, you have misrepresented yourself, the "offender," and the emotions. The negative emotion is already present (like the Loch Ness monster that lies just beneath the surface, ready to snatch you up and drag you down at any moment) and is triggered in the moment but is not created or caused in the moment.

It's like when Iron Man asks the Incredible Hulk what his secret is, and he responds by saying, "My secret is, I'm always angry." When we have full sandbags, the negative emotions are always there, present, and easy to reach, lying in wait for the next trigger to have a reason to express the unpleasant feeling.

Thus, not only are you misrepresenting these experiences, but the negative emotions are reinforced and perpetuated by accompanying thoughts, drama stories, and emotions.

The truth, rather, is that your sandbag has been triggered. Because you have dragged that sandbag around into adulthood with you, you have practiced certain negative emotions and reactions related to specific types of situations for many years, even decades, and are practiced at responding in specific negative ways and with specific negative emotions.

A more joyful and intentional strategy is to learn to poke a metaphorical hole in each sandbag so the sand can begin to leak out. And at some point, you can empty each sandbag completely. I will share more on how to accomplish that in a later chapter, but for now, it is important to know the role that sandbags play in your life.

Let me give you an example of how this has shown up for me.

When Chris and I first started dating, we were great at letting our sandbags cannonball into one another. Often, I would perceive (make up a story) that Chris was not helpful enough around the house. Never mind the fact that I almost never asked for the help and support I wanted—and if I did, it was with a resentful and sarcastic tone that oozed out after I was already triggered and spitting various sandbags of upset at him (*blush*).

This group of sandbags stemmed from well-worn paths; they were learned, conditioned, and programmed with very deep roots. I learned patterns of anger, blame, and control as it related to romantic relationships, though the old versions of these patterns more closely mimicked addiction rather than genuine, *unconditional* love. When I became triggered in this way, Chris would unleash his most easily accessible sandbags and learned patterns of submissiveness, emotional shutdown, over-trying and pleasing, and the corresponding emotional sandbags of fear of conflict, rejection, and abandonment.

One day I got upset with Chris because he was sitting at his computer while I was packing our bags to go on a hike. The anger sandbag I carried at that time was starting to spring open like a bag of microwave popcorn because of my perceived story about him "not caring about me and not wanting to help me because I was not important enough to him." (Can you hear the payoffs of self-pity and martyrdom?) Normally, when I became upset and began huffing and puffing and dramatically stuffing things into our backpack, this would trigger Chris to literally spring up and ask how he could help me and then proceed to try very, very hard to be helpful and sweet as an effort to turn things around before I *completely fell off the emotional cliff!*

This situation, however, played out differently. Chris had recently been learning about boundaries while working with his coach. So instead of scurrying about and then waiting on me to go for a hike, he walked out the door and went on a hike without me. He refused to put up with our old patterns. At first, I felt the pain of the triggered sandbags of my own rejection, abandonment, and betrayal. Yet, this situation woke me up big time, and I chose to surrender (a practice I had already begun to learn to engage in).

I knew, the same as Chris, that I no longer wanted to blame, argue, or fight. We wanted a truly unconditionally loving partnership. This opened the door for us to eventually eliminate conflict completely, take one hundred percent radical self-responsibility, and practice unbridled truth-telling and vulnerability instead. It opened doors to beautiful connection, and partnership as each of us took ownership of our sandbags and emptied the sand from them and now live inside of a harmonious, conflict-free, blame-free, unconditionally loving relationship.

This is why today, Chris and I do not argue, fight, or have conflict in our relationship. We understand that any and all negative emotions are a consequence of our OWN sandbags and can only be solved by personal action and surrendering of the internal negativity. Any other perspective is that of blame and an abdication of personal responsibility. As such, we have simply reprogrammed and reconditioned our chosen practices toward truth, unconditional love and care, deep vulnerability, and service.

Taking ownership of each and every emotion is a direct path to happiness. In this way, you elicit well-being from within instead of seeking outside of yourself that which can only be discovered and embraced within.

I cannot say this path has always been easy—certainly not. In fact, at first, I was so entrenched in the sandbags and roots of negative emotions that I was not sure achieving this level of love and peace was possible at all. I often felt that, even though I knew the truth of the roots of negative emotions, somehow, others were still responsible for how I felt. This concept behaves like an odd paradox at first. But then, as you settle into this fresh understanding, it is quite empowering. To know that nothing external can control you, your emotions, your experience of life...well, there is nothing like it. And to further know that you are one with all things and all people and that our human struggles are one and the same is quite comforting and allows for grace and compassion to grow and extend to all, no matter the circumstances. This is what it is to love unconditionally and to live for love.

Here is another example of how this might show up for you.

Let's imagine that currently, you are quick to experience hurt feelings—or more commonly characterized as having your feelings hurt easily by others.

Perhaps, then, you arrived at adulthood with a sandbag of hurt feelings or oversensitivity, betrayal, or abandonment. That collection of sandbags then has the capacity to trigger sadness, resentment, or blame easily. There were likely dozens of experiences you witnessed or encountered growing up that mimicked the ways in which you feel hurt today. Feeling hurt or offended by others' words or actions was likely modeled for you by close family members or friends or even on television shows. Perhaps your mother modeled feeling hurt when your father did not come home at the time she perceived was the "right" time, or maybe he did not pick up his things off the floor after showering, and your mother had a story that he must not care about her or else he would clean up after himself, or maybe your father was sensitive and had his feelings hurt easily when your mother did not give him praise or complements in the ways or frequency he wanted.

You see, there are innumerable stories that we learn to tell to justify all means of upset.

Own Your Happiness

Parental or caregiver modeling teaches us not only how to fill negative emotional sandbags but also that others are responsible for those sandbags and, therefore, our happiness. Individual happiness is so very personal and divine, yet we give it away like free condoms at a health fair. Because of this modeling, you learned how to be triggered by the same or similar situations or experiences and play them out today.

Your brain has become wired to think A+B=C. In this case, "A" represents a parent, "B" represents the situation that is blamed, and "C" represents hurt (or other negative) feelings. In your home, ideas like this were learned and taught as "truths," meaning that they would be universally true among all people, families, and situations. Yet, in my home, this A-B-C "truth" did not equate to hurt–it equaled anger. I was taught that this was the truth. So, for example, my mom was late very frequently; I learned from the rest of the family that when mom was late, we were supposed to be mad and offended and give out silent treatments, yelling, or frustration for this "crime."

So, if both are taught as universal truths, which one is accurate? Should we be angry or hurt at lateness? Should we be resentful or hurt when clothes are left on the floor?

I would suggest D, none of the above. In fact, why would anyone in their right mind interpret a habit of lateness as something to be hurt or angry about? In fact, another person's lateness has nothing to do with anyone but the person being late. I would challenge you to examine your sandbags and their accompanying beliefs and practices from a broader perspective and with an open heart.

In reality, the real truth is that dad probably just had stuff to do and forgot to pick up his clothes, or maybe clothes on the floor did not bother him. Acts like this are usually benign. Maybe he was under a lot of stress at work in trying to provide for his family, and getting home on time meant he might lose his job or did not make enough money, or he felt valued at work in ways he did not experience elsewhere, making work a strong value. This kind of recontextualizing is an invaluable practice in creating internal peace and happiness. If you are going to tell yourself a story, it might as well be contextualized as something that feels good instead of upsetting.

In your situation, and mine, the problem stems not from the actual lateness or clothing on the floor, but from a person choosing to *interpret* the lateness and clothing on the floor as offensive, hurtful, anger-inducing, and so on.

The *choice* to feel hurt came from mom's sandbag of hurt (or anger, or other sandbags). And she learned from her family to interpret the situation as hurtful based only on other or similar fabricated stories and beliefs. Thus, it got passed on to you, and you now have the choice to pass it on or to powerfully transform and transcend.

Interestingly, when Chris and I began dating, he was essentially always late (we are very inclined to choose romantic partners who mimic growing-up patterns). This beautiful cycle provides each of us opportunities to heal, grow, and empty sandbags together. By this time, I had learned a great deal about surrender and decided I would apply it with a full and open heart. So instead of taking Chris's lateness personally or verbally brow-beating him about the lateness, I simply surrendered. I let the lateness be his to solve or keep—whichever he chose was okay with me. I accepted him and loved him whether he was on time or not (and time is an illusion anyway!). I simply kept a book with me at all times, so when I was ready to go before Chris, I engaged in one of my favorite activities while I waited! Or, if I really wanted to be somewhere at a specific time, I simply gave Chris a loving kiss goodbye and drove myself so he could arrive when it was right for him—this actually happened a couple of times!

But wait! Here is the amazing part of this story. Within twelve months of treating Chris with one hundred percent unconditional acceptance in this particular area, treating myself as one hundred percent responsible for my own experience of life and emotions (i.e., radical self-responsibility), and letting go of any stories about taking personal offense for Chris being late, Chris stopped being late ninety-nine percent of the time.

THIS is the gift and magic of surrender and acceptance and owning your experience of life. There are thousands of examples where this principle has made space for healing in our relationship and in the lives and relationships of dozens of clients!

In truth, very few people actively or consciously try to do or say things that are intended to hurt or upset others.

Like those in your growing-up environment, most people carry unconscious, hidden, and very sneaky limiting beliefs and payoffs that are inclined to keep us stuck and maintain very full sandbags of negative emotion. This cannot shift until you decide to take radical self-responsibility for your experience of life. This includes catching yourself in stories (in unwanted negative emotions), identifying the payoffs, and being willing to surrender and recontextualize.

For me, I had the most difficult time taking radical self-responsibility, recontextualizing, and surrendering anger as it related specifically to protecting others. With the best intentions, I learned from my family (and falsely believed) that anger was *justified* if it had to do with the protection of animals, family, friends, children, or the elderly. And though many of you are likely mentally *arguing* that anger is a natural response toward grievances against animals, family, friends, children, or the elderly, I can perhaps offer a different perspective.

Ask yourself, what value does anger bring to the table? If anger (or any negative experience) inspires you to take more powerful or empowered action, then great, use it. But you could also witness unjust behavior, recontextualize it, and take loving action from the space of radical self-responsibility.

In my case, I was stuck in this particular sandbag of negative emotion because my family had a confusing relationship with protection. If family members perceived a threat toward people or animals we love, the learned behavior was to respond with anger or outrage, or promote some kind of punishment, and to say things like, "I will kill them if they..." or, "I will kick their ass if they...."

This translated to mean, in the example of A+B=C, that Protection + Anger = Love. Thus, a perceived family "truth" I learned was that in order to love or be loving toward someone or an animal, you must also wield anger and possibly aggression. But in truth, this is a prideful response that can be recontextualized. Love has no opposite. Love needs nor wants for anything. Love is complete and needs nothing to help be whole. Love stands on its only legs on solid ground. As an example of recontextualization, if you want to protect someone or something, in nearly all cases, you can simply flee (I'll share an example of this shortly).

Are you beginning to see how the negative sandbags of emotion fill up over time? Do you see how family *truths* are often actually the unconscious practice of limiting and untrue beliefs and behaviors that have been mimicked for generations?

Anyone can and will find ample justifications and excuses for negative emotions and outbursts in daily life, should they be looking for them.

Because of this "family lesson," I used to haphazardly practice envisioning what I would do to someone if they hurt someone I loved or my dog. I would envision, for lack of classier terminology, coming at them like a spider monkey and kicking their ass! Then one glorious day, while I was asking the Divine for the truth about why I had been having so much seeming difficulty surrendering this particular vein of anger (especially since I had been dedicated to peace and love for years by this point), the truth hit me like a ton of bricks. It was quite simple (as all paths to increased joy and love are), actually. In the end, I needed to recontextualize and uncouple my "real self" from the two concepts—love and anger. If someone were trying to hurt my dog, I could simply pick her up and run away. I could act as a shield as best as I could at the moment. This would be a loving action. And on top of this, I learned that these kinds of unloving, violent mental visions were perfectly orchestrated by ego/mind/small self to perpetuate "unlove" within me. The crafty ego will find any possible inlet to maintain a stronghold.

This beautiful moment then encouraged a powerful dissection of any and all thoughts connected to negativity. I decided to begin combing through three-plus decades of beliefs, experiences, trauma, abuse, and the like and reframe them to include ONLY LOVE.

Of course, this is amazingly simple. But here is the thing. Even when you are consciously dedicated to changing your life for the better, old limiting beliefs tend to be quite sticky. Programming runs deep, and the ego/mind/small self is a crafty enforcer of the "status quo." I believed that punishment was part of love. It is not. I now have the gift of understanding that punishment is never appropriate and is not of love under any conditions. Punishment is always born of anger or aggression of some kind.

Another common example I see of unleashed sandbags of anger and resentment is something we have all probably encountered when driving, as I've previously mentioned. The limiting beliefs and reactions that arise when someone cuts you off, and you say to yourself or others in the car, "That car tried to run us over (kill us, etc.)." Beliefs like this can be difficult to release. It "seems" justified to practice anger under many circumstances. What this means is you hold a belief that another person knowingly and willingly tried to attack you, so it must be justified to _ _ _ _ _ (flip him off, get pissed off, swerve at him or her, etc.). And while it is possible for another human to attempt to harm or attack, the number of times this actually happens versus the number of times you think it in your head is hundreds of thousands of times to one.

Honestly, this idea is quite silly when you think about it. I mean, when was the last time *you* were driving and "tried to kill another car full of people?" In truth, all drivers are focused sometimes and distracted at other times. Drivers drive well and make mistakes.

All drivers are experiencing their own sandbags, doing their best with the tools and awareness they have in a given moment, and responding accordingly.

It is up to each individual, however, to choose to align with old programming, mistruths, and limiting beliefs to perceive an attack where none exists (like, "my husband is trying to make me miserable," or "my boss is trying to ruin my life"), or to simply understand that ALL "drivers of life" are sometimes focused and other times distracted—but usually totally focused on being the star of their own life stage! It is the epitome of narcissistic pride to continue along with any beliefs about the perceived injustices happening to you.

Just as we discussed perfectionism versus excellence, the real truth is that all people are ALL doing their very best at any given time with the tools, wisdom, and awareness they have at that moment. And even when you do not particularly like *their* best effort, it is not for you to judge—it is for you to be radically self-responsible for your own sandbags and experience of life...and to do your increasing best to live for love and look for others' goodness, share grace and forgiveness, and stop looking to be offended.

Aren't we each human? And aren't each of us perfect and in progress? With talents, gifts, strengths, weaknesses, and a variety of different programming and upbringings?

Yes, even when we are driving!

The real issue here is that when a negative emotion arises, a primitive trigger button has been pushed. For example, you may feel sad because you did not get enough time with your partner this weekend. Once triggered, your brain reaches into the bank of neurotransmitters and says, "Hey, this situation seems very familiar; it is time to react!"

The sadness or rejection emotional siren(s) goes off, and a cascade of issues pours out.

At this point, any number of behaviors, feelings, and reactions can be elicited based on what you have learned to practice over the years (shutting down, lashing out, zoning out on social media, overeating, overdrinking, etc.) and on what sandbags you are dragging around.

In addition to the negative emotion and related action(s), there is also a victim payoff, like righteous indignation, poor pitiful me, or the sweetness of perceived deserved blame, punishment (i.e., silent treatment or shaming), and anger for "him/her doing this thing *to* me."

The ego loves a good victim payoff and in fact, thrives on it. The ego will gleefully lead you astray at any and every turn possible. So, the trigger is the "event" to which you attribute blame for your emotional sandbags. The practice is the emotional reaction. The payoff is whatever ego "reward" you get for practicing the pattern.

The interesting thing about being triggered into negative emotional sandbags is that the ego-mind-body-emotion connection perceives a physical threat that then incites the "fight, flight, or freeze" reaction and practice, even when no physical threat actually exists. Unfortunately, due to the perpetual practice of carrying triggered sandbags, many, if not most, people have overactive fight, flight, and/or freeze responses.

The payoffs, in this case, are the accompanying flood of neurotransmitters and other chemicals (adrenaline, cortisol, serotonin, dopamine, endorphins, and so on) due to conditioning during perceived traumatic circumstances growing up and the filling of sandbags.

I am still working on rewiring my brain-body-spirit-emotion connection in order to calm stubborn fight-or-flight reactions that were learned and imprinted from childhood traumas. For example, if I am in bed under the covers and Chris is lying on top of the blankets, and the dogs snuggle in beside me on top of the covers and on the opposite side, I can, in an instant, well up with a sharp panic, which used to turn to rage (a now empty sandbag). As a child, I was held down and zipped up in sleeping bags as "entertainment" for family members. Acts like this create well-worn paths and sandbags in the brain-body-spirit-emotional connection and take time to empty, recontextualize, and surrender permanently.

During adulthood, in what are otherwise playful and joyful moments with my husband and dogs, the brain might, in an instant, tap into the old physical threat of being trapped under the covers, even though no threat exists. With focused practice on letting the sand out of the sandbag, this happens less frequently and with less intensity. The point is, the body's memory system and its accompanying sandbags are quick to say, "FIGHT OR RUN LIKE HELL!" Freezing has never been my thing.

It is important to note that couples often come together with differing or opposite temperaments and wounds. I am naturally passionate and as fiery as the day is long, while Chris is as steady as a mighty oak. While freezing is not my go-to reaction, freezing is Chris's go-to response when his sandbags are triggered. He was conditioned (and his temperament encourages) to emotionally shut down or freeze when triggered or feeling attacked or afraid.

Let us look at a few additional examples so this idea can become increasingly clear to you.

Think about the ways in which you might react to different people doing or saying essentially the *same* thing. For example, your partner, boss, and best friend each left a towel on the floor in the bathroom. Let's assume this usually triggers your sandbag of irritation, frustration, or even resentment when the perpetrator is your partner. So, you carry a sandbag of irritation related to a belief that partners "should pick up their towels" that you likely learned was a "universal truth" from your family unit growing up. In your case, the trigger is "towel left on the floor." One practice is "feeling irritated" due to your sandbag of irritation. The payoff is "righteous indignation" and "being the victim of your partner's crime or betrayal," thus, a secondary practice is indulging in "telling your partner off" or "withholding care."

But let us flip this. How would you respond to your friend or boss leaving a towel on the floor? Do you unleash the same wrath? Likely not. Even if there is a twinge of the irritating sandbag stringing open, you will simply pick up after your buddy or boss and probably tell yourself a different story than the one about your husband, like, "Oh, s/he just forgot." Therefore, it is not a "universal truth" that "leaving towels on the floor" has to irritate you or equate to a betrayal of some kind. The truth is, you carry a sandbag of irritation based on untrue beliefs of yesteryear.

You might have several "logical" reasons for suggesting a justification for lashing out at your partner, but not your boss. But the truth is, you have a sandbag full of anger (irritation) and another one full of resentment, and you are on the lookout for justifications and excuses for unleashing the sandbags for short-term satisfaction, release, or justification of the mental drama stories that already exist in your mind.

You may take some things more personally than others and therefore become triggered in this way or that. Then, you may deny or suppress when something has to do with a boss or friend because this, too, is how things were modeled at home. It could have just as easily been modeled that when you feel upset, you share your concern (with whoever is involved) in a calm, loving manner while asking the other person to help brainstorm a great win-win solution.

And if this is not your current habit, you can certainly shift to practice that idea anytime moving forward.

Like everyone else, you, too, are doing the best you can with the tools and awareness you have currently—and this is truly perfect. And you can shift if or when you like. No need to worry or feel bad about current sandbags; like everything else, these are just practices, and practices can be changed at any time!

To take this concept one step further, think about the dramatic stories you tell yourself about your partner leaving clothes or towels on the floor: "S/he doesn't give a crap about me," "S/he thinks I have nothing else to do but clean up after him/her," "S/he doesn't care about my feelings at all." When these dramatized thoughts come onto the scene, they are used to perpetuate the unleashing of the sandbags. Drama stories trigger more negative emotions and justify behaviors like lashing out, thus continuing the cycle of upset.

In truth, your partner is likely forgetful and absentminded, does not notice those kinds of details, or is not bothered by the same things you are. This might simply be a difference in preference. It is not right or wrong to leave or not leave the towel on the floor—it is simply a different way of looking at a particular idea or situation. Differing opinions are not something to disrupt happiness over; they are things to accept or try to understand. Situations like this need not be taken personally (even if intended to be). Yet your primitive conditioning sets you up to perceive certain things as an attack of sorts and to have specific negative emotional sandbags that are ready and looking for an outlet at all times.

In effect, the vast majority of lashing out, upset, drama, and conflict serve only as excuses to blame or justify sandbags that have sprung open and indulge the associated egoic payoffs while simultaneously keeping you stuck in painful cycles, disconnection, and lacking in emotional liberation.

So...let's get liberated from negative emotions!

Depersonalizing Negative Emotions

I like to describe negative emotions using the sandbag analogy because it helps to depersonalize emotions. Instead of saying "my loneliness," "my anxiety," or "my hurt," we can begin to say, "the sandbag of loneliness," "the sandbag of anxiety," or "the sandbag of hurt." Can you feel the difference between the simple act of changing how you describe it?

The key is to stop taking ownership of that which you do not want in your life. As soon as you use the words "my," "mine," or "I," the ego wants to take possession and keep whatever the object of "my" affection is, no matter how misery-making it might be.

A fun and wildly interesting practice is to spend two full weeks (or a lifetime!) without using the words "me," "mine," or "I." You will be surprised at the difficulty and the rise in inner peace and personal awareness!

Depersonalizing anything and everything is a monumental gift of emotional freedom. In my old life, I was trained to be very easily offended. So when I first began the journey of depersonalizing, I kept this mantram top of mind: "It is not about me." This worked for thousands of applications!

Through no real fault of your own, the "sand" in any given sandbag is simply stored up negative energy that was never released but instead was denied, suppressed, repressed, or projected onto others. But you have the power to change your experience at any moment. You can, at any time, decide to cut holes in sandbags to let any or all grains of metaphorical negative emotional sand trickle out bit by bit...

Removing Negative Emotions

Would you enjoy developing the ability to remove the vast majority of heavy negative emotions and sandbags and the negative responses, reactions, and emotional weapons that accompany them?

What if I told you that, depending on how willing you are to engage in a very simple practice, you could drastically reduce and eventually eliminate multiple layers and types of negative beliefs, perceptions, experiences, opinions, and emotions?

I am not talking about *managing* negative emotions. This is not an "emotional management" course! I mean, literally, deflate or dissolve emotions like anger, hurt, resentment, loneliness, pain, frustration, anxiety, sadness, guilt, shame, remorse, humiliation, failure, depression, and fear.

Feeling doubtful? Well, it is possible.

I have dedicated my life to spiritual evolution and, thus, to eliminate the vast majority of negative emotions and emotional states. There are plenty of people who have achieved this goal—people who are dedicated to emotional and spiritual evolution and to being abundantly happy, loving, liberated, and joyful in each moment. I can say unequivocally that it is possible to get rid of the sandbags you carry that are chocked full of negative emotions and the cascading experiences, perceptions, judgments, beliefs, opinions, behaviors, and actions that accompany each sandbag.

If I can do it, and if so many of my clients can do it, YOU can too!

You don't need to lug around any negativity if you do not want to. In a perfect emotional world, when a negative emotion arises, it would vanish quickly because a) you have so successfully learned to accept all things and all people as perfect and in progress in each moment, b) you have mastered recontextualization and come from a place of unconditional understanding, or c) negative emotions might periodically crash in like a wave, then recede just as effortlessly because they are being surrendered instantaneously.

Emotional waves may crash softly or powerfully at times, but they can still recede quickly. In this analogy, practicing allowing emotions to crash in and then letting them recede quickly is what it means to be emotionally free. This happens when you are still instead of getting on the mental bandwagon of ceaseless dramatic thoughts designed to keep the drama alive and fuel the ego/mind/small self. Because I used to live consistently in various states of negative emotion, it continues to feel like a *miracle*, and I stand in awe of experiencing negative overwhelm only on rare occasions and rebounding from them effortlessly (most of the time!).

Healing sandbags requires intention and practice. Oftentimes, the support of a professional life coach and/or a spiritual coach, along with deep spiritual practice, is needed to heal, rewire, and reprogram the body-brain-spirit connection.

I personally have worked with amazing coaches and spiritual teachers and have read hundreds of books to assist in my own healing and spiritual evolution journey over the years. It has also made an enormous favorable difference to be going through this kind of healing and spiritual transformation in tandem with my darling husband and my two best girlfriends. There is no need to go it alone—seriously, be brave and get the support you need.

Take Loving Action!

1. Grab your notebook or journal and write about how you are feeling right now. Take your time and become clear about your *current* feelings, the ones that are always there below the surface, whatever they might be—the positive and the negative.

2. Next, make an ironclad decision and commitment to do what it takes to empty your sandbags.

3. Then take a moment to create a strong visual of the metaphorical sandbags that are being carried: sadness, anger, grief, pain, frustration, confusion, fear, terror, anxiety, rage, sorrow, disappointment, greed, envy, jealousy, disgust, misery, vanity, emotional shut down/paralyzation, unforgiveness, pride, helplessness, insecurity, humiliation, embarrassment, hostility, inferiority, superiority, bewilderment, guilt, shame, loneliness, weakness, victimhood...and so on. It can be helpful to spend a few moments each day when you wake or just before you fall asleep going over the day's events, locating moments where you experienced unwanted negative emotions, "seeing" that particular sandbag, and breathing as you envision grains of emotional sand trickling out, bit by bit.

4. Now, choose one single action that you intend to practice or remain aware of that will help you cut a hole in one or more

186

sandbags so the negative emotional energy can trickle out permanently, igniting the fires of emotional liberation. For example, depersonalizing and practicing saying "it's not about me" each time you feel offended.

Key Takeaways

- The roots of our emotions and mental habits begin and are shaped by the people who raise us.
- Being programmed simply means that, consciously or unconsciously, you have adopted a belief by which to run your life.
- You can examine any positive or negative result, consequence, or experience in your life and reverse engineer it to locate the belief that leads you to the thoughts, feelings, and behaviors that produced those results, consequences, and experiences.
- Because literally every single thing you think or believe has been programmed from somewhere, you have the power to decide what you want to keep, what you want to change, and what you want to delete!
- It is important to note that sandbags can be either managed, which is rooted in most traditional psychotherapy modalities, or emptied, which is marked by specific spiritual teachings and coaching modalities.
- Through no real fault of your own, the "sand" in any given sandbag is simply stored up negative energy that was never released. But, you can, at any time, decide to cut holes in sandbags to let any or all grains of metaphorical negative emotional sand trickle out bit by bit.
- Healing sandbags requires intention and practice. Oftentimes, the support of a professional life coach and/or spiritual coach, along with deep spiritual practice, is needed to heal, rewire, and reprogram the body-brain-spirit connection.

CHAPTER 7

The Art Of Emotional Escapism

Emotional escapism is where people act consciously or unconsciously to avoid the emotion they are feeling at a given moment.

As previously discussed, taking radical self-responsibility is a key step to achieving emotional liberation and sustained happiness. But, as you might imagine, this is sometimes easier said than done and might include a lifetime of practice (or perhaps several lifetimes!). Just as we all collect sand in our sandbags along the way, we also learn to simultaneously attempt to avoid feeling the growing weight of the bags upon our backs (in other words, negative emotions, and emotional pain). Avoiding the negative emotions that often accompany life is very high up on people's unconscious "to-do" lists. However, attempting to escape from them is a fool's errand, unfortunately. If you could avoid or escape the pain in any meaningful way, then you (and everyone else) would already be sustainably joy-filled, content, peaceful, and pain-free!

Alas, each and every attempt to avoid pain simply adds negative emotional sand to the sandbags and deeply prolongs and heightens our suffering. It is important that, along with learning tools to help empty sandbags, we also learn how to let go of *resisting* them and the pain they bring. Pain comes with being a human, but suffering is a choice.

Suffering emerges and adds sand to the sandbags when one resists negative emotions. Fear arises and causes us to say, "Feeling fully will break me, so I must avoid it at all costs." Though it may seem counterintuitive at first, what truly relieves one of suffering and the buildup of emotional pain is letting go and entering into a state of surrender. Instead of allowing negative emotions to crash in like waves, feeling each one fully, and then watching them dissolve and release, people are conditioned to avoid feeling emotional pain and instead collect their painful feelings in their ever-expanding sandbags.

For some, feelings can be perceived as something so frightening, something so overwhelming and threatening, that they choose to stay stuck in their heads for fear of total collapse, fear of being truly seen by others, fear of appearing weak or vulnerable, fear of having needs or needing support, and countless other fears. **So instead of actually feeling one's feelings, people develop sneaky, deep-rooted, strategic ways to avoid feeling altogether.** In fact, there are five basic internal mechanisms discussed in this chapter that most people deploy in their efforts to avoid emotional and mental pain and, as a result, perpetuate their inner suffering. These mechanisms are thinking, numbing, unconscious avoidance, expressing (lashing out), and projection.

It is common to "want" to avoid pain or suffering, which is the main reason humans go to such creative lengths to avoid feeling at all. However, when we feel fully and learn to let go as negative experiences/thoughts/feelings arise, they softly dissipate like morning fog on an emerging sunny day. The way to stop feeling crappy so often is literally to feel things in the moment they present, then to let go of resisting the troubling or even painful feelings, and finally to surrender to and let the feelings go. To BE with and surrender to emotions in each moment as they arise is the most efficient way to dissipate them.

Once this practice is integrated into one's life, suffering is incredibly rare, and abrupt emotional pain is very short-lived—in most cases, just a few moments. This is an enormous secret to emotional liberation. And at the same time, when you learn to let go of negative emotions as they arise, you simultaneously clear the way for unbridled and consistent joy, play, peace, clear intuition, and creativity to take their place.

Why Eliminate Escapes?

Each method of escape, or attempting to avoid feeling, is also a way of abdicating radical self-responsibility instead of taking full ownership. The trick oftentimes is striving to gain an increased awareness of when you've engaged in escape mechanisms and the rewards of each payoff.

As you become increasingly practiced at taking responsibility for how you choose to experience life, including how you feel and the content of your thoughts, you will be more available and open to feeling emotions more fully, including pleasant and joyful emotions, which are usually tamped down by negative sandbags. Additionally, when you carry full sandbags, they leave very little space for feeling great, alive, energetic, and inspired. As you empty your negative emotional sandbags, you will also be able to let go of and surrender your escape habits permanently. This is a beautiful gateway to consistent emotional peace and joy.

Humans think approximately 60,000 thoughts per day. Eighty-six percent of said thoughts are destructive or negative for eighty-ish percent of the population. One overarching goal for inner growth and peace is to reduce the overall quantity and drastically improve the quality of your thoughts and, therefore, your emotions. This is possible with all of the tools you are learning, especially as you grow in awareness and become less haphazard and unconscious in your thinking.

Over time, this translates into an overabundance of peace, love, joy, amazing calm, beautiful creativity, inspiration, and a deep connection to all living things. Additionally, in the absence of unwanted thoughts, you will have thousands fewer unwanted emotions as well!

It's a win-win. The cycle of negative thoughts spurring on negative emotions and negative emotions spurring negative thoughts (chicken or the egg?!) and their corresponding escape patterns diminish with the intentional raising of consciousness and the surrendering of emotions, drama, thinking, and payoffs. Dr. David R. Hawkins says, "Ignore thoughts. They are merely endless rationalizations of negative feelings."

No truer words! If you simply observe your thoughts for a single day, you will find this to be abundantly true—and surprising. Both feelings and thoughts can be protected, nurtured, matured, and practiced in truly fruitful ways.

Feelings and thoughts work together to spontaneously curate this unfolding cascade of experience we call life. **The way you feel and think about *anything* predicts the way you will think and feel about *everything*.** This is a profound sentiment. It begs the question, what are you thinking and feeling? (This bends us back toward practice makes permanent.) And when a life experience occurs, and you do not like said experience, ask yourself, "What have I been thinking and feeling to propagate said experience?" Whether the experience is preferred or not preferred, it is a valid and helpful question to engage anytime.

Honestly, this is a huge reason I wrote this book—to help you understand that negative feelings are something you can transcend and thus eliminate, and secondly, that YOU have the power to create and experience ANYTHING you can dream up in this life, from emotions to career.

This is what it means to live liberated.

A primary goal for gaining power over your attention and feelings is to enable you to stand in emotional softness and freedom, to interrupt and stop the drama stories, to escape patterns that lead to cycles of pain and suffering, and to become increasingly present (or alert) so you can feel emotions without clinging to the negative payoffs, thus increasing emotional freedom bit, by bit, by bit.

In this chapter, you will learn to understand better the power you have over your thoughts and other escapes and defense mechanisms, how you can begin leveraging thinking and other skills you have been practicing to shift gears and support your overall goals, vision, values, divine direction, and, most of all, to enable you to live for love, from business to the bedroom!

Why Is Escape So Appealing?

Escaping, although it causes more trouble, in the end, is something we are drawn to do for a couple of reasons. First, escaping is an easy, well-worn path that you learned to take early in life. And secondly, the emotional, physical, physiological, and even spiritual payoffs are what makes escaping seemingly worth the self-sellout and self-dishonor activities that inevitably follow suit.

Escaping and numbing out to avoid painful feelings is the crux of addiction of ALL kinds. Addiction sneaks up on people. Escaping and numbing emotional (or physical) pain is engaged for the purpose of avoiding feeling. For example, using gambling to avoid the pain of financial struggles feels good and can elicit highs, just like alcohol or zoning out on social media. But at some point, it becomes a want, and then a desire, and then an all-consuming craving—an itch that cannot be scratched. Eventually, it perpetuates into a practice that is immensely difficult to stop because of the perceived comfort. In fact, feel-good neurotransmitters are released before the escape activity is even started—as you drive to the bar in anticipation of that first drink, the mood is lifted. Or, as you pick up your phone to open Facebook, your mood begins to shift. And so it can be with alcohol, drugs, spending money, food, work, exercise, sex, helicopter parenting (i.e., enabling and codependency), relationship addiction, or anything else that is done in excess or from a place of seeming as if there is "no choice."

One of the main reasons that escaping is so addictive is because of the neurochemical payoff one experiences in the escape sequence. Because feeling genuinely uncomfortable emotions may register in the brain as a "threat," the brain also may mistakenly register "escaping" as a protective mechanism. In return, a neurotransmitter called dopamine is released, which is more or less one of the main "reward" chemicals in the brain. Thus, you receive a payoff—a reward!—for escaping, and you actually do feel better for some period of time and to some degree. This is why escaping seems so appealing and why it may be difficult to release. Just as with any addiction, eventually, the brain requires more and more dopamine to feel good, safe, or secure when escaping from emotions.

This is also why the community of support groups like Alcoholics Anonymous is so advantageous. There are different, healthier payoffs that come in the form of unconditional acceptance and support. I have not experienced alcohol addiction in my life, but I have attended AA groups just to experience beautiful and unconditional support! I believe the twelve steps are for everyone. Nowadays, there is an "AA" group for just about any kind of escape you can think of, so please, if you have a desire for connection, belonging, and unconditional support and acceptance, any spiritually based group, might be a GREAT option, including AA.

Even though letting go of escape mechanisms may seem like work and requires devotion and dedication, it is also filled with the most extraordinary sense of hope.

Let us take an in-depth look at the defense mechanisms that were likely the best actual protective mechanisms you could muster as a child but now only masquerade as protective mechanisms as an adult. This way, you can be armed and ready to release the core defenses and embrace tools that allow you to empty your sandbags, permanently freeing yourself from many negative emotions and experiences.

Thinking: The Original Gateway Drug

I call thinking "the original gateway drug" because thinking is the most readily available defense mechanism and was the first line of defense against feeling when you were a child and did not necessarily have any other methods of escape or numbing out available as adults do with food, alcohol, TV, drugs, sex, social media, gaming, over-working, and the like. Most thinking is no more than an endless parade of dramatized, melodramatic stories driven by conditioned, learned, or fabricated opinions, beliefs, positions, and ideas. Most thoughts are comprised of self-loathing practices, justifications, judgments, guilt, martyrdom, control tactics, or efforts to make others wrong, incompetent, or otherwise less than others. Thinking is also a way to stay stuck in a victim payoff position due to not knowing how to handle and release the negative emotions that come up.

The mind or ego is fueled by the negative and takes secret pleasure in the suffering that negative emotions and upsetting situations bring. Take gossiping, for example. There is nary a soul who would argue that gossiping is a positive or loving act. Conscious or unconscious guilt always accompanies gossip. Yet, because there is a morbid payoff of sorts (as there is with all negativity), people persist until there is a conscious decision to stop this habit out of deep love for others.

I am sorry to say thinking, or at least the majority of thought content, is ego-driven emotionality that is intended to overwhelm. Thinking easily leads to triggering other forms of escape later in life.

This is why I say thinking is the *original* gateway drug. Disruptive, destructive, and manufactured interpretations, along with plain ole false thinking, can and does trigger self-destructive cycles of all kinds.

For example, feeling bad encourages destructive thinking, which encourages more negative feelings, which encourages more elaborate stories, justifications, and blaming—then more negative feelings or even states of depression or anxiety...and on and on the snowball rolls, gaining more and more mass and momentum.

It is important to recognize that most of the thinking that happens in the mind is just an endless series of dramatic, unnecessary mental stories. The good news—as we have already discussed in previous chapters—is that you can change and diminish, or in some cases, eliminate, your thoughts and feelings with intention and practice.

You can learn a ton about where you need healing simply by collecting as many thoughts and mental stories as you are willing to capture over a three-to-five-day period. This activity can reveal what you currently practice from a mental-emotional standpoint, thus illuminating what you might prefer to practice.

People believe that what goes on in their minds is uncontrollable, or worse, that they are the sum of their thoughts, or their thoughts reflect the truth of who they are.

This is false and highly limiting.

What is uncontrollable is the fact that thoughts form in repeating succession. Most people will never stop the mind from producing thoughts, and that is okay. There are a few exceptions to this statement related to those with extremely advanced spiritual consciousness or who are at advanced levels of enlightenment.

Yet, while the production of thoughts is more difficult to stop, the content, quality, and quantity of thoughts can be shifted, chosen increasingly deliberately, or even completely transformed in many cases. This takes practice, commitment, and discipline.

Dramatic and negative thinking is primarily the result of an unchecked stream of consciousness that is given *unconscious* permission to perpetuate dramatic, aggressive, sad, guilty, fearful, and otherwise victimized or negative thinking and feeling. More often than not, dramatic stories are told over and over and over to ourselves and then shared with others to justify further negativity and upset.

Dramatic stories (story is an interchangeable term for thoughts) are very different from solution-focused thinking or solution-seeking conversations. They are nothing alike.

Here's an example of a thought process full of dramatic storytelling: "I can't believe he couldn't manage to remember to pick up dinner. He doesn't care about me at all, and if he did, shit like this wouldn't happen. I do so frickin' much around this house: laundry, grocery, cooking, finances, basically everything, for gosh sake. But, no matter what I do, it's never enough. I'm just so angry. And all I do is diet and eat healthily, well, most of the time...and I'm still a heifer. What gives? Of course, even if I were a supermodel, I doubt my husband would notice me since work is his only priority. Why doesn't he just marry his job? I'm so sick of all this! I'm exhausted. I just want to get away, Hawaii, maybe? No, that will never happen, I'd need at least two weeks off to be able to enjoy myself, but I could never leave my business for that long. Who would run the place? I have to do everything there too, or else the whole place would fall apart...Geez, how did my life get so stressful? I just feel like crying. I want to crawl in bed, cover my head, and never come out."

Whew! Now that is a rough, dramatic story. But one that is very familiar to many.

Do any of the parts sound familiar or similar to stories you tell yourself or share with others? When was the last time your thoughts went down an unconscious rabbit hole similar to this one?

I am sure you do not have to reach too far back to find one! Do not worry, though—it happens to everyone. An undisciplined mind, and therefore undisciplined thinking, is extremely inclined to run away with your emotions, leaving you more upset, more overwhelmed, and more apt to be depressed and anxious.

The Origins of Thinking to Escape

Thinking—or losing oneself in thoughts and drama stories—is the first way individuals learn to escape as children. Escape what, you might ask? Escaping from feeling difficult experiences that are interpreted as emotional pain and suffering.

Somewhere along the way, children learn (or are programmed or conditioned) to perceive negativity or negative feelings—and sometimes even positive feelings—as *bad, inappropriate, or naughty*. They then learn to suppress, oppress, deny, project, or express feelings that are deemed overwhelming, unwelcome, or inappropriate. In time, projecting unwanted and denied feelings onto others becomes a practice in place of taking radical self-responsibility. People come to believe that negative feelings—or feeling deeply and vulnerably—are experiences to fear, hide and are too painful or even threatening.

It just so happens that as children, the only real escape available—or perhaps the only way children can exert personal power (or perceived control) in ways that feel potentially empowered—is by going deep into their heads to *think* (or tell dramatic stories that paint their experience in a favorable, self-protective light). This is why it is so beautiful to have open communication with children and to teach them tools (such as the ones taught later) from a young age. In this way, children do not dive so deeply into all manners of escape later in life. Instead, they can be set up to live for love and be present and more emotionally empowered from the start. The well-practiced pattern of "thinking escapism" is carried alongside the many sandbags and into adulthood.

This illuminates why the vast majority of adults have a habit of getting so "stuck in their heads." I hear it all the time from clients: "I overthink everything," "I get so stuck in my head," or "I can't sleep because I can't turn my brain off." Overthinking, overdramatizing, over-worrying, being overly afraid, over-perfecting, and so on are trademarks of thinking as a way to avoid feeling fully and, therefore, literally dissolving the upset at that moment. Likewise, thinking, toiling, replaying, recounting, going over mental checklists, thinking about "what I should have said," considering "what I wish I hadn't said," and the like are chief ways to distance yourself from feeling fully in the moment, processing cleanly, and ultimately surrendering the negative energy associated with negative emotions.

Now let us look at the most common ways of avoiding emotions.

Numbing Out

Have you ever gotten hammered drunk or eaten yourself practically into a food coma after a breakup? Have you ever dove headfirst into a vat—or two—of Ben & Jerry's ice cream after a crappy day? Or perhaps you have treated your phone like heroin, checking every few minutes, wondering if it is, perhaps, "not working," while waiting impatiently for a new love interest (or a new job or new client) to check in or ask you out for another date? How about this—

have you gone on a "retail therapy" shopping spree to find new stuff to feel better momentarily?

These are examples of ways in which one attempts to escape or numb out and avoid tough and painful experiences and feelings. Numbing to escape can include (but is not limited to) any of the following:

- Overworking
- Overconsumption of alcohol, food, or drugs
- Erratic or emotional spending or shopping
- Hoarding or collecting unnecessary items that rarely, if ever, get used
- Escaping into social media or internet research
- Pornography or other sexual escapes
- Chronic attention-seeking from the opposite sex or same-sex
- Exercise or fitness
- Obsessive or compulsive food behaviors
- Obsessive or compulsive behavior regarding romantic relationships
- Work/business/career

Honestly, virtually anything can be a way to numb, escape, or become an avenue to try to avoid feeling altogether. Understanding your own versions of numbing requires great and courageous self-honesty.

Of course, some numbing mechanisms, such as shopping, for example, are more "socially accepted" than others. But in the end, the addictive properties and intention behind why someone might avoid feeling make each practice essentially the same.

Escaping also indulges the ego-driven payoffs we have discussed previously—victimhood, martyrdom, guilt, failure, self-pity, perceived helplessness, and even citing one's life as filled with "bad luck" (a common offshoot of victimhood). This ball of wax works in tandem and is part and parcel of emotional sandbags.

What are your go-to numbing vices? What feelings do you try the hardest to avoid experiencing? What emotions seem just too overwhelming to indulge? Even if you are not exactly aware yet, grab your notebook and take a swipe at answering these questions. You might need to lean over and grab courage by the hand to help with this vulnerable exercise.

Unconscious Avoidance

Unconscious avoidance encompasses behaviors like pretending, suppressing, repressing, oppressing, avoiding, projecting, and straight-up denial of feelings or experiences. This defense mechanism can be a bit tricky to uncover because of its unconscious nature. We learn to actively hide emotions, and we do so most often unconsciously. Denial, for example, is, in and of itself, a hidden or unconscious avoidance tactic—hidden even from, or especially from, one's self.

This is why my clients—or really anyone—are seemingly unaware of their own emotional sandbags (at first). Likely, as a result of reading this information, you will begin to see others' sandbags pop open even before you recognize your own. Do not be alarmed by this—it can be a solid avenue for recognizing and taking radical self-responsibility for your own bag of tricks. But when someone denies, projects, or represses feelings of grief, anger, and so forth, therefore giving the feelings space to fester on the inside and propagate drama stories, at some point, the feelings will emerge. All emotions eventually float to the top, regardless of any crafty avoidance tactics.

This is often made transparent when the seemingly "calm, cool, and collected" person suddenly blows up over something trivial.

This happens because repressed emotion can only bubble for so long before it boils over, and the lid springs off and whacks someone in the nose. People bottle it up and bottle it up and eventually explode into escape devices or into bigger emotions like tears, anger, violence, or even depressed states. Unconscious avoidance of emotion is never a winning solution. But it happens innocently because people just do not know what else to do.

Another form of unconscious avoidance is the art of eggshell dancing, like tip-toeing around others, not saying what you mean or meaning what you say, not setting appropriate boundaries, or even a lack of asking for what you want and need for fear of upsetting others. This is where the art of pretending comes into play.

Let's say, for example, your partner tends to use bullying as an emotional weapon. Because of the "elephant in the room," you might be inclined to walk on eggshells in an effort to "not disturb the beast." If the beast remains calm, then you have effectively succeeded at not having to feel the pain of his/her wrath! This may seem, on the surface, like a way to protect yourself (and your partner), but in the end, you are simply acting out of suppressed or denied fear and avoiding honoring yourself with authenticity, self-love, and strong boundaries. The problem is the fear is still there, lying beneath the surface, waiting to be triggered.

In what ways do you use unconscious avoidance to avoid feeling pain, loneliness, rejection, upset, or other feelings?

Expressing

There are numerous methods of expressing emotion as a way to avoid feeling. Bullying, controlling, manipulating, yelling, sometimes crying, lying, physical abuse, sharing drama stories, venting, gossiping, complaining, passive aggression, and any other emotional weapon are all forms of expression to avoid feeling.

These expressions of avoidance, depending upon which one, are often mistaken for "healthy communication" or "necessary sharing." Yet rarely is expressing emotions healthy or productive because they are viewed from a position of blame—and without radical self-responsibility (i.e., not pointing fingers), you will continue to stay stuck in negative emotional states.

First of all, most people do not *share* emotions. They *express* them while telling dramatic stories that are emotional. When a person tells dramatic stories, they get upset, angry, exasperated, or resentful. Not to mention, dramatic, emotional stories are usually rooted in judgmentalism, gossip, complaining, or other harsh or negative positionalities.

Next, these dramatic stories are intended to get the receiver on your side but not to accept responsibility or actually experience what one is feeling. Thus, no matter who you are telling the story to, the story is always slanted in a way that attempts to gain compliance, approval, or even a sense of belonging. When this happens, you are not only avoiding experiencing your own feelings but also avoiding a tough conversation with the person you are upset with that could result in a solution. This is where we go awry. This is why thinking, because it translates into drama stories, is the original gateway drug and why expressing is a way to avoid feeling.

If you are expressing, then you are not feeling or experiencing your emotions, which means you cannot eliminate or transcend them either. Being dramatic, judgy, gossipy, and complain-y is a cheap substitute for feeling and releasing your negative feelings once and for all. Of course, this requires a desire to solve versus a desire to practice emotional payoffs like attempting to gain compliance, approval, favor, or a sense of belonging.

This is an enormous shift. Stopping yourself from engaging in these very well-worn practices is NOT easy and requires great commitment to love, peace, joy, and radical self-responsibility.

In what ways do you express your feelings in unhealthy ways in an effort to avoid feeling them or for the purpose of making it someone else's fault (blame) so you do not have to be responsible for resolving them—or the situation—yourself?

Sharing Emotions Versus Expressing

Sharing emotions or feelings is simple and less dramatic. Sharing sounds like this, "I feel sad," "I feel angry," "I feel overwhelmed," or "I feel rejected." As you can see, there is nothing dramatic here and no long, drawn-out stories that include ulterior motives. (Even if the ulterior motives are unconscious, you are still trying to escape feeling and instead indulge in a victim payoff.) This is a way to own your inner experience, so you do not have to escape. Owning is a step toward processing fully and letting go.

Expressing stories is dramatic, overly emotional, slanted, and inevitably exaggerated.

The next time you begin telling a loved one a story that is rooted in upset, take a step back and really listen to yourself. Take note of your dramatic flair and exaggerated emphasis to prove a point, get your desired reaction, or gain sympathy. There are hidden motives behind all drama stories. Please note this does not necessarily mean that you need to stop telling stories—it means you need to pay attention to your motives. Is it a fun and playful tale meant to entertain and be silly or even be a little outrageous? Or is it a story that is meant to escape feeling and therefore ensure that peace remains at bay?

You can practice asking yourself, "What am I trying to get, and what am I trying to avoid and escape from?"

Often, the act of speaking one's mind (or giving someone a piece of your mind) stems from an unconscious sandbag of pride, anger, or another negative emotion. There is usually an underlying, pressure-filled message that stems from aggression or powerlessness.

This tactic is completely different from the self-protection skill of heart-centered sharing, which occurs from a place of radical self-responsibility and personal ownership of your experience. This is a common trap that parents get stuck in. They host limiting beliefs that say, "Kids must respect and comply." Yet, then parents may say things that are not always rooted in integrity or love, which are often expressions of negative emotional sandbags.

Children are to be stewarded with wisdom and love at the forefront of all interactions—a tall order for sure, but certainly within reach. In this way, be it with kids, spouses, dogs, co-workers, or anyone else, compliance and respect need not be demanded. After all, vying for compliance and respect is merely a control tactic and an effort at asserting dominance, all a mask for sandbags that you are responsible for emptying. We cannot try, nor do we have any business trying, to force anyone to do anything for any reason. Power and empowerment are wielded from within.

Unfortunately, this is a false sense of parental control, dominance, and pride and is usually a parent's way of escaping from feeling emotions surrounding fear regarding his or her perceived parental shortcomings or fear of their children's future. Perfectionism, too, (also based in fear and control) can drive many parenting pitfalls. The truth is, each person can simply do their very best and give attention and intention to healing, loving unconditionally, and evolving—and this is more than enough.

It is best to let your journey be yours, let kids' journeys belong to them, and let anyone else's journey belong to them. It is favorable to help, support, guide, be a sounding board, and to love, care, and allow *consequences* to flow naturally.

You can learn to be quite careful and on high alert regarding what is expressed in times of upset. If you feel upset in any way, the temptation to escape will be present. You are better served by using one of the skills that will allow you to process and let go of the negative emotion so you can continue emptying your sandbags for good!

While there can be great power and value in stating, "I feel _____ (happy, sad, angry, frustrated, scared, etc.)," it is important to understand the difference between being vulnerable and avoiding emotion through expressing, lashing out, blaming, or trying to assert dominance or control. Expressing emotion usually consists of blaming, the core and most popular emotional weapon (followed closely by sarcasm, passive aggression, guilt-tripping, shaming, and other emotional weapons that are outlined in more detail in a later chapter). The ego goes to great lengths to rationalize and justify any negative action or emotion, so we must be quite vigilant to consciously increase awareness bit by bit and process and release negative emotions.

What do you see as the difference between sharing and expressing emotions?

Projection

I was so very thankful when I came to understand the concept of projection. In doing so, you instantly know what you need to heal. Understanding projection is the most efficient way to point you toward what needs to be healed within.

Why?

Because every single word you say and think is a reflection of how you see yourself.

The most simplistic way to begin catching yourself in the escape mechanism called projection is to notice when you *think* you see something wrong in or with another person. What you are actually seeing is what you unconsciously do not like or accept about yourself or what you judge and condemn within yourself.

This can be a difficult pill to swallow at first. But in the end, it is quite nurturing and empowering. There are times when what you are projecting onto others might also be true for them, but it is certainly true for how you view yourself in some capacity. I find it extremely fascinating to listen to others speak. In a very short time, people share every fear, insecurity, self-judgment, and any other sandbag or limiting belief they carry, and you can see this simply by paying attention to what comes out of their mouths.

For example, any effort to criticize, judge, or belittle another person is the operating definition of projection. It is equivalent to holding up a mirror to one's own perceived shortcomings. What you criticize in others, you find icky within yourself. What you belittle or complain about in others or gossip to others about, you fear or judge yourself. And what you judge or condemn others for, you judge and condemn in yourself. Each time you criticize, belittle, gossip, or judge another, it is a direct reflection of a perceived personal flaw (and a sandbag filled with negative emotions and limiting beliefs) that you fear or that brings you shame—these have NOTHING to do with others, literally nothing. It is all just one big reflection of how and where you find yourself "not good enough." And by the way, your inner perfectionist loves to engage in the art of projection!

Projection is a wildly accepted social practice and often a pillar of social connection. It consists of gossiping, complaining, judging, criticizing, and attempting to leverage you as superior when you actually feel inferior. Projection can also be considered a method of repression or denial due to its unconscious nature.

For example, let us pretend your boss tends to micromanage everyone in the office, and it drives you crazy. You constantly complain to your co-workers about your boss being "such a control freak" and purposely go out of your way to seem laid back and relaxed to the employees who work under you. You might also be complaining or gossiping, and therefore projecting, as a way to attempt to "make her look bad" so your lack of courage in setting a boundary with your boss is not illuminated. After all, the victim does not take courageous action. Otherwise, the very definition and payoff of victimhood would be null.

As you gossip, complain, judge, condemn, or criticize, you actively avoid feeling the undercurrent of your insecurity, fear, rejection, or pain. Unconsciously, with projection, we often rationalize that if a person is "bad," then I am "good" in comparison. In the example above, the boss was described as "bad" so you could look good or receive sympathy for "suffering the wrath of such a *bad* boss." When in reality, the only thing you are a victim of is the lack of courage to talk with your boss, explain how you feel perceived as untrustworthy, and ask how you can collaborate moving forward to reach a place of increasing autonomy. This is what it is to be solution-focused, *courageous*, and living for love!

In this scenario, with projection, you likely have an insecurity or fear of losing control or are insecure about your controlling tendencies, and you project it onto your boss. In your case, you might use the expression to convey your own inner "control freak" or "micromanager," perhaps not exactly by micromanaging employees, but instead with your spouse, kids, diet, exercise regimen, or keeping your house excessively tidy.

Can you see how there is an unconscious avoidance of feelings here? To project "your stuff" onto others gives you a free pass at the moment to either *not* feel your inner goings-on or to *not* face and take radical self-responsibility for that which you are projecting (calling out) in someone else, and, as a result, not heal that personal inner space.

All hidden, unhealed inner spaces keep us from living for love to some degree.

Projection also tends to bring with it the tendency to view life in a polarizing manner: good-bad, right-wrong, black-white, success-fail. Thus, in the case of the example above, if you consciously or unconsciously believe that your boss is "bad" for his or her micromanaging tactics, then you get to claim to be the "good" one in this scenario. If your boss "fails" at being a leader, then, in turn, you get to claim to be "successful." However, underneath the surface, projecting "bad" and "failure" onto your boss indicates that you find yourself to be bad and a failure as well. In the practice of projecting, you attempt to shine a light elsewhere so you do not have to handle, solve, or accept your shortcomings. And the projecting is just a ruse, a false attempt to feel good at the expense of others, and a way to assert control.

Practicing polarization and projection tends to lead us more easily into practicing criticism and judgment of ourselves and others. To practice self-honor (self-love, trust, and compassion) allows you to choose to develop the conscious position of leaning into the idea of positive and negative *preferences* versus strict polarized thinking that only allows for a "one or the other" way of looking at the world (i.e., good or bad, right or wrong, success or fail).

When you practice having preferences rather than polarizations, it simply means that you can be happy either way, with either option. You may prefer apples, but oranges are okay too. This way of navigating life makes everything from business to the bedroom far more peaceful. Whereas the polarized vantage point is all about good or bad, right or wrong, and success or failure. You either win, or you lose. Preferences, on the other hand, allow for softness and acceptance.

You can begin leaning into preferences and saying things like, "I prefer to delegate tasks to my team and allow for a system of accountability," or, "I'd prefer Mexican food tonight, but I am happy with a burger if you wish," or, "I'd prefer you pick your things up off the floor, but I love you dearly, even when you don't."

Leaning into preferences allows you to honor yourself and others more effortlessly. We accept any and every situation as it is and can lean toward a preference with ease rather than with the emotional attachment or upset that polarizations bring. Thinking in polarized ways is extremely common for high-achieving women and is very fertile ground for rampant sandbag explosions such as perfectionism! High achievers LOVE things done "my way" because that is the perceived "right way." Such an emotionally immature way of seeing the world, other people, and their actions is emotionally exhausting, controlling, frustrating, and in the end, futile!

Projections are tricky, especially when woven with polarized thinking, and can be difficult to catch at first. But, if you are willing to tune into your words or even record yourself for a day or two, you will quickly catch within yourself what is aching to be healed, transcended, and released.

The Role of Limiting Beliefs

Limiting beliefs are just that, limiting! Limiting beliefs perpetuate all manner of escapes because they are rooted in lies, fabrications, or misunderstandings of things you learned as a child or were programmed to believe. They include opinions, positions, perceptions, judgments, and perspectives.

They limit awareness, courage, vulnerability, connection, flexibility, loving service, kindness, energy, joy, potential, success, and excellence. Limiting beliefs then encourage rigidity, resentment, being stuck, pridefulness, division, fear, and anger.

People are extremely emotionally attached to their beliefs because they are viewed as "me, mine, my, or I." Whatever the ego mind claims as "mine" in any way, it is also willing to fight for it in any conceivable way.

Limiting beliefs flow through the mind by the thousands each and every day, which means you are acting on and navigating your life based on a great number of lies and conditioned ways of doing, being, living, relating, and, of course, believing–which should quickly explain the innumerable negative feelings that spring out of your negative sandbags at the first sign of a belief being challenged. Limiting beliefs keep you stuck in negative, disruptive, or destructive practices, thoughts, and negative sandbag cycles.

Limiting beliefs are, arguably, the root of much, if not most, conflict, personally and on a global scale. People are quite practiced in the art of self-centeredness and are overly focused on "me, mine, I, and my."

Self-centered fighting looks like these examples of limiting beliefs:

- "I" want something "you" will not give.
- "You" never see "my" point of view.
- "You" don't understand "me."
- That is "my" opinion, and "you" are wrong.
- "You" don't love "me" the way "I" want to be loved.
- "I" said to do _____, and "you" didn't do it.
- Those _____ belong to "me," and you ruined them.
- That is "mine," put it down.
- "My" political, religious, family, educational, and moral views are right, and "yours" are wrong.

Limiting beliefs not only encourage self-centeredness and division between you and others, but they also encourage internal division as well.

- "I" am not enough.

- "My" thighs are way too big.
- "I" don't make enough money.
- "She" is smarter than "me."
- "I" will never match up to "him."
- "They" have more patience than "me."

Limiting beliefs drive you emotionally and propagate grave division. They encourage you to hold tightly to opinions, positions, past drama, future fears, and current upset—even if they have zero bearing on the truth or your current life. I know people who have held grudges and no longer talk to loved ones for "crime" (differing perspectives and opinions) from decades ago. Yet, what possible good or happiness could come from holding onto limiting beliefs from the past? What amazing and liberating joy might you be missing out on in this very moment because you choose to hold fast to limiting beliefs, opinions, perspectives, or perceptions?

Whatever your beliefs are, you tend to follow them blindly—this is a distinct area of practice to look into with a very curious eye.

Additionally, people rarely think to question beliefs of any kind. Whatever your beliefs are, you will inexplicably align your life experience with them and literally design your life around them. Let us look at a few examples of how this all unfolds.

Limiting Belief Example 1: My husband is lazy.

If you believe that your husband is lazy, you will create experiences that leverage him as lazy so you can continue to buy into this belief. You might be in the habit of doing "too much" around the house, so your husband does not have to take an equal role in home (or child) care—this way, your limiting belief can be upheld. This might also be referred to as a self-fulfilling prophecy.

When you act on limiting beliefs like this, you then need to tell additional drama stories to ensure this belief stays afloat. Soon, you have convinced yourself that your partner does not love or care about you at all. Otherwise, he or she would not be lazy and would help you more.

Limiting Belief Example 2: I'm dumb.

If you believe you are dumb, you will be in the habit of doing or saying dumb things for the sole purpose of propagating this belief. If you believe you are dumb, you may unconsciously choose not to engage in philosophical or "deep" conversations with other people because it is out of your depth (or so you think). Instead, you only talk about surface-level "fluff" and rarely (if ever) share your intellectual ideas. If this limiting belief was not present, you would believe your thoughts and ideas are valuable, valued, and worth sharing.

Limiting Belief Example 3: People are bad.

Under this limiting belief, your mental focus will be tuned to all the negatives in the world, and perhaps even spend time with people who are unkind. And the kicker of a limiting belief like this is that you, too, find reasons to behave "badly," as you have defined "bad."

If someone drops a ten-dollar bill on the ground and you hold the belief that people are bad, you pick it up without trying to return it. Someone else will just pick it up and keep it anyway, so you may as well have it. You think the person who dropped it was probably a bad person too and doesn't deserve to have the money returned.

Limiting beliefs are also judgmental statements that encourage polarized thinking and behaving, blaming, and efforts at making yourself look "good" and "right" while attempting to make others appear "wrong" and "bad." These ideas are untrue, no matter how many additional thoughts are used to justify such positions.

Take Loving Action!

Move Away from Escapisms By Moving Toward Inner Liberation

It is helpful to begin catching yourself in the act of undisciplined or negative thinking, speaking, or escaping. It is this negativity that sends you down fruitless paths.

You think a thought (drama story), believe it, feel terrible, melt into one of your various escapes, and then sink further into sandbags of, say, guilt, shame, or anger. And so the downward cycle goes...

Perhaps you might stop reading for a moment and take a few minutes to note what you believe to be your primary "gateway thoughts" and escape mechanisms.

Now make a note of thoughts, beliefs, perceptions, opinions, judgments, ideas, and concepts that could be shifted, changed, surrendered, or let go if your mind were more disciplined and focused in a guided and intentional manner. Eknath Easwaran, a beautiful spiritual teacher and author of many of my favorite books, talks about this as the difference between a horse who is driving a run-a-way carriage and a horse and carriage being driven by a very conscious driver. Which one are you? A haphazard, wild, driverless carriage, or a conscious, careful, and wise driver of your mind and ego?

Once you catch yourself in the act of negative thinking, escaping, and dramatic storytelling, you will want to have tools on hand to divert your attention, reclaim control of your wild horse, and proceed intentionally.

Interrupting old patterns and injecting new intentional practices is a fantastic way to make great progress.

Here are five gorgeous tools you can try to practice interrupting old, unwanted thoughts and limiting beliefs. In this way, you will be encouraged to indulge less frequently in the five ways of avoiding feelings. I encourage you to practice all of these tools in ways that honor and strengthen your resolve. Be cautious of trying all five at once, though. You might need to give your inner perfectionist a bit of a lecture and remind her that one ounce of progress is always superior to perfection that is never attained!

1 - Breathe

Stop and breathe before you engage in an escape.

In this way, you are training your mind. Even if you block the practice and payoff of an escape with only five minutes of breathing, you are interrupting the cycle. And perhaps the next time you are triggered and head for an escape, you will breathe for five minutes and then feel totally calm and no longer have the desire to escape into food, alcohol, work, or social media.

It might seem too simple, but slow, conscious breathing is very effective for interrupting unwanted patterns and practices, as well as strategically and *consciously* engaging, letting go, and surrendering unwanted emotions and behaviors.

You could begin by setting alarms two or three times throughout the day as a reminder to breathe and then a two-minute timer for the actual breathing session. When your timer goes off, stop what you are doing, sit still, and breathe deeply. Breathing deliberately into your stomach while expanding your rib cage, sides, and lower back is a beautiful and calming practice that can help reset emotions and thoughts in favorable, healing, and liberating ways.

There are literally dozens, if not hundreds, of books dedicated to the art of conscious breathing. Please feel free to find one that feels good to you.

2 - Meditate

Learning to meditate transformed my life, especially as it related to emptying sandbags while simultaneously revealing the peace and love that was already within, as it is with you.

I adore meditation and aspire to remain in a sort of meditative state as I navigate day-to-day life, moment to moment. More and more, my days are filled with peace, joy, and love, from the second I open my eyes and thank God for the day ahead to the second I close them and thank God for another day of love.

Yet, this has not yet been perfected! Which is why I continue to meditate!

There are dozens of meditation techniques, from transcendental meditation to traditional Zen Buddhist meditation or progressive muscle relaxation (which I used to teach to young athletes). I started twenty years ago with traditional Zen Buddhist meditation. Now, I am devoted to three forms:

The first is used in the morning and is a traditional form of sitting meditation called passage meditation.

Second is a form of letting go that I use all throughout the day at the first sign of being triggered. This is a letting go and surrender meditation.

And finally, I sit in contemplation in conjunction with morning journaling, and at various times throughout the day, sometimes while hiking or cycling.

Paulo Coelho said, "All you have to do is contemplate a simple grain of sand, and you will see in it all the marvels of creation. Listen to your heart. It knows all things because it came from the Soul of the World, and it will one day return there." Such heartfelt truth resides in this quote. Everyone is different, so honor yourself as you grow into a meditation practice.

3 - Mantram

I am not an expert in a way where I feel adept at teaching this amazing skill of mantram repetition, though I do use it daily—all day in fact. This is a newer spiritual skill for me, and I am deeply in love with it. It grips my heart with love and devotion and moves me into a place of surrender almost instantly, and the experience grows more powerful and profound by the day. For me, repeating my mantram over and over quickly moves me out of any negative trigger to the very intentional payoff of love and surrender.

I encourage you to read *Passage Meditation* by Eknath Easwaran to better understand the role that a mantram (more frequently referred to as a mantra) can play in calming the seemingly endless chatter of the mind. This book teaches the reader how to choose a mantram and use it every day.

What I will comment on briefly is the confusion around mantras. Most people think that a mantram/mantra is interchangeable with an affirmation. They are quite different and provide very different consequences. While affirmations are a lovely tool to call upon at times, repetition of a mantram is the difference between a beginner gymnast and a five-time Olympic champion.

4 - Journal

Like meditation, there are countless ways to journal. You can create a gratitude journal, a dream journal, a travel journal, a "catch negative emotion sandbags and limiting beliefs" journal, a feelings journal, or a journal with any other topic or intention. You can write in a stream of consciousness, bullet points, stories, or fragments. You can journal in the morning, throughout the day, or in the evening. You can journal as if speaking with your higher self, God, the Universe, your best friend, Source, Allah, Buddha, Christ, Krishna, anyone else, or no one at all!

But like meditation, the gift lives within the consistency of practice.

The main purpose of journaling is to RELEASE your thoughts, feelings, stories, and payoffs onto paper so as to become clear about what is tripping you up or masquerading as mind/ego "truth." Journaling can also serve to help free you from your sandbags! Getting ideas and feelings out of your head and heart and onto paper is cathartic and freeing, and it ultimately provides a positive payoff and a platform for recontextualizing and surrendering.

At first, you will want to journal for much less time than you think you "should." Spending five minutes each day is better than spending twenty minutes avoiding it because it feels like an overwhelming time commitment. Progress over perfection, remember?

I do encourage you to have an element of deep appreciation added to each journaling session. Gratitude and appreciation trigger unique centers of the brain that add efficiency in healing, awareness, and emotional and spiritual growth.

To get started, grab your notebook and make a couple of notes as to when, where, and why you might begin the practice of journaling.

Key Takeaways

- Emotional escapism is where people act consciously or unconsciously to avoid the emotion they are feeling at a given moment.
- If you could avoid or escape the pain in any meaningful way, then you would already be sustainably joy-filled, content, peaceful, and pain-free!
- To BE with and surrender to emotions in each moment as they arise is the most efficient way to dissipate them.
- As you become increasingly practiced at taking responsibility for how you choose to experience life, including how you feel and the content of your thoughts, you will be more available and open to feeling emotions more fully, including pleasant and joyful emotions, which are usually tamped down by negative sandbags.
- Feelings and thoughts work together to spontaneously curate this unfolding cascade of experience we call life. The way you feel and think about anything predicts the way you will think and feel about everything.
- Thinking is "the original gateway drug" because it is the most readily available defense mechanism. Disruptive, destructive, manufactured interpretations and plain ole false thinking can and does trigger self-destructive cycles of all kinds.
- Every single word you say and think is a reflection of how you see yourself.
- It is helpful to begin catching yourself in the act of undisciplined or negative thinking, speaking, or escaping. Interrupting old patterns and injecting new intentional practices is a fantastic way to make great progress.

CHAPTER 8

Let Go & Surrender

The practice of letting go is the ultimate tool that helps remove sand from sandbags and lead you to liberation. Liberated living means to be free of the shackles of overwhelming and negative emotions—to no longer be controlled by negative emotion sandbags or any other self-imposed emotional weapons like escape mechanisms, selling yourself out, drama stories, and the like. Liberated living is to remove the barriers to love, one by one, so all that remains is your divine essence. When negativity is surrendered, increasingly higher levels of consciousness are available, meaning there is more room for love, joy, and peace to be embraced, lived, and shared.

You really can learn to live in such a way where feelings (positive and negative) flow in and out effortlessly and without attachment—to let feelings crash into your emotional shore like a wave, then recede softly and with increasing immediacy. People experience slumps, stuckness, paralyzation, numbing, escaping, and various forms of stress, anxiety, and depression only when they become attached to something they want, then latch onto a cycle of negative thoughts and emotions, and let THEM take you for a wild ride. Like a child throwing a tantrum at the grocery store for not getting a candy bar, so it is with the emotional overwhelm cycle. This cycle can be quite dramatic or painful, or even traumatic.

You will be hard-pressed to find a better way to achieve increasing levels of love, joy, and peace than to surrender through the practice of letting go.

Beginning Your Letting Go & Surrender Practice

When you first begin letting go and surrendering, there is a tendency to forget to practice, sometimes for many days, weeks, or even months in a row. I first learned about this practice in 2001. I dabbled with it for nearly a decade before a serious commitment was made. Next, I practiced weekly (not yet daily) for a few years. Then it became a daily practice in 2014. And in the past three years, letting go and surrendering has become an all-day, everyday practice. A literal constant practice or state of surrender guides my day-to-day living, emoting, connecting, and communicating. The now meditative practice of letting go and surrendering IS my life. This is a spiritual dedication and devotion to God and the evolution of lovingness (Source, Divine, Allness).

Beginners often start with periodic efforts at letting go and surrendering. Certainly not ideal for emptying sandbags efficiently, but better than not practicing at all! However, as your practice unfolds, be gentle, compassionate, and loving with yourself, as this will make space for expedited and increased practice and, therefore, efficient and effective sandbag depletion.

Remember, surrender, in its most simplistic terms, means to be fully present with a thought or emotion without trying to make it become something else or eliminate it. It truly means to simply be with it.

I began practicing letting go and surrendering to emotions and thoughts many years ago as a form of meditation. This seems to work well for many people. Eventually, and with dedicated practice, one can learn to let go of *pretty much anything* in a matter of moments.

The Basic Technique Of Letting Go And Surrender

Letting go is the practice, and surrender is the state of mind and spirit or consequence of the letting go of practice. The most transformative solution, as well as a beautiful, divine, healing, and peace-inducing practice, to transcend negative feelings and sandbags is to let go and enter into deep surrender.

The overall goal is to surrender TO the emotion itself. The practice is letting go of resistance and attachment. When a negative or icky emotion comes up, the instinct is to use one of the escapism techniques (i.e., numbing out), which is the practice of actively resisting an emotion. Resisting it may seem like a way to get rid of the emotion, but what it actually does is shove it below the surface and add sand to the sandbag. To surrender to emotion is to feel, embrace, and accept the emotional state fully, and by doing so, you allow the emotion to flow in and out like a wave. Rather than grabbing a beer or scrolling on your phone endlessly when upset, letting go means stopping and feeling what you are feeling and being with the emotion without trying to change it. When an emotion is surrendered, sand flows out of the sandbag, and it becomes lighter. The more you begin to let go, the easier it becomes.

The technique itself looks like this:

1. Identify the emotion associated with an unwanted thought, story, payoff, defense mechanism, emotional weapon, or limiting belief that you would like to transcend or eliminate. This can be an emotion in the moment of an emotional storm or an emotion still lingering from a past upset or wound.
2. Stop what you are doing and sit, stand, or lie still.
3. BE with the negative emotion fully.

4. Do not TRY to do anything with the emotion–simply be with it fully, surrender TO the emotion and experience.

5. Let go of the emotion without trying to get rid of it. Breathe and repeat, "I am letting go and surrendering," until the experience either softens or dissipates completely.

Sounds simple enough, right?!

Honestly, nothing could be more simple.

This technique IS practice. Letting go and surrendering can be the most liberating practice of your life if you build in dedication and devotion. It will require practice and dedication to experience ongoing emotional freedom and emptying of the negative emotional sandbags.

A common mistake I see with people who are new to this practice is to ignore the fact that everyone is deeply attached to their negative emotions and grossly resistant to letting them go. Paradoxically, even though people say that they want to be happier, they are in NO hurry to give up the payoffs like self-pity, victimhood, self-righteous anger, and so on. Most people are not even aware they are indulging in such payoffs and avidly resist owning the negative payoffs for a very long time.

At first, you will wonder:

- Is this working?
- Am I doing it right?
- This isn't working.
- It feels too hard.
- This is a waste of time.
- My resentment (loneliness, self-pity, pride, fear) IS real and justified *this* time.
- I don't want to do this.

All of this mental banter and suspicion is merely ego resistance. The ego will attempt to thwart your efforts to maintain a stronghold–to keep you attached to negativity and negative payoffs. The only thing you need to be concerned with is continuing to practice the technique. Continue to stop, breathe, surrender to the emotion, and let go.

Clients often avoid this simple practice for long periods of time because of its simplicity or because they are not yet ready to relinquish the payoffs associated with negative feelings and emotional states.

At times, we would rather savor the sweet victory of justification, the charge of being right, righteous indignation, self-pity, victimhood, or seething resentment, than feel good, loving, or happy.

Sounds silly perhaps, yet exceedingly too true. Otherwise, why would one remain stuck in an emotion like anger for years, even decades? I know people who have literally been angry and resentful for decades about perceived "wrong-doing" by others. Of course, this is a projection, but their mind has them convinced that someone "did them wrong," thus giving a justification for maintaining the anger sandbag. What is the point of this negative feeling if not for a negative payoff? On the other hand, when one is *willing* to be happy, you simply say, "Well, I'm sure Bob was doing his best at the time. I don't prefer his actions (words, etc.), but I accept and love him anyway." You do not even have to spend time with people who do not align with your lifestyle or values, but you can choose to love anyone and everyone.

The payoffs for avoiding surrender and letting go can seem and feel very appealing. The rush or high of anger and justification may seem very sweet at the moment. For example, hitting children elicits the illusion of power and control. (Though, classically, hitting is referred to as "spanking" because, mentally and emotionally, the word "spank" or "spanking" has the illusion of being okay or justified.) The righteousness of being right or condemning and judging others seems victorious to the ego. Yet, you can never escape the guilt that inevitably accompanies any and every negative emotion, word, or action, though this guilt is usually unconscious. This might be a good time to remind you that judgment is of no value and can also be surrendered. Self-love and self-compassion are far superior pathways for feeling good and emptying the sand. The attention received by the martyr or the helpless victim also seems so good and often even too supportive to give up.

It can be necessary to let go of resistance to the surrender and the letting go technique itself, as well as surrender the payoffs to unwanted feelings. You must decide to surrender not only the emotions and their sandbags but also the payoffs. You can decide to make a stand for true happiness and to do so in ways you may have never experienced before. Thus, it is paramount to rely on faith and hope that such happiness and contentment, beyond your current experience or even your imagination, exists. The alternative is to maintain the status quo.

There is no right or wrong choice here—it is simply a matter of two choices that lead in two very different directions. One keeps you stuck or spiraling. The other moves you forward. The conscious choice is yours and is available multiple times each day.

You have the opportunity to be one hundred percent responsible for your experience of life in any way you choose!

The Basic Letting Go Technique Expanded

For your benefit, the five steps of the surrender technique are expanded and explained in the following section. Often, additional clarity will help the logical mind latch on to the importance of the practice.

1. Identify the emotion associated with an unwanted thought, story, payoff, defense mechanism, emotional weapon, or limiting belief that you would like to transcend or eliminate.

    At this stage of practice, it is important to become curiously and consciously aware of any given moment in time when you feel emotionally icky in some way. This can seem like a barrier due to remembering to catch yourself. We are in the habit of feeling an icky emotion and then getting so caught up in the story, the drama, and the escapism techniques that we forget to be aware of how we are feeling. This piece, too, is an evolution. You can begin by asking the Universe to show you these moments and to reveal the truth of the negative emotional experience (so you can take radical self-responsibility for the negative experiences and programs that come into your conscious awareness).

2. Stop what you are doing and sit, stand, or lie still.

    This step often feels like the biggest barrier to practicing the letting go and surrendering technique. Life feels too busy, or the task at hand feels too important to pause. Yet, it is this pause, this pattern interruption, that helps shift you spiritually, emotionally, and neurologically.

    You are welcome to sit, stand, or lie still as you practice. Most people seem to have the most success initially by lying down. In fact, a girlfriend and I came up with the word "nap-ser-tation," as the practice of letting go evolved into a meditative practice which often ended in a very blissful nap!

3. BE with the negative emotion fully.

    This step is where resistance often comes into play. I like to teach clients to think of resistance as a thin piece of glass that stands (often invisibly) between you and the liberation experienced by letting go. The resistance is the part of the egoic mind that says things like, "This is a waste of time," "I'm not doing it right," or, "It's not working," thus working to convince you to abandon your quest for happiness, peace, and contentment. This is where you will need to lean into courage and conviction—it requires great courage and conviction to persist in the face of uncertainty.

Your only job is to set up a consistent practice regardless of the resistance and drama stories. To be beautifully present with any negativity and even welcome it into your awareness so it can dissipate and run out of fuel.

4. Do not TRY to do anything with the emotion—simply be with it fully, surrender TO the emotion and experience.

This element often feels awkward. I mean, isn't the whole point of the practice to eliminate negative emotions and to empty those annoying sandbags, so joy and peace become increasingly prevalent?

Well, yes!

BUT, during the practice, it is important to suspend any attachment to feeling good or getting rid of the emotion. It is paradoxical, as all highly illumined concepts are. To be in the moment with and to welcome the negative emotion, to be courageously still WITH each negative emotion—that is where the power of the technique lies. This is what it means to surrender TO the experience. To get out of the habits of escaping negativity, to let go of projecting, numbing, lashing out, storytelling, and the like. This is what it means to be completely radically responsible for YOUR experience of life. And in this, life will be transformed, and joy elevated. It is a beautiful progression and evolution.

5. Let go of the emotion without trying to get rid of it. Breathe and repeat, "I am letting go and surrendering," until the experience either softens or dissipates completely.

Again, this part of the practice is devoid of any DESIRE to get rid of any particular or difficult emotion. In fact, this specific desire may be the first thing you surrender when you catch any negative emotion. If you find yourself wanting so badly to stop feeling something like grief or anger or alone-ness, first let go of the wanting, the resistance, and then let go of the other negative feeling that you caught. Being present with the experience and suspending any trying is key. This might seem confusing because it is yet another paradox, but after you practice for a few weeks and then a few months, the process and results will become increasingly clear.

Additional Access Points To Letting Go & Surrendering

Interestingly, as simple as the process of letting go and surrendering is, many people avoid it for some period of time. Or they get stuck in mental scenarios like, "Am I doing it right?" or, "Is it working?" thus allowing the fear of doing it wrong to serve as a barrier! Because of the many objections and roadblocks that seem to accompany resistance to practice, I have developed a few "surrender hacks" to override these challenges and encourage practice.

In each of the following surrender hacks, the defining factor is awareness and acknowledging that awareness in conscious thought. Meaning the gateway to letting go and surrendering all that blocks your divine inner sun from shining is noticing, *at the moment*, a trigger, limiting belief, escape mechanism, self-sellout, telling a dramatic story, or eliciting a negative emotional sandbag that you no longer want to practice. This is the ongoing jumping-off point.

Hack #1: Engaging The Imagination

Imagination can be a wonderful tool. After all, it is used countless times throughout the day as a weapon that tells upsetting dramatic stories, so why not use it to your advantage?

If it is helpful to your process, take the time to spend a few minutes each day visualizing letting negative feelings or experiences blow over you like a warm spring breeze—or sometimes like a ninety-mile-an-hour gust of wind! Either way, allow feelings to blow over without grabbing on to take a wild ride. Play with engaging your imagination to create a visual representation of the emotions and how you want them to behave moving forward.

Let us pause for a moment to engage in a visualization practice exercise.

Think of any emotion (happy, resentful, angry).

Now, visualize the emotion in various contexts, like the wind example. Perhaps you would like to imagine negative experiences crashing in like a wave and receding just as smoothly, or perhaps blowing over you like a cool breeze, or even floating by like an autumn leaf on a gorgeous river. You might see or even feel happiness blow over you. You might see and feel anger crash in like a wave and recede back into the abyss with elegance and effortlessness. Or you might experience a feeling of resentment floating on by like an autumn leaf passing by into the infinite.

Now consider which metaphor worked best and was most easily accessible. This is a beautiful access point to learning to let go of and surrender negative emotions. You might need to practice each visualization a few times to learn which one best serves you. When you learn to let your emotions come and go, you no longer need other escapes, like overthinking, alcohol abuse, spending or eating addictions, men, sex, or even work. With practice, painful emotions dissolve faster and faster. Ultimately, you will begin to have experiences where negative emotions no longer arise at all.

Hack #2: Shifting Attention

Once you catch yourself in the moment of a trigger, limiting belief, escape mechanism, self-sellout, dramatic story, or diving headfirst into a negative emotional sandbag that you no longer want to practice, you can consciously shift your attention. But first, note the truth of the experience as to ensure you do not delve into something like denial or projection.

You can shift your attention to the emotion and the truth of the emotional state and then how to lovingly proceed. You could say, for example, "Wow, I am totally stuck in a sandbag of frustration because I was telling myself a story about how the world is full of terrible people and is completely unsafe." Admitting the feeling and story is the acknowledgment needed to successfully shift toward letting go and surrendering. Next, you will simply breathe and remind yourself that you do not want to feel frustrated and that the story is just that—a story with no basis in reality. Then shift your attention further to something helpful. Perhaps you could call a friend to connect, pull out your laptop and write a new blog, focus intently on love, send someone a card or email of gratitude, create a new belief about how people are always doing their best, or how everyone is perfect and in progress, just like you!

Shifting attention away from a practice that no longer serves you and toward something that does is a way to surrender that particular practice, even if just for a moment.

Hack #3: Tune Your Radio To Acceptance

Again, your jumping-off point here is when you catch yourself in the act of a negative experience—anything you perceive as upsetting, icky, or unfun! Once you have caught yourself in a moment of emotional overwhelm, you can choose to tune your mental and emotional radio to acceptance. After all, acceptance in any and every moment is the only sane choice.

231

At any given moment, whatever IS can either be accepted or resisted—there is no third option here. Resistance means eminent sandbag overload and heaviness on your shoulders. Acceptance means peace and mental and emotional clarity—acceptance lightens the load of all these sandbags. When you accept a given moment, thought, feeling, situation, or circumstance, you will have a far easier time taking action or making decisions that impact your future in preferred ways.

Acceptance means embracing any given moment or situation as "okay" simply because it is what is in a given moment. If you are feeling down in the dumps, then accept that for that moment. Accept that all four seasons parade through your body, mind, and spirit.

This can be a difficult concept to comprehend, so I will provide a couple of examples. Over the past twenty-plus years of coaching, I have worked with innumerable people who have suffered from chronic pain or chronic illness (I *used* to be one of these people, and on both fronts). When you experience chronic discomfort to any degree, be it mild or extremely severe, the dominant practice for most people is resistance of all kinds—frustration, suffering, irritability, upset, apathy, depression, anxiety, helplessness, self-pity, victimhood, and certainly all brands of fear.

Because of the upset associated with chronic conditions, acceptance can seem, well, ludicrous! You might be wondering, "How or why would I want to *accept* pain, suffering, or illness?" Because that is the current reality. Acceptance of a given moment, or series of consecutive moments, does not mean you are signing up for a life sentence of suffering—it means you are aligning with the present moment. To be aligned with the present moment means you are aligned with truth rather than having your mind filled with *illusions* of the past or potential future (which is a form of escapism). Acceptance gives birth to letting go, which leads to surrender.

Acceptance can be sort of an emotionally healthy version of resignation. Like when a person is diagnosed with a fatal illness, at some point (hopefully sooner than later), they accept that death is coming, which of course, is coming for us all! Once acceptance is embraced, joy and peace follow, suffering subsides, and life is lived in the present, drinking in every delicious moment. In fact, this is the time when spontaneous healing (i.e., miracles) takes place.

Like many before me, I am actively using letting go and surrender to heal many physical conditions. The first to be surrendered was chronic neck pain, which I had struggled with on a daily basis since I was a young gymnast. And then chronic tendonitis, autoimmune dysfunction like insulin resistance, bloating, and so on. I'm currently working to surrender and heal chronic sinusitis and a couple of other digestive issues. A first step to healing is often acceptance of what is present in a given moment. For me, surrender worked where traditional medicine did not. Over the years, I have spent well over seventy-five thousand dollars on any and every kind of expert, pain relief specialist, chiropractor, physical therapist, functional medicine doctor, health coach, and other professionals. A few things were supportive and somewhat useful for relieving symptoms, but nothing was curative. The letting go technique, alongside some holistic medicine, has *cured* many ailments and diseases I experienced.[1]

Acceptance is a beautiful practice and gives birth to a great deal of peace, contentment, happiness, and increased energy. It positions you to let go of what is standing in your way of surrendering and being in a surrendered state.

---

[1] If you would like to learn more about healing the physical body through surrender, you can read *Healing and Recovery* by Dr. David Hawkins.

Let Go Of Resistance

It can be helpful to look at resistance as similar to a glass ceiling of sorts. It seems invisible and insurmountable until scrutinized. This glass ceiling of resistance acts as a thin but seemingly strong, immovable layer of concrete that stands between you and a blissful, peaceful, surrendered state. This resistance used to show up for me most often in the form of, "I don't feel like taking the time to let go right now!" or, "I have too many other things to do right now and don't have time to just stop everything and surrender." This kind of glass ceiling has the illusion of being very justified, reasonable even. I mean, seriously, there is work to do, dinner to prepare, kids to bathe, and laundry to fold! So really, who has time?

There will be a piece of resistance available to latch onto instead of letting go and surrendering if that is your choice. But what could be more valuable to yourself, your family, your co-workers, teammates, or friends than taking a few minutes to let go of the resistance (i.e., dissolve the glass ceiling) so you can then move on to emptying your sandbags? In this way, you can connect with and approach difficult communications with clarity, care, and love. Not to mention how good you will feel being rid of the negativity. There is no better gift. This is the gateway to permanent emotional liberation. The fact that I do not blame my husband for ANYTHING has totally transformed our marriage. But before I could let go of blaming, I had to let go of the resistance to the justification of blaming!

Once you decide that, indeed, you would like to be increasingly happy and to empty your sandbags and surrender their payoffs bit by bit, the next step is an evolving surrender practice.

A Mega Turning Point

I'll never forget the time I discovered the true power of letting go. It was a major turning point in my life and in my relationship with Chris. In an earlier chapter, I shared the story of when Chris left to go on a hike without me. He set a boundary and chose not to give me the emotional payoff of my unloving behavior. He chose to go on the hike rather than scurry around, trying to make me happy and not be "in trouble" when I was upset.

I could not believe what had happened. I felt totally abandoned and left for dead (speaking of dramatic stories!). I was crushed and shocked, and in total disbelief. After all, this was not how the cycle was supposed to go. Chris was supposed to be sweet and caring and ...

Alas, he was gone.

So, I did what any strong, independent woman would do. I sat down on the floor and cried like a baby! I sat there thinking the absolute worst. *He is going to leave me. We are going to end up divorced like our parents!*

The crying went on for thirty or so minutes before I gathered myself up off the floor. I decided to do the thing that always helped reset me—listen to a great audiobook and learn something new! So, I grabbed my phone and earbuds and turned on *No More Mister Nice Guy* by Robert A. Glover. This is a book about men with Chris's temperament. I figured, what the heck—I could learn more about him and try to see what was up with him and our relationship. This way, I could fix him and our relationship (oh, the irony)! After all, I knew how to work hard, try hard, put on my perfectionism hat, and scoop up the accountability for *both* of us. That makes sense, right? I mean, I was the coach here; obviously, the problem was not *me*, but certainly mine to solve!

Yes, I hear you laughing as you read...

I went to lie in the grass. As I lay there breathing and listening, I just could not concentrate. So, I tried my second calming activity—meditation. This was a great feeling. I was calming down, feeling relaxed, and even beginning to experience some peace. All of a sudden, it felt as if something had dropped on my chest like a ton of bricks. I sat up quickly and heard a voice that said, "It's time to let go and give up trying."

My first thought was that this voice must not know me very well since my whole jam in life was controlling, overtrying, and perfecting.

But this moment of surrender ended up being the most liberating and relieving moment of my life. And within a few minutes, I was totally on board. I had no idea (yet) how the heck I would achieve these seemingly, very lofty objectives or who I even was without these facets of myself, but I was willing to do what it took to feel this idyllic sense of relief, liberation... surrender.

Eventually, Chris returned, and to his very pleasant surprise, I hopped up, hugged and kissed him, and told him I was planning to do whatever it took for us to be happy. Chris made the same commitment. For the first time, Chris and I put down all of our emotional weapons, took off our armor, and shared our hearts. I can honestly say that this often NEVER happens in a relationship. People usually get divorced or break up BEFORE they are willing to take this radically vulnerable and self-responsible step.

This seemingly painful few hours then served—truly served—as the biggest stepping stone for what ultimately became an unbelievably juicy transformation. This was our first commitment to radical self-responsibility. I am beyond thankful that Chris was brave enough to set that first and oh-so-important boundary.

After this experience with Chris, I realized just how beneficial it was to practice letting go and surrendering on an increasingly regular basis. I began spending time each day lying on the sofa (or wherever) and breathing *into* the various thoughts, feelings, and body sensations that had anything to do with feeling upset or triggered.

Anger was the biggest sandbag I carried. It also took the longest to empty/surrender.

Now that this sandbag is essentially empty, if anger does begin to bubble up, I am able to let it go and surrender it within a few moments in nearly all cases. Anger is, thankfully, no longer my brain's first course of action. Additionally, the frantic, dramatic thinking that used to accompany negative emotion is at an all-time low and continues to dwindle bit by bit.

There becomes a time when you no longer need to connect with your partner or friends to complain, rant, or rave about any *perceived* situation. Instead, emotions, perceptions, and opinions are felt and surrendered. It does, however, lead you to do a great deal of rearranging in life, as once this is gone, you might not have much else to talk about—which can be difficult to navigate at first. But, with some creativity and willingness, you will find far more interesting and heartfelt ideas to connect about and discuss.

Take Loving Action!

Planning for letting go and surrendering efforts is key. Here is a roadmap to get you started. Feel free to engage any or all of the access points outlined in the hacks on the previous pages.

1. Begin by carving out two to five minutes each morning and each evening to practice letting go and surrendering. Perhaps just as your eyes open in the morning and just before falling asleep at night, or anytime you can practice consistently. Most people will not remember to practice letting go during the day at first, thus, planned practice periods are usually necessary.
2. Next, bring to mind a thought, idea, experience, conversation, or situation from the day (or the day before if it is morning) that resulted in feeling negative in any way.

3. Now sit with the feeling and emotional experience and breathe. You might find where you are sensing the negative emotion in your body and place your focus or hand there.

   Be prepared for your mind to wander. This means nothing, and there is no reason to become frustrated or throw in the towel. It is part of the process. Just see thoughts wash over you like a warm breeze, give a giggle to the sheer magnitude or ridiculousness of the thoughts, then bring your focus back each time you become conscious of your mind wandering. Suspend all self-judgment or condemnation. Becoming distracted might happen a hundred times during a five-minute letting-go session, but who cares! It may eventually lessen with practice, or maybe not. It makes no difference. Let the mind do its thing in the background of the letting go practice. Do not be tempted to let a wandering mind become an excuse for stopping the practice.

   Some days will seem easier than others. Humans are fickle creatures. Just keep at it. I have been practicing surrendering and letting go for many years, and there are random days when my mind seems to be a bucking bronco! On other days, it is as still as a mountain. Neither means anything. Thus, feeling annoyed with a busy mind only serves as resistance or the illumination of an annoying sandbag that needs to be surrendered—and you can begin that particular letting go session by surrendering to *annoyance!*

4. Once you have practiced the above for at least thirty days, you can begin practicing letting go of and surrendering to negativity *in the moment* versus only during your two designated practice periods. This simply means that you become still with the feeling or situation that is going on in the moment instead of going all drama queen on your own ass (or someone else's)!

This is an important step in the progression of emptying sandbags. Choosing to stop what you are doing in any situation, then breathing into a feeling, being with the feeling, and not trying to chase it away or make it anything else is a key piece of the *peace* that accompanies surrender.

This is where creating a living, breathing commitment to happiness steps in. And you begin actively *choosing* surrender, and therefore calm, love, and peace in place of drama, upset, angst, pride, resentment, self-loathing, justification, aggression, and so on.

5. Continue with your morning and evening practice periods, and add an additional five minutes whenever you wish. I encourage people to practice morning and night for five minutes each for at least thirty to sixty days before adding time. This way, you will be more inclined to be trustworthy to yourself on a more sustainable basis.

   Remember, this is a new habit and will take some time to integrate. As you see results, which usually happen almost immediately for most people, you will be encouraged to persevere.

6. Keep practicing. There will likely be times when you feel the technique is not working, you think you are *done* needing to use this skill, you do not have time, or you do not feel like sitting still. Trust me. Your mind will come up with a thousand excuses NOT to practice feeling your feelings, surrendering to them, focusing your attention on your body where the feeling sits, and ultimately letting it go. Yet, the more you practice, the more grains of sand trickle out of the long-standing sandbags. There is a cumulative or compounding consequence with surrendering and letting go. The more time you spend surrendering and letting go, the less potent emotional experiences will be when

triggered, and they will arise less frequently. Interestingly, some days you will sit with an emotion, and it will lessen only slightly—other days, it will completely vanish. Accept both scenarios as positively fantastic.

Note that this practice is a lifetime commitment. You will likely experience surges of improved emotional well-being. You may notice all at once that you have not been upset about [fill in the blank] for weeks, when in the past, that particular issue would upset you on a near-daily basis! You will uncover experience after experience where you are lighter, more loving and patient, and increasingly less affected by the same ole' things that used to bother you.

At first, you will feel like you have no idea what the heck you are doing. This is not a problem at all. Surrender and let go of the questions regarding "am I doing it right?" and move on. The only goal is practice, practice, practice!

7. Keep a journal of your progress. It is WAY too easy to throw the baby out with the bath water with this new practice. Thus, keep a diary of daily progress and wins. This will help you in times when your ego mind is trying to convince you that "no progress has been made, this is all a big waste of time, and you are a loser who will never stop feeling terrible!" Yes, the mind (ego) will try, but you will not succumb!

One last note, if you begin feeling resistance to this technique or to feeling any particular emotion (grief, loneliness, etc.), first sit with and surrender to the resistance and then move to the feeling. The main goal of surrender is to stop, be still, and surrender TO the feeling. The goal is NOT to chase it away, even though the result of surrender is often that the feeling dwindles. This technique will serve to diminish the various ways in which you have learned and practiced avoiding, denying, suppressing, oppressing, or escaping from feelings in negative ways.

Key Takeaways

- The practice of letting go is the ultimate tool that helps remove sand from sandbags and lead you to liberation. Liberated living means to be free of the shackles of overwhelming and negative emotions.

- When negativity is surrendered, increasingly higher levels of consciousness are available, meaning there is more room for love, joy, and peace to be embraced, lived, and shared.

- Surrender, in its most simplistic terms, means to be fully present with a thought or emotion without trying to make it become something else or eliminate it.

- The most transformative solution to transcend negative feelings and sandbags is to let go and enter into deep surrender.

- The ego will attempt to thwart your efforts to maintain a stronghold—to keep you attached to negativity and negative payoffs. The only thing you need to be concerned with is continuing to practice the technique. Continue to stop, breathe, surrender to the emotion, and let go.

- Your only job is to set up a consistent practice regardless of the resistance and drama stories and to be beautifully present with any negativity and even welcome it into your awareness so it can dissipate and run out of fuel.

- When you learn to let your emotions come and go, you no longer need other escapes. With practice, painful emotions dissolve faster and faster. Ultimately, you will begin to have experiences where negative emotions no longer arise at all.

- Acceptance means embracing any given moment or situation as "okay" simply because it is what is in a given moment.

CHAPTER 9

Emotional Weapons

Emotional weapons are used for conflict and fighting with yourself and others—they are a "skill set" that you learned from those who had the strongest influence on you as you grew up. As you moved from formative to adult ages, you adopted these skills ("emotional weapons") in your own unique style and learned to use them (unknowingly) *against* yourself and loved ones to ensure others do not get too close, so you do not have to be *too* vulnerable. In the end, the ego/mind utilizes emotional weapons as a false sense of self-protection, which is why I call them "weapons."

Why do we use these weapons, you might ask? Because closeness, deep connection, and raw vulnerability are perceived by the mind/ego to be totally unsafe and scary as hell!

Client Case Study: Maria

When speaking with a new client, Maria, the other day, she shared with me how she was really frustrated with how her husband prioritizes his life, work, and family.

Here's what she said: "My husband Eddie makes himself so busy that he doesn't even have time for us—not for me and not for the kids. It feels like he doesn't care and that we're not as important as his work. Because of his lack of care for us, I now have grown to behave in ways that I really don't like, and that, quite frankly, makes me sick to my stomach. But I do it anyway because I feel so hurt and resentful and am unsure how to stop or what else to do. I'm just so mad at him all the time. This leads me to make snide and sarcastic remarks. Like when Eddie says that he's exhausted, I will come back with things like, 'Well, if you came home once in a while, you might have time to rest.' And then I huff out of the room. Or, I will withhold sex or accidentally 'forget' to pick things up at the grocery that he specifically asked for. I really hate who I have become in our marriage and who we are becoming together. And honestly, my anger is really starting to impact the kids as well. Shawn, I am at a loss. I just don't know what to do."

Can you relate to any of Maria's heart-felt struggles? To summarize, here are the key challenges Maria and I are working through to solve together:

- Her husband seems to be constantly consumed with his job and therefore does not have time or energy left for his family.
- Maria feels she has to be bossy, naggy, or somehow upset in order to get the help and support she wants from Eddie or for him to come home even one time per week at a "reasonable" hour.
- She tries really hard to set schedules and reminders for him, but they are usually ignored.
- She attempts to give constructive feedback about the home and stuff with the kids, but it always seems to turn into a fight and then into sarcasm or meanness.
- Maria has all these great ideas for how the family can work better as a team, and Eddie seems not to care.

Needless to say, Maria feels very alone and like she doesn't really have a partner in parenting, in the home, or in their marriage.

Does any of this sound familiar?

If it does, please know you are not alone.

I could totally empathize with her because so many of my clients struggle in similar marital situations.

And I want you to know that it does not have to be this way.

At the root of Maria and Eddie's relationship challenges is the use of emotional weapons, which I will illuminate in a bit.

When you see the phrase "emotional weapons," do you envision something like an alien invasion, nuclear bombs, or maybe even a zombie apocalypse?

Well, truthfully, emotional weapons might be just as dastardly— at least on an emotional level.

Why you might ask?

Because emotional weapons promote emotionally charged (even emotionally abusive at times) negative sandbag explosions that temporarily withhold love toward others and/or yourself and puke negativity and volatility all over you and those closest to you. Emotional weapons serve as specific ways to sell yourself out and simultaneously put on armor to emotionally defend and protect yourself.

Emotional weapon is a phrase I coined over the years of working with individuals, teams, and couples while witnessing the fascinating ways in which people ensure self and emotional isolation. They creatively block vulnerability and connected collaboration from occurring because emotional weapons set up an emotionally *unsafe* environment that breeds mistrust and disconnection. Emotional weapons are used in place of healthy vulnerability, authenticity, deep connection, trust (in self and others), emotional safety, and healthy self-love skills. Thus, as you learn and apply raw, unbridled vulnerability through self-love skills, authentic self-expression, and healthy self-protection skills, you will naturally use emotional weapons less and less.

245

This is truly great and healing news!

Let us dig deeper into this idea.

Emotional Weapons Overview

Emotional weapons reflect a specific combination of internal and external emotions and behaviors that occur consciously at times and unconsciously at other times. At their core, emotional weapons are designed (unconsciously) to push people away (i.e., reject or abandon before being rejected or abandoned), erode relationships, break trust and emotional safety, and compromise or eliminate the availability of vulnerability, connection, collaboration, and unity. Unconsciously, humans believe they are "safer" in emotional isolation, and the use of emotional weapons serves this end.

These underlying motives are, of course, untrue.

Emotional weapons are rooted in:

- Lies
- Limiting beliefs that drive defensive, mean, or cruel actions and words
- Self-sellout through the inevitable guilt that follows the use of emotional weapons
- Numbing out with booze, drugs, television, pornography, overworking, over-exercising or trying to over control food
- The endless dramatic thoughts and mental stories that cascade when you are triggered

As you saw with Maria's story, she found herself exhibiting some emotional weapons (though she had no idea the dynamic that was unfolding at first) in the form of snide comments (anger and sarcasm), withholding sex (emotional punishment), and intentionally leaving her husband's items off the grocery list (passive aggression).

The magnitude of pain, suffering, and calamity that results when emotional weapons are unleashed can be significant and cyclical and erode emotional safety and trust until a relationship dissolves completely, and divorce or breakup becomes inevitable.

People typically learn emotional weapons from the people in their growing-up environment and then unleash them throughout their life. Emotional weapons are used when a person feels overwhelmed, helpless, or powerless when they do not know another method of getting their way or getting their needs met, when they feel they have been unfairly or unjustly treated, or when emotionally triggered and a sandbag pops open. When emotional weapons are triggered into action, you tend to do, be, and feel in ways that are conditioned and programmed into your consciousness during your formative years.

That is, of course, until you decide and commit to taking beautiful, radical self-responsibility and choose to consciously change old patterns and replace them with new, loving practices.

In the next few sections, you will find descriptions of each emotional weapon and loving actions you can take to encourage radical self-responsibility, lay down your emotional weapons, and replace them with loving skills for you and your loved ones. There are variations of the emotional weapons I list, but the following descriptions will give you a significant framework for understanding and dissipating them.

As you learn about each, note which emotional weapons you engage most frequently. Do your best NOT to engage in self-shame, condemnation, or guilt as you read—practice sharing self-honor skills instead. Like all negativity and unwanted habits, emotional weapons can be changed, replaced, and surrendered completely with practice.

Also, do your best to maintain *self-focus* as you read. It can be very tempting to let your mind wander and be overly concerned about how other people in your life might use the various emotional weapons instead of remaining focused on you and your journey! You have zero control over others, so let those thoughts go, as well as any associated control thoughts.

With increased healing, wholeness, and raised levels of consciousness, the favorable impact you have on others expands exponentially—it is actually quite marvelous. As you lay down your emotional weapons, it becomes exceedingly difficult for others to continue using their emotional weapons. Inevitably, as you lay down yours, your loved ones will most certainly try to push your buttons for a while to get you to fall back into your typical conflict role, but this behavior will soon subside. Even better, encourage your loved ones to read this chapter with you—it will completely transform any or every relationship you have.

But remember, YOUR main goal here is to work to develop YOUR radical *self*-responsibility skills and become an increasingly healed, whole, and liberated version of yourself. For this, you are also to be praised and congratulated!

As you read, let this be a beautiful time where unconditional self-love and compassion flow within yourself to your utmost capacity. As you read about each emotional weapon, consider what you might not be able to receive from or cultivate with others as a consequence of pushing others away through the use of emotional weapons while they still exist in your life.

You literally miss out on the most amazing pieces of what makes life juicy and relationships safe and joyful when emotional weapons are in play. Emotional weapons are a significant piece of drama and chaos that Chris and I worked to eliminate so our relationship could become wildly vulnerable and deeply connected. You may not realize it, but when you use emotional weapons, you push people away *strategically* but unconsciously. This typically occurs because you are afraid to be vulnerable, engaged, and connected for fear of being rejected or abandoned and do not yet know how to lay down the emotional weapons.

Why Are Emotional Weapons So Harmful?

Emotional weapons are harmful for the following key reasons:

- Emotional weapons are used as an effort to control others.
- Emotional weapons are used to get your way or gain compliance from others at any cost.
- Emotional weapons trigger shame within yourself and others (the lowest level of emotional energy humans experience, and which is most aligned with being stuck, depressed, suicidal, alone/lonely, apathetic, and underachieving).
- Emotional weapons ensure the impossibility of cultivating sustainable connection, vulnerability, closeness, collaboration, and unity with others—coincidentally, the couples I coach all around the world reach out to me to build, reinvigorate, or deepen these particular relationship elements most often.
- Emotional weapons crush emotional safety and trust in relationships.
- Emotional weapons provide additional (albeit false) evidence that others are untrustworthy, emotionally unsafe, and unreliable.
- Because emotional weapons are reactionary defense mechanisms, they serve as a false sense of security and are cheap replacements for meaningful conversation and self-honor skills.
- The increased use of emotional weapons over time is responsible for the end of relationships.

Reap The Benefits Of Laying Down Emotional Weapons

I am guessing the benefits of removing emotional weapons are becoming fairly transparent. But let us take a look at the most valuable benefits of removing emotional weapons anyway, just for fun.

- The embracing of radical self-responsibility and, therefore, a rise in self-confidence, empowerment, and happiness (being that happiness is found and cultivated ONLY from within).
- An enormous sense of relief, peace, and unity is experienced internally and with others as you lay down your emotional weapons bit by bit.
- Increased ability to share genuine and vulnerable connections in the absence of emotional weapons.
- You will receive far more of what you want as you lay down your emotional weapons (support, help, care, compliments, adoration, etc.).
- An enormous reduction in emotional stress and overwhelm will ensue as you lay down emotional weapons.
- Freedom to become more and more of your authentic self-unfolds.
- A sense of true belonging and having a place in this world— this is HUGE.
- The ability to communicate openly, candidly, and especially fruitfully with anyone, anytime, anywhere will unfold as you replace emotional weapons with new loving skills.

There are numerous other benefits and nuances of benefits that you will joyfully experience as you lay down your emotional weapons. And now, without any further ado, let us meet the various types of emotional weapons.

Seven Dominant Forms Of Emotional Weapons

Here is a list of the seven most common emotional weapons that will be detailed ahead. There are numerous offshoots of each of the following emotional weapons, but these seven are at the core of most emotional suffering.

1. Blaming and shaming
2. Emotional shutdown
3. Anger
4. Right-fighting
5. Passive aggression
6. Emotional punishment
7. Criticizing and belittling

Emotional Weapon 1: Blaming and Shaming

Blaming is the most frequently used emotional weapon and is used by all until you decide to lay this weapon down and replace it with any or all of the living for love skills that you are learning.

Blaming is the exact opposite of taking radical self-responsibility. Instead, blaming is the art of abdicating responsibility and the habit of assigning fault to something or someone other than yourself.

Blaming is the quickest and surest way to play the victim and give all of your power away in an instant. In this way, you feel awful and usually angry (emotional weapon number three) or defeated. Yet when you are engaged in blaming, you feel one hundred percent justified in your negative emotions and ensuing words that nearly always induce shame because you are the victim and someone or something else is the perpetrator. When you are blaming and therefore shaming, you view yourself as the victim and the other person as the perpetrator of a crime against you.

No wonder there is a deep lack of emotional safety and trust, right? When you believe in a given moment that you are the victim of an emotional crime and your loved one is the perpetrator, it is impossible to feel safe and trusting. Make sense?

All forms of blame are a combination of dominance and victim tactics born from feelings and beliefs of powerlessness and an unwillingness to hold yourself radically responsible for your role in a given situation. Blame is accompanied by some combination of aggression, anger, shutdown, shaming, and/or frustration, even when masked or expressed with sarcasm, a smile, or a laugh. It is the sense of powerlessness and lack of willingness (or know-how) to own your lane that you will want to address at a deep level in order to trade this emotional weapon with loving communication skills.

A sense of powerlessness is like the virus, and the shaming, anger, or other complementary emotional weapons that accompany blame are, in effect, symptomatic expressions of the underlying feelings of powerlessness. The lack of willingness to own your role in any given exchange is a learned skill. When you believe, fallaciously of course, that the other person in a conflict exchange is responsible for the pain you are experiencing, lashing out or retaliating is inevitable and is the only "reasonable" response according to the mind/ego. The juicy payoff is righteous indignation and justified anger or fury.

Blame is a common way to get to play the victim and abdicate responsibility. Blame says, "If you (the other person or people) would do (be, act, or speak) the way I want you to, then I could be happy (satisfied, feel good enough, feel important or valued)..." and so on. Of course, the latter can only be cultivated from within. As stated before, happiness is a one-person, inside job! You may have experiences that you do not prefer, but inner happiness, contentment, and well-being, or lack thereof, is *soul-ly* your responsibility.

The most joyful thing about blame is that, in its absence, there is no more conflict, and arguing becomes impossible.

You might want to read that sentence a few more times and sloooowly!

Here it is again. The most joyful thing about blame is that, in its absence, there is no more conflict, and arguing becomes impossible.

What a gift, right?

Laying down blame is a significant reason why Chris and I have had just a handful of very small arguments over the past several years. And I can say, as someone who used to be a total blame and anger addict, this is one of the most joyful "accomplishments" of my life.

In the absence of blame, there is nothing to argue about. In fact, I challenge you to get into an argument with someone, anyone, without placing blame of any kind—not on yourself and not on another person, group, situation, or anything in between. I get pushed back frequently on social media and during talks when I share the fact that Chris and I live in and practice a harmonious, conflict-free, blame-free marriage. People find it very difficult to believe that we do not argue. But it is quite simple. We do not blame one another...for anything. Therefore, there is no fighting or conflict available. We have simply outgrown the usefulness of emotional weapons, thus conflict as well.

With the practice of radical self-responsibility and self-love practices, blame dissolves over time. Chris and I each made a conscious decision to never blame one another for *our* individual experience of life, for our results, for our sandbags, not for anything. I assure you, this was not easy—at first. Laying down blame required great discipline, committed practice, grace for frequent failure in the beginning, and great patience for ourselves and each other while navigating brand-new territory. This is a radical approach to living for love and living in a marriage environment of lovingness. It took radical dedication and commitment for three or so years to completely eradicate blame and other emotional weapons, thus conflict, from our marriage. Conflict dwindled systematically over time as we shifted and changed from the inside out. There are few life endeavors or commitments more valuable than this one. Personally, I would not trade it for anything.

Blaming and shaming are control tactics and a way to attempt to get others to behave differently or gain compliance of some kind. It is a dirty and cruel trick. Blaming and shaming triggers guilt in others and actually makes them LESS likely to change long-term, but more likely to try harder in the short term out of fear of being punished with shame again.

Blame and shame are used for the purpose of gaining compliance, winning, trying to appear superior, or abdicating responsibility and playing the victim. Most of the time, blame and shame are nothing but a projection of your negative programming and old fruitless habits of communicating. It is a way of expressing one's own self-doubt, insecurity, or lack of self-love by blaming "it" on another, then shaming them for the action or words: and then assuming that the problem lies outside of yourself. Blaming and shaming are the opposite of radical self-responsibility. And it is never, never, never your job to try to get others to change by using these (or other) emotional weapons.

Usually, when people use blame of any kind, it is because they feel disconnected, unheard, rejected, abandoned, unloved, undeserving, or unimportant. This results in pangs of inner pain and anguish. And when pain and anguish have been elicited, it somehow seems like a good idea to hold others responsible for that pain and anguish instead of looking within to heal it permanently by using the lessons you are learning in this book.

In nearly every situation, pain and anguish are self-conflicts to heal. They are inner reflections of old programs and learned negativity, not external reflections of others' actions or words. For example, you could never be rejected or *rejectable* because you are perfect and divine. But you can *feel* rejected or abandoned if you believe you are rejectable and abandonable and that someone you love might leave you or stop meeting your desires and needs. There is no disconnection, as all things are one. Nor could you possibly be unlovable, undeserving, or unimportant, except as a story or illusion in your mind.

You are divine essence. Therefore, suffering or inner anguish can only be an illusion rooted in stories, limiting beliefs, programs, and emotional sandbags. As such, you and only you, with divine grace, are responsible for igniting a path toward healing and true inner happiness.

When you become practiced in self-honor and self-love skills, emotional weapons like blaming begin to dissolve rapidly. When you turn the light on, the roaches scatter, or when the sun rises, the fog lifts—so it is with healing. As we remove obstacles and trade them for truth, divine essence and love emerge.

For all of my childhood and into my late twenties, I was a big yeller, door-slammer, silent treatment giver, and blamer *(blush)*. I behaved a great deal nastier than I like to admit. I grew up with family members who were often aggressive, angry, enraged, violent, and loud, thus, yelling and blaming were the main forms of generationally learned communication. My parents, too, grew up with aggression and yelling and violence, and so the cycle went. Just like other sandbags, emotional weapons are rooted in the growing-up experience.

Remember, there is no value in *blaming* our families and childhood experiences for current adult habits. You can simply choose to stop the cycle and behaviors you no longer wish to exhibit. Then, align with intentionally chosen practices and new behaviors and patterns that produce happiness and joyful payoffs.

Take Loving Action: Lay Down Blaming & Shaming

The first order of business is to let go of playing the victim and decide that you are an active participant in every single moment of your life. You are a powerful human—powerful beyond your wildest dreams, really!

You may want to revisit Chapter 4 on radical self-responsibility to help you continue practicing taking one hundred percent radical self-responsibility for your role in whatever is unfolding in any given moment. Essentially, there is never a time to blame but only times to recontextualize, check in with your values, practice self-honor, walk away to surrender for a few moments—anything to take empowered action for yourself.

You are not a victim—you are a volunteer in this life! How awesome and powerful is that?!

When you feel like blaming someone for something, ask yourself, "What was my role in this situation? And how can I shift my actions to impact it in the future?"

When getting sucked into a blame cycle, it is also fabulous to remind yourself that you are always doing your best (and so is everyone else, even if you do not like your or their best in a given moment) and you are working to "upgrade" your body, mind, and spirit in the future.

Emotional Weapon 2: Emotional Shut Down

Shutting down emotionally is akin to a deer in headlights: frozen, unable to move, think, or even breathe sometimes. From a limbic system perspective, emotional shutdown mimics the "freeze" and "fawn" spaces of the "fight, flight, freeze, fawn" trauma cycle. In truth, all emotional weapons are trauma responses. When in emotional shutdown, one experiences a feeling such as powerlessness, paralysis, or deep fear. This occurs when a person is at a total loss, afraid that anything they do or say will be the wrong thing and make matters worse. The inner experience is akin to cowering, hiding in a corner, or covering one's head as a child, fearing being hit or beaten. It is a serious situation and deserves great care and compassion.

Emotional shutdown used to be Chris's go-to emotional weapon. Before I knew better and understood his trauma responses, I would meet his shutdown with anger, coincidentally the worst possible response to encourage someone to open up...ugh! Yep, you guessed it—I had a lot of guilt to surrender once I understood this dynamic. So, please have grace and compassion with yourself regardless of which side of this coin you tend to land on more frequently.

Shutdown is indicative of putting on emotional armor, albeit very quiet armor. Putting on emotional armor and keeping others at arm's length is at the core of all emotional weapons. It gives the illusion of protecting the heart. Of course, this is fallacious. The heart wants to be open, vulnerable, and knitted together with the entire Universe—yet, not many come to understand this truth.

Emotional shutdown is a way to build emotional walls to keep others from getting too close or experiencing the kinds of hurt you experienced as a child or in abusive relationships. Again, like all emotional weapons, the feelings and practices are deeply rooted in fear, guilt, grief, and anger sandbags, which can be emptied and healed at any time through the letting go technique and the other healing practices you are learning here.

Once in tune with one's self, people who shut down realize that the experience feels like an emotional collapse into a deep, vast pit of grief. They feel tongue-tied and utterly afraid to use their voice (or sometimes even afraid to move). During a period of shutdown, inadvertent silent treatments are given, often with diverting of eye contact or a head held low. Each of these is possible and may or may not occur in tandem. Emotional shutdown is indicative of being filled with complex, confusing, frustrating, and sometimes angry emotions yet, feeling completely incapable of speaking, sharing, opening up, or even self-protecting with healthy boundaries.

Again, emotional shutdown was the dominant emotional weapon my husband entered our relationship with. It started out being incredibly frustrating for me to experience as his partner, and it nearly always elicited an angry outburst when his shutdown arose.

When you shut down, it feels like someone pushed an "off" button to your mouth and body with no ability to press the "on" button until the whole situation has "blown over" or there is a pattern interruption (i.e., a friend phones, your partner shuts down too, etc.). Often, when the opposing partner shuts down, the first partner begins traditional fawning habits like trying to be sweet, pleasing, or other things to reconnect–this, too, is a trauma response used in an attempt to mitigate being left, punished, rejected, or abandoned.

It is truly a heartbreaking cycle and inner experience.

The shutdown cycle looks like this: Person one displays emotion that feels overwhelming to person two. This triggers an emotional shutdown in person two, in which emotional collapse ensues. Person one then becomes even more upset, trying desperately to get person two to engage (because they believe that their engagement means that they care, and person one is desperately afraid that they do not). The person who is shut down often emotionally retreats even more when faced with additional anger, hostility, or volatility...with increasing volatility being triggered in person one...and so repeats the cycle of increasing volatility and increasing shutdown. I can attest–this cycle truly sucks!

This cycle perpetuates until one or both parties recognize the cycle, own their respective roles, learn new communication skills, engage in healing, and utilize techniques like surrender. Then you will each be enabled to choose to participate in increasingly productive, inviting, and loving ways.

This is how all the emotional weapons are, in effect, cleaned up.

Take Loving Action: Lay Down Emotional Shutdown

If you are prone to shutting down when emotional overwhelm grips you, start by journaling. Just two to three sentences are more than enough in the beginning. At the first sign of overwhelm, even if you are in the middle of a conversation, grab your journal and write any detail you can describe the experience. This may feel awkward or even inappropriate at first, so you might want to let your partner or friend, or family member know what you have learned and that you may need to simply turn and walk away to journal for a few moments. In terms of practicing intentionally versus haphazardly, stopping in the middle of any unwanted behavior, cycle, or habit is key. This way, you can at least get your feelings and ideas on paper and out of emotional purgatory! You may even be able to share some of the feelings with the person you are interacting with through email or a letter to get the ball rolling and move away from the gripping paralysis of emotional shutdown.

What is most important is that you stop depriving yourself of the emotions and thoughts that are in your heart and mind (even if you cannot currently recognize or name them). If emotional shutdown is prone to occur during specific situations or conversations or with specific people (like a romantic relationship), let them know ahead of time that if or when shutdown begins to unfold, you will simply say, "I am going to go journal for a few minutes." This way, you are both prepared and setting sail to healthier and more vulnerable connection and conversation, and from a larger perspective, becoming increasingly emotionally healthy.

Setting better boundaries, speaking your mind, and asking for what you want are nearly always required skills in this process. These skills will be covered in the next chapter. Remember the story shared previously about the fateful day when Chris went on a hike without me? He was very prone to emotional shutdown and emotional collapse. Gaining the courage to set that first boundary totally set our relationship on a fresh and beautiful trajectory. A joyful new trajectory is quite indicative of what happens as you begin to interrupt emotional weapon habits and replace them with intentional practice, vulnerability, and self-love.

Emotional Weapon 3: Anger

Anger is perhaps the most volatile emotional weapon. Of course, everyone experiences anger to some degree, as well as its cohort's frustration, aggression, irritation, annoyance, and sometimes violence. Anger does frequently get results, but it leaves a lot of damage in its wake. When anger is afoot, connection, vulnerability, trust, and emotional safety are impossible, which is the exact reason to lay anger down as quickly as possible.

Anger ensures that a truly close relationship is impossible. This is because the people who receive the anger are always holding back and walking on eggshells, afraid to do or say the wrong thing and trigger the anger, blame, and shame cycle. These are the three musketeers and always come as a trio.

This can be difficult to hear, but again, this is a place to lather on self-compassion, not self-abuse or self-loathing. Give yourself grace as you work to lay down anger and pick up loving communication tools. It is actually quite common to become angry with yourself for feeling anger. It is okay to feel anger—it is what you do with it that matters most.

As you might be picking up by now, anger (plus blaming and shaming) used to be my most prolific emotional weapon. I arrived at adulthood with a great deal of anger that needed to be laid down and transcended. I can attest that removing at least ninety-eight percent of the anger I used to carry, experience, and unleash legitimately feels like a miracle—and a gift beyond measure!

Anger is oddly useful, and it does get results. Anger is used for one's own gain and stems from feeling powerless. Please read that again. When someone who is prone to anger feels powerless, anger is ignited. Anger is used for the following reasons:

- To gain compliance from others
- To feel superior
- To get one's own way
- To prevent others from sharing an opinion or doing something his or her way
- To scare others
- To control others
- To bully others

The thing is, no one wants to admit to feeling powerless, but it is extremely powerful to melt into this level of vulnerability. I used to control Chris and gain his compliance in a million ways—ugh. Especially when I needed or wanted his help. I did actually believe that he should just know when I wanted help preparing dinner or cleaning up afterward. But how could he? For the first two years we dated, I joyfully did all the cooking and cleaning. And then, one day, I started to feel angry and resentful for his lack of help. And because he did not "just offer," I felt helpless. This was when my anger began to emerge.

Instead of simply asking for support, I got super pissed off and began shaming him. Over time, all I had to do was let out an aggressive sigh, and he would literally JUMP up to see how he could support me. But, by then, I had already stewed in my juices and was ready to unleash a lot of drama, cruelty, and disconnection between us.

Does any of this sound familiar to you?

If anger is one of your top three emotional weapons, do not beat yourself up as you lament how it is used in your family or with friends—just commit to laying it down as quickly as possible.

Take Loving Action: Lay Down Anger

Literally, all of the lessons that you have learned thus far will be helpful in laying down anger, but there are two that are clutch.

The first and most courageous step you can take in laying down anger is to begin calling a spade a spade and admitting, at least to yourself in the beginning and then to your loved ones later, "I feel powerless."

Next up is surrender. Surrender is the most powerful and efficient elixir for not only laying down anger, but transcending it. We are not in the business of suppressing anger or managing it—we want to lay it down completely. If anger is merely being managed, it is always just beneath the surface, ready to pounce. Thus, engaging in the letting go and surrendering practice can be life-changing.

Remember, take your time, give yourself great patience, and stick with working to lay down anger, even if it takes the rest of your life! It is completely worth it, my friends.

Emotional Weapon 4: Right-Fighting

Do you find yourself struggling to win conflicts? Do family, friends, children, or co-workers wonder why you insist on "always being right?" Does the conflict you engage in typically end with you having the last word and with others feeling bullied, punished, frustrated, or otherwise far *less* than encouraged, validated, and cared for? And do your disagreements frequently escalate to shouting and anger? If you have said yes to any of these questions, you might be practicing right-fighting.

Right-fighting means that you typically work very hard to win arguments, even when you doubt your own view. Right-fighting usually involves utilizing other emotional weapons to get your way or to enforce compliance. Accompanying tools include defensiveness, bullying, blaming, and/or anger when others do not agree with your opinions, position, stories, or beliefs. There is an insistence on having the last word and a refusal to back down from conflict to ensure winning or being right, regardless of potential damage to a relationship.

Those exhibiting right-fighting behavior are masterful at turning situations around and laying blame on others in their effort to win and be right. At the core of right-fighting are pridefulness and competition, and of course, deep insecurity—all of which are unfavorable expressions and negative sandbags that make closeness, vulnerability, trust, and emotional safety essentially impossible to sustain.

At the heart of right-fighting is an accumulation of sandbags that encourage stories of being unheard, unimportant, unworthy, rejectable, abandonable, unlovable, and undeserving. Therefore, there is an attempt by the right fighter to puff up during conflict to "win" or "dominate" in an effort to feel worthy, lovable, deserving, accepted, important, and validated instead of cultivating these truths from within—the only place they actually exist. Right-fighting is always a losing battle. If there is only one winner in any conflict, there are really only two losers. Winning or dominating is degrading, humiliating, and shaming and severs connection in those moments while, at the same time, chipping away at connection permanently. The illusory payoffs of right-fighting (pridefulness, justice, superiority, etc.) can be surrendered anytime you are willing to experience increased genuine connection, collaboration, and joy.

Right-fighting habits include emotional punishment and withholding of love and care. Because a right fighter's main goal is only to win (and to feed the underlying lie that winning equals lovable and worthy), s/he often forgets what the argument was even about. Like a dog with a bone, the only goal is to win. These destructive behaviors present in varying degrees for right-fighting practitioners. For example, many people, especially couples, frequently argue about things like who is remembering a certain situation accurately (which, by the way, if people knew how faulty memory actually is, they would give up these fights immediately!).

Right-fighting uses any means necessary to gain compliance or agreement. Usually, a right-fighting practitioner will pair up romantically with someone they can fairly easily dominate or win arguments with. This was certainly true for Chris and me. Chris would avoid conflict at any price because it shook him to his core to feel anger being expressed toward him, so he would back down and give me my way immediately. I lovingly refer to this type of couple dynamic as the "tornado and the inchworm." I myself am a *recovered* tornado, while Chris is a *recovered* inchworm! If you want to learn more about this relationship dynamic, please feel free to join our Reimagine Love Facebook Group.

In essence, a right-fighting practitioner has their personal perceived lovability, value, and worth attached to the outcome of being perceived as right in a given matter. This is usually an unconscious process. This person desperately wants to feel valuable, loved, and worthy but does not yet know how to courageously tap into and nourish him or herself with the great wealth of love that already fully exists within every being.

The metaphorical "fight to the death" for right-fighters is all but eminent when they engage in "battle."

Unfortunately, fighting to win provides only short-term satisfaction and is accompanied by guilt, fear, sadness, and shame.

People do not really feel good (albeit justified) about beating another person, spouse, or child down emotionally—but no matter the consequence or emotional damage, the internal payoff seems worth it at the moment. The right-fighting cycle is disheartening and damaging to relationships. But the perceived comfort of being "agreed with" is powerful (in the same way people find temporary and false comfort in overeating, overworking, or overdrinking). It is similar to the addictive process described in the escapism chapter.

Right-fighting ultimately leads to dependency upon others' agreement for self-esteem boosts, therefore, bullying others into submission becomes an ingrained habit. Right-fighting is a draining roller-coaster of conflict, hurt feelings, justification, guilt, shame, and growing resentment. Because right-fighting patterns are ultimately one-sided, producing a consistent winner and loser, the cycle and its effects often present as abusive and traumatic to the receivers.

Learned submission and low self-esteem on the part of those who interact with right-fighting practitioners are all but inevitable and present in varying degrees.

I get that this emotional weapon can seem glum, and it is. But recovery from anything is always possible. Try not to worry—there are plenty of ways you can trade right-fighting for beautiful new, loving skills. And remember, if this particular shoe fits you currently, give yourself grace—you learned this program, and you can unlearn it.

Take Loving Action: Lay Down Right-Fighting

Laying down right-fighting is amazingly powerful and healing for yourself and all the people you interact with. A softening of body language, mental drama, spirit, and tone of voice are wonderful gifts to give yourself and your loved ones.

The first step in letting go of right-fighting is owning the fact that you are absolutely lovable, worthy, and valuable simply because you are! As you continue practicing self-honor and self-love skills, this truth will be reinforced and believed more and more.

Leaning into courage is also key. It requires great courage to catch yourself in the moment and acknowledge that you are merely fighting for the purpose of winning at the expense of others.

Thus, deep, unwavering self-love and compassion will be required, especially during times when you forget and bulldoze others. In these situations, it is IMPERATIVE that you go back and say the words, "I'm sorry," every single time. Without this step, you will not want to stop the right-fighting. Remember, being wrong is egregious to the right fighter—knowing that you will have to apologize later will stop you from going down this road in most cases!

Right-fighting can take a while to lay down, so give yourself plenty of time and grace and remember to be courageous and apologize each time you mess up!

Emotional Weapon 5: Punishing

In short, punishment as an emotional weapon emerges when one person is feeling hurt or attacked in some way, then elicits the desire to hurt or attack the other person in return. It is a "tit for tat" situation. Whether the *perceived* crime against you was accurate or intentional or not, there is a desire to hurt another simply because the hurt is being experienced personally; as a result, deliberate punishment is enacted. Additionally, the hurt being experienced can be blamed (emotional weapon number one) on another, thus justifying the unleashing of emotional punishment.

Punishing can consist of a variety of expressions, like purposely "forgetting" to do something that was asked of you (also a passive-aggressive emotional weapon behavior detailed below); withholding care, affection, or sex; giving someone the silent treatment; bullying; or saying something that you know will sting, offend, or otherwise trigger upset and hurt.

Punishment says, "Because I am hurting, suffering, and in emotional pain, *you* will be too!"

Punishment springs into action typically when the anger sandbag is triggered. It is mean-spirited retaliation tied to feeling helpless and, therefore, angry. Punishment of any kind is never appropriate. Punishment is born of anger and aggression, whereas consequences are shared within the context of care and love. There is no third direction here.

Consequences are innately positive and rooted in love—always. Punishment is rooted in aggression and the desire to get revenge and induce suffering. This is how we can easily tell the difference. In our coaching programs with parents, they are encouraged never to act until they can come from a place of love to ensure they deliver consequences and refrain from emotional weaponry. This is a key path to raising emotionally well children.

There are numerous other forms of punishment, including avoidance or intentionally withholding care or kindness of any kind. Verbal attacks like blaming, shouting, throwing things, punching walls, violence of any kind, or other forms of bullying are forms of punishment as well. Punishing can also include physical punishing like pestering, tickling when it is unwanted, intimidating, picking on, scaring, and so on. Any form of bullying, withholding, or intimidation counts as cruel punishment and is an especially fine line with the parent/child relationship. Children are often treated as property and have little to say about their bodies. For example, tickling can turn quickly to terrorizing simply because they do not have the strength to escape. I have actually seen parents tickle until a child is crying and then laugh—this is never, under any circumstances, okay.

Terrorizing, intimidating, taunting, overpowering, demoralizing, pressuring, alarming, or scaring another human are ALL forms of bullying and punishment and are never acceptable, even when disguised as so-called "play." **If EVERYONE is not having fun, then it is NOT play–it's *punishment or cruelty.***

Once again, if you find yourself to be a practitioner of punishment (as I used to), please give yourself grace and compassion and look for opportunities to practice love and unconditional kindness toward yourself and others.

Take Loving Action: Lay Down Punishing

This action is extremely simple but also difficult when attempting to put it into action. The goal here is to practice unconditional kindness at all times, toward all of life, and surrender the desire to make others pay for your pain. Your pain arrived "fair and square" from experiences you collected along your path, and they are yours now to heal. Even when punishing feels justified, your negative emotions are never about the other person and are always yours to surrender.

When you have a mindset of kindness, two things happen. First, you become mindful that everyone deserves unconditional kindness at all times (including yourself, first and foremost), no matter what the perceived mistake might be. And secondly, without practicing something like unconditional kindness actively and diligently, punishing yourself and others will continue.

Neither you nor anyone in your life deserves punishment. Grow the courage to express and share grace.

Emotional Weapon 6: Passive Aggression

Passive aggression is just that, a passive form of aggression. Those who practice passive aggression actually fear and deny expressing or experiencing outward anger. Thus, because they carry so much anger, it emerges as passive aggression.

This gem of an emotional weapon can be extremely difficult to recognize and even trickier to catch. On top of this, those who practice passive aggression often have zero interest in owning up to it. This is where pridefulness is a significant hindrance, and as the saying goes, "pride goeth before the fall." Additionally, passive aggression is seemingly easy to justify or dismiss by the practitioner, as well as those on the receiving end.

People who use passive aggression utilize teasing, snide comments, and sarcasm. They say hurtful things and pretend they are a joke. Here are a few examples:

- "Oh, I was just joking; why are you so sensitive?"
- "Why are you so sensitive all the time?"
- "Can't you take a joke?"

Passive aggressive, emotional weapons often come across (or try to come across) as funny or entertaining on the surface, while under the surface, a great deal of anger, hurt, or even rage is being masked. Using sarcasm or teasing in an effort to disguise passive aggression as playful or fun is common. Sure, some teasing can be playful, but sarcasm stems from anger. There is a distinct line that is easy to cross because sarcasm is frequently celebrated and often thought of as witty.

Usually, when a person behaves passive-aggressively, speaks sarcastically, and even teases or jokes, what he or she actually needs to do is speak their mind and heart vulnerably, set a brave boundary, or share candidly with another person.

And for the person who is on the receiving end of passive aggression, seriously brave boundaries need to be set. The rule of thumb is if someone else's words are not loving and feel icky, a boundary of some kind is needed.

Unfortunately, when boundaries are set, the person who is behaving passive aggressively or sarcastically often responds like I shared above, by turning things around and acting offended or surprised at the response to their behavior, stating things like, "Geez, can't you take a joke?" or, "Why are you so sensitive?" or, "I was just kidding." But when the practitioner of passive aggression and sarcasm becomes radically self-honest, they will find a great deal of denied and suppressed anger. What is needed in its place is a wild amount of self-love, compassion, and vulnerability. Passive aggressive communication erodes emotional safety and trust and places an enormous, emotionally isolating wall between him or herself and others.

Passive aggression is damaging and usually ends up having an abusive impact on others, especially spouses and children. Here is a short list of common passive-aggressive behaviors, characteristics, and tactics:

- Gives subtle insults wrapped in a joke or a laugh
- Withdraws and avoids instead of sharing desires, wants, opinions, or needs
- Saying things like "fine," "you pick," "I don't care," or "whatever..." in order to stop or avoid a discussion
- Procrastinates or completes tasks intentionally poorly or inefficiently (note that passive aggression is not the only reason for procrastination)
- Pretends to "forget" things for others they really just don't want to do/get, or they believe are unnecessary or the other person is undeserving of
- Placating, agreeing, or pretending to be compliant while knowing they have no plan to change a particular behavior or situation
- Chronic lateness, especially to events that are important to loved ones

- Lying about where they are, telling half-truths, withholding information, or lying in general
- Giving the silent treatment, being sullen

Family members who live with practitioners of passive aggression and sarcasm usually learn to walk on significant eggshells, lose confidence, doubt their sanity in some ways, and live in emotional fear. Being around passive-aggressive people generally feels uncomfortable, but it can be difficult to put your finger on why because they seem like nice people who you think should be perceived as "funny" but really are not. They just feel sad, alone, and angry, even if they are not willing or ready, or capable of admitting it. Passive-aggressive practitioners live in a great deal of shame, which is why their feelings come out in this way, "as a secret," so to speak.

Once you learn about these behaviors, it becomes easier to understand the underlying discomfort associated with spending time with these humans. This particular emotional weapon is challenging because the person who practices passive aggressiveness and sarcasm rarely presents as coachable or willing to look in the mirror to embrace or embody needed changes. Over the past twenty-plus years of coaching individuals, business leaders, and couples, I have found that a deeply passive-aggressive dynamic is one of the least sustainable relationship models. Though, by the time the end of the relationship comes about, there is usually a great deal of emotional damage and a serious need for healing for the partner who has been on the receiving end. Being on the receiving end of a passive-aggressive relationship feels brutal—and again, it leaves a great need for deep healing, self-love, and self-compassion. I encourage anyone in this situation to hire a great coach who has experience in this realm—our team is prepared to support you or you and your partner in this domain.

Take Loving Action: Lay Down Passive Aggression

To be very honest, passive-aggressive habits can be challenging to chip away at and ultimately transcend because such practitioners do not often present as coachable (though often they say they are). But healing is VERY possible when their hearts are fully in. This archetype is usually extremely intelligent, which is part of why this emotional weapon works so well for them. There are two important pieces of learning to overcome passive aggression.

First, you must acknowledge that this habit stems from a great deal of hurt from your growing-up experience that needs to be addressed and healed. People who practice passive aggression learned somewhere along the way that expressing anger is very wrong and you are a bad human if you do so. This makes complete sense as to why they turn the anger inward and into veiled jokes, sarcasm, teasing, mistruths, and outright lying.

And second, if you use this particular emotional weapon, you must be completely willing to learn to share and connect with raw, fearless, unbridled vulnerability as you practice communicating bravely in sharing your heart, feelings, and ideas with others with radical honesty—and with love and care. This commitment is paramount to recovering from this emotional weapon.

A passive aggression practitioner has a great deal of difficulty, excruciatingly so, sharing their honest feelings and heart. Vulnerability is brilliant medicine for diminishing all emotional weapons, but with this one, in particular, it is very important to practice sharing vulnerably, receiving any and all consequences, and then learning to lean into surrender when your vulnerability is not received as you would like. This way, you learn that you are actually okay (you will survive and thrive over time) when you share your heart, feelings, and other sensitive ideas with loved ones, no matter the outcome.

Emotional Weapon 7: Criticizing and Belittling

Criticism and belittling reflect one's own negative self–beliefs. Those who specialize in this emotional weapon tend to practice perfectionism and be very hard on themselves and others. They give the impression that "nothing is ever good enough" and often believe it. Criticizing and belittling others is the equivalent of holding up a mirror to one's own perceived shortcomings and projecting them upon others. Their thoughts and opinions are never about anyone other than themselves. What you criticize and belittle, you actually view as wrong within yourself in some way. What you gossip about, you fear or judge within yourself. And what you judge, you condemn in yourself. Criticizing and belittling are forms of judgment and condemnation. Each time you criticize, belittle, gossip, or judge another, you merely reflect perceived personal flaws that you fear or that bring you shame. It has nothing to do with the other person.

People criticize and belittle because they feel bad about themselves and perceive themselves as flawed, broken, unworthy, unlovable, or undeserving, and for NO other reason.

I had a client once who, for a while, would come to every call with a story about how someone in her office was an idiot or lazy. She would go on and on about how this person was always late to work, said stupid things in meetings, and would leave early whenever she felt like it. I let this ride for a couple of sessions and then began to ask her about some of the issues. It turns out she was late to the office at least as much as her co-worker and often missed meetings altogether. She really struggled in these areas. And up until then, she had not realized that the way she criticized and belittled her co-worker was really a projection of how she felt about her own shortcomings.

Fortunately, this client was very coachable and was willing to do what it took to start practicing a higher degree of integrity and lay down the emotional weapon of belittling and criticizing.

Belittling and criticizing as an emotional weapon is designed to divide, alienate, or push others away. This happens by perceiving something about another person as wrong, bad, or otherwise unacceptable or problematic and, therefore, not worthy of love, care, kindness, compassion, or grace. Ultimately, criticizing and belittling others winds up leading you to feel alone, sad, and isolated. It is coincidentally one of the four horsemen of divorce, as noted by the Gottman Institute.

Take Loving Action: Lay Down Criticizing and Belittling

To begin laying down the emotional weapon habit of criticizing and belittling, you will first need to turn inward and look at the perfectionistic habits you practice that are spurred on by shame. Perfectionists are excellent at this emotional weapon. It stems from being so good at criticizing and belittling oneself, which is then projected onto others.

As such, a very efficient way to begin laying down this emotional weapon is to replace it with deep, delicious, delightful self-compassion and self-love.

Of course, this practice is really a symptom of rejecting oneself or fragments of one's self. But, as you become increasingly dedicated and practiced at radical self-responsibility, self-honor, self-acceptance, and letting go, you will simultaneously become more loving and accepting of others, flaws and all. You can begin intentionally focusing on and seeing others through the lens of what you love, admire, or appreciate about others and, therefore yourself.

When you notice yourself criticizing or belittling (or gossiping or complaining about) others, take the opportunity to grab that pointer finger and either turn it around or point it into a mirror! This way, you can practice courageous, radical self-responsibility.

After all, picking out and naming what you deem "wrong" with another is an illumination of your own issues.

Feel free to revisit chapter one on self-honor. And if you have been practicing this already, you have a beautiful head start!

A Happy Ending

As you can see, emotional weapons are a paradox; they are quite simple on the one hand and seemingly complex on the other. And while there are dozens of additional nuances of emotional weapons, these examples give you a framework to begin laying them down. Take a moment and use your imagination to envision how life might be different in the absence of emotional weapons.

Remember my client Maria from the beginning of the chapter? To show you how impactful it can be when you lay down your emotional weapons, let me tell you a little bit about how we turned this around for her in just fifty minutes.

- We outlined effective ways to communicate with her husband so she could get more of what she wants.
- I gave her simple scripts to get her point across by sharing with love and care without getting her point turned back around on her.
- We came up with a plan for how to get him to buy into taking a more active role in their family so everyone would feel valued and connected.

Here's what happened next:

She emailed me three days later, telling me how receptive he was when she shared all of this with him.

"OMG, Shawn, I can't even believe these words are coming out of my mouth. He was so open and actually sat and listened without getting defensive. And he even helped brainstorm ways he could get more involved."

Even though I literally work with clients on these kinds of challenges every day, I almost could not believe how fast this turned around! You can have these kinds of experiences too!

Nothing brings me more joy, often to the point of tears than when I see a client have a big breakthrough or share a success story about how she does not have to try so hard to get what she wants in BUSINESS, LIFE, OR LOVE!

Take Loving Action: Lay Down All Of Your Emotional Weapons

What follows is one additional loving action to get you working toward laying down all emotional weapons as a collection of habits you have been programmed to practice and engage when you feel negatively triggered in any way, large or small.

Laying down emotional weapons that are used against yourself and others will have a beautiful, transformative impact on your entire experience of life. This is a powerful action that naturally builds emotional safety, trust, and vulnerability in relationships with yourself and others.

Guard Your Lips

From here on out, give yourself and others the gift of guarding your lips with deep, heartfelt vigilance! What does this mean? It means embracing total integrity with your words and thoughts. It means to speak less, breathe and surrender more. It means that you strive to focus on what you can do or be or say that honors you and that you release being concerned with others. And to never again begin a thought or statement with sassy and harmful words like "you," "he," "she," or "they." For example:

- You made me feel (mad, sad, and alone).
- You make me crazy (angry, frustrated).
- You hurt me.
- You are mean (terrible, a jerk).
- He / they hurt me...
- You are awful.
- They did ____ and made me cry...

And so on.

This type of language is a complete abdication of radical self-responsibility and begins a cascade of back-and-forth emotional weapon launching. Do you see how using emotional weapons perpetuates victim payoffs, pity parties, discouragement, disconnection, lack of trust and emotional safety, and all-around problem-focused communication?

Special note: I do get that sometimes other people's words and actions can be cruel or thoughtless. You are always allowed to set boundaries or remove yourself from others' lives. But you do not have control over them, and it only creates more upset and feelings of powerlessness within yourself when you unleash emotional weapons. Please know that it IS so very possible to let go of feeling so impacted by others and that your inner and outer mental and emotional safety can be claimed by you alone.

Identify the Emotional Weapons

To close down this chapter, I invite you to get super clear on your most prominent emotional weapons so you can begin laying them down quickly. Please consider the following four questions.

1. Which three emotional weapons do you engage most frequently?
2. What are you trying to gain by engaging in each one?
3. Why would you like to stop using each emotional weapon?
4. Of the tools you have learned in this book, which tool would you like to use as a replacement for each emotional weapon so they can be laid down?

Take a couple of minutes to consider these questions and write your responses in your notebook. How will you and others (family, friends, spouse, co-workers) benefit when you have released and replaced emotional weapons with habits and practices that are fruitful, joyful, and loving? Do your best to come up with five juicy benefits.

Key Takeaways

- Emotional weapons are used for conflict and fighting with yourself and others—they are a "skill set" that you learned from those who had the strongest influence on you as you grew up. Emotional weapons serve as specific ways to sell yourself out and simultaneously put on armor to emotionally defend and protect yourself.

- As you learn and apply raw, unbridled vulnerability through self-love skills, authentic self-expression, and healthy self-protection skills, you will naturally use emotional weapons less and less.

- Like all negativity and unwanted habits, emotional weapons can be changed, replaced, and surrendered completely with practice.

- As you lay down your emotional weapons, it becomes exceedingly difficult for others to continue using their emotional weapons.

- The ability to communicate openly, candidly, and especially fruitfully with anyone, anytime, anywhere will unfold as you replace emotional weapons with new loving skills.

- Laying down emotional weapons that are used against yourself and others will have a beautiful, transformative impact on your entire experience of life. This naturally builds emotional safety, trust, and vulnerability in relationships with yourself and others.

CHAPTER 10

Self-Love Skills

Let's finish our living for love journey by sending you off with four juicy self-love skills. The development and practice of self-love skills are deeply transformational. These skills demonstrate to yourself and others that you find yourself worthy, valuable, and deserving of love, care, and kindness through your own courageous actions. Simultaneously, self-love skills teach others how they are permitted to treat and interact with you. Additionally, as you practice self-love skills, you grow your courage in gorgeously powerful ways.

Along the way, your perceived self-value and worthiness amplify!

The fun thing about applying and practicing self-love skills is that once you have a bit of experience under your belt, people tend to stop pressing your buttons. Thus, you only really need to stand firm with them for a *season*, so to speak, until you master each self-love skill. As you begin, be mindful that while setting up and practicing self-love skills, it will likely feel quite challenging at the start and will require commitment and courage. Not to worry—this season is short-lived. The fruits of the initial discomfort will result in a simpler, freer, and happier life inside and out.

Most people need to practice these four skills a lot at the beginning, but if you practice them for a period of time, you will need to use them only sporadically for the rest of your life.

Here are the four key self-love skills that work well for everyone to learn:

- Clear boundaries
- Speak your heart
- Ask and receive
- Just say no

Clear Boundaries

Let's begin with the basics—clarifying and setting boundaries. Boundaries are all about determining what you will and will not give or receive or what is related to your expectations of others and yourself.

Examples of Clear Boundaries

- I'm sorry, but I cannot meet with you at that time. When during our business hours of 8 am to 4 pm will work for you?
- I want to hear about your work day. I will be free to give you my full attention in 15 minutes (or a specific time).
- Sure, you may borrow our lawn mower. We've cleaned it and gassed it for you. We'll appreciate your returning it the same—clean and with the tank full.
- If you put your clothes in the hamper, I will wash them for you.
- You may go out to play as soon as you make your bed and finish your homework.
- We can deliver your month-end reports by the 5th as long as we receive your data by the 25th of the month.
- I will be happy to give you feedback, but only when you request it.

- I love you and will love to have a conversation with you as soon as you become calm.

Do you see how crystal clear these statements are? Can you see how they set up an invisible fence? Oftentimes, boundaries are shrouded in guilt, shame, tip-toeing, eggshell walking, enabling, and codependency. Defining clear boundaries is a loving action toward yourself and others. If someone asks for a favor and you truly want to do it, say yes. If you do not want to or do not actually have the time, make it clear that you are not available. Explain that, although you would love to help, you cannot help this time, but maybe the next time. But make your "no" very clear.

Why do clear boundaries seem so difficult to set?

It seems difficult to set clear boundaries because

- There is a strong inclination for most women to put others' needs and feelings first.
- Women are not always in tune with what they actually want and need.
- Pleasing others seems easier and more available.
- Women do not feel deserving.
- Women feel afraid or anxious to set clear boundaries.
- Women do not have practice or experience setting clear boundaries.
- You believe setting clear boundaries will jeopardize relationships.
- Clear and direct boundaries were not modeled when growing up.
- It seems "mean" or rude to set clear boundaries.
- Enabling or codependent habits get in the way and cloud judgment.

If you feel any version of the above, don't worry, it is very common. We all feel these ways at times. Women are raised to be pleasing perfectionists, thus raised to NOT have very strong self-love skills!! But with practice, you can learn to say no without feeling guilty.

Speak Your Heart

Speaking your heart is deeply and gorgeously vulnerable. It gives others permission to "see" you or to "see into" your heart and spirit.

Speaking your heart first requires you to know your own heart, which encourages vulnerability and radical honesty (which are also practices). This can be far more challenging than first glance might indicate. Women can be so concerned with others' needs and wants that knowing one's own heart is often difficult.

You might begin by tuning into one simple question and asking it throughout the day: "What do I want or prefer at this moment?" Numerous clients I work with seriously struggle with answering this simple question, be it about food choices, movie choices, business actions, relationship decisions, parenting choices, and anything in between. Without being tuned into the nuances of your own preferences, it is quite difficult to speak your heart intimately, deliberately, and lovingly.

This is why the whole process is an effort toward self-exploration and vulnerability.

Here are a few examples of how to speak your heart. Feel free to adopt them to your own style and come up with your own unique ways to share your heart with loved ones.

- Sharing the deepest and most vulnerable emotions with others can seem incredibly challenging (even to admit them to one's self), yet it can be incredibly nurturing and connecting. Try saying a statement like the following: "I am feeling very overwhelmed" (alone, ashamed, angry, humiliated, afraid, terrified, and so on).

- To share a past story of abuse, pain, or trauma is often a heart-centered and courageous endeavor.
- Asking for help, support, or encouragement are beautiful examples of speaking your heart.
- Openly sharing perceived failures, mistakes, and stumbles, too, requires vulnerability and courage.

While most applications of speaking your heart actually involve speaking, eye-gazing is a nonverbal exercise that takes vulnerability to a whole new level. Eye-gazing is a wonderful way to "speak your heart" without words. When I work with couples (onsite for retreats or virtually), they are encouraged to begin a daily ritual, for at least eight weeks, of setting a two-minute timer to simply sit still and stare into one another.

This exercise is shockingly challenging at first. Couples feel so seen and vulnerable that it can literally seem unbearable. Many, many sandbags are inclined to spring open, yet it is the most beautiful experience. Couples first face the fear of judgment (i.e., "Is my partner staring at my wrinkles, looking at a pimple or age spot, does he or she think I am ugly," and so on). This gorgeous exercise accentuates one's own self-judgments, which are then projected onto the other, assuming that s/he, too, must be judging.

Yet, with time, it is nothing short of magnanimous to be truly seen and loved for every fiber of one's being. Feel free to practice this exercise first in the mirror—an equally powerful exercise. Looking into one's self can be just as vulnerable and might even feel painful at first. Try self-eye-gazing first while surrendering, letting go of judgments, and allowing unconditional love and compassion to radiate outward from your heart. Practice for several weeks, and then try it with another person.

Why does speaking your heart seem so difficult?

Simple! Because it is so darn radically vulnerable, and being vulnerable scares the shit out of people! Speaking your heart requires a boatload of courage, and, quite frankly, people would usually rather play the victim, throw a pity party, or indulge in some other form of negative payoff.

In place of speaking one's heart (or sharing any of the self-love skills), people are far more practiced in the arts of inserting blame, accusations, judgment, projections, right-fighting, pridefulness, criticism, anger, resentment, and the like.

Unfortunately, people do not often speak their hearts because they do not deem themselves worthy or deserving of the care and support that typically accompanies speaking one's heart. Speaking your heart comes from a deep softness, self-compassion, and unbridled humility—the trifecta of LOVE.

Ask & Receive

Asking and receiving are very near and dear to the heart. I used to have a painfully difficult time asking for what I wanted and needed—I genuinely did not believe I was deserving, as so many of the women I work with in my private coaching also believe. Yet, when I did not receive that which I desired, I would frequently spew anger and resentment onto those whom I perceived "should" have been meeting my (essentially secret) needs and desires. This kind of upset, pride, and resentment springs forth from a place of desperation. Underneath is a little girl desperate to be cared for, yet not courageous enough to supply herself with care, nor bravely ask for it from others.

This is where a new practice steps in.

We must practice until proficiency and then master all that is needed to build belief in self-love, ironclad worthiness, and unbreakable value and deservingness.

Here are several examples of asking for what you want:

- Would you grab me a glass of water?
- Can you make dinner tonight?
- Will you give me a hug (pat my back, cuddle me...)?
- Could you give me a bit of encouragement about...?
- Can you help me with _____ on Saturday morning?

Why does asking for what you want seem so difficult?

Again it circles back to four main roadblocks: 1) A lack of practice, 2) assuming others should "just know" what you want, 3) a lack of courage to behave vulnerably, and 4) not feeling worthy or deserving of support.

It can feel quite uncomfortably vulnerable for many to admit that they cannot meet every need and want of others and that they are very much human and NEED, want, or appreciate help sometimes!

Just Say NO

Saying no can be pure magic, totally transformational, and...a little or a LOT scary!

Saying no often means taking a bold stand for yourself, your time, your energy, your contribution...and even your sanity! You are allowed to say NO, to anything, anyone, anywhere, anytime, simply because you want to say no or do not want to do what is being asked or expected of you.

Repeat after me: "I can say a big juicy 'NO' to anything, anyone, anywhere, anytime, simply because I want to say NO or because I do NOT want to do what is being asked or expected of me."

Whew! How is that for empowerment, self-love, and reclaiming your time, energy, and sanity?

Women are historically quite poor at setting this particular boundary. Women are often socialized to be hospitable, accommodating, subservient, and helpful to the detriment of one's self. Thus, this two-letter word can be quite an obstacle to climb over. Fortunately, here again, you will just need a bit of practice!

Examples of saying no:

- No, I have a prior engagement.
- No, but thanks for asking.
- No, thanks for thinking of me.
- No, I don't have the bandwidth for that right now, but perhaps next month.
- No.
- Nope.
- No ma'am!
- No sir!
- No, thank you!

Do you see how none of these ways to say no come with an excuse, rationalization, explanation, story, or lie?

You do not need any excuse, rationalization, explanation, story, or lie in order to say no. You just need to say it. And you say it simply because you can, and you are deserving and worthy of doing what honors you, your time, your health, your energy, and so on.

Why does saying NO seem so difficult?

Well, one likely reason is that you have a ton of practice saying yes when you want to say no. Therefore, you have little practice saying no.

Secondly, saying no can have the illusion of being or sounding "mean." Remember, this is a story that hosts a big ole' sandbag full of guilt. Both are to be let go of and surrendered to the Divine. You may need a great deal of practice with letting go of stories like this on your way to feeling great about saying no.

And then, of course, there is the piece regarding vulnerability. Saying no, especially in the beginning, seems quite vulnerable. It might take you several tries to say no to various obligations before you actually say no!

And, just like the other self-love skills, not feeling worthy or deserving of guarding your time, energy, or sanity can stand in the way of saying no.

Visioneering

A natural byproduct of choosing a crystal clear path is visualization (also referred to as visioneering, imagining, or daydreaming). This is an excellence-driven habit that I strongly encourage you to develop. Visualization supports bringing what you desire to fruition more effectively and efficiently.

Visualization encompasses several powerful benefits, the least of which is the fact that the brain-body-emotion connection does not know the difference between something that is real and that which is vividly imagined.

Thus, when you visualize an intended outcome over and over, the brain starts building neural pathway "bridges," giving the illusion of actual experience and therefore growing confidence.

I use visualization to imagine successful, warm, joyful, loving speaking events. The vast majority of the time, speaking events then unfold as I had imagined them or better.

Visualization is a beautiful gift.

When I was working to eliminate various aspects of anger, I visualized over and over how I wanted to feel and respond in certain situations and how I wanted to share unconditional love and kindness instead of aggression, sass, or self-righteousness.

That, too, began to unfold better and more quickly than I had envisioned.

I invite you to spend time daily envisioning, daydreaming, and imagining your clear visions, intentions, and defined practices coming to fruition.

Envisioning a clear path of any kind (positive or negative) increases the odds of it coming to fruition. Even if you are not totally conscious of a vision, when you give it enough energy, the Universe conspires to bring your vision to you.

Accidental Visioneering

Sometimes, visualization does not always turn out favorably, and we have to be very careful and have clarity with what we allow our minds to practice.

Have you ever spontaneously or accidentally envisioned something catastrophic? Here are some examples:

- A policeman coming to your door to announce that your lover has been killed in a car accident
- Your child getting cancer or being kidnapped
- Being attacked by a stranger
- Seeing your business or marriage go down in flames
- Tripping and falling down the steps
- Your computer getting stolen and losing all of your precious writing

In my old life—the one filled with fear and overwhelm—I used to envision these kinds of catastrophic events all the time, then subsequently see some of these happen. Okay, who am I kidding—they *all* used to happen, and I don't even have children!

The variety of possible catastrophic visions are endless and startling! Interestingly, catastrophic visions happen far more often in people prior to getting on an increasingly clear and intentional path where vision and value alignment reign supreme.

Why does this happen? Why do our brains have a tendency toward catastrophic visioneering?

Numerous possibilities and potentialities add to this phenomenon.

They include a combination of childhood events and parental norms, personality/temperament, brain function, trauma, hard wiring, and even innate "fight, flight, or freeze" responses designed to keep us alive.

Regardless, being blindsided by rapid-fire visions, or what I like to call "popcorn catastrophic" visions, used to occur for me daily. And, lacking clarity, I was completely unclear of why this was a problem and that there could be a better way to live.

If you pay attention, this likely occurs multiple times each day in your own mind and imagination.

Eventually, I found this mental habit to be darn annoying, especially because sometimes the content of a particular vision would stick with me all dang day!

Over time, however, as I began to practice life with more and more self-honor, unconditional love, and intentionality and as I sought to heal old wounds and build visions of love, peace, truth, and joy, the negative and unconscious visioneering began to miraculously vanish.

I cannot say that I am completely immune to negative popcorn visions. But these days, they are few and far between.

It is valuable to note that your version of the negative unconscious, popcorn visions, can often be tied in some way to your deepest fears. Knowing this can be favorable as it helps identify spaces where healing is needed. So, take note of these negative visions, be curious about them, and use them to catapult you toward a clear vision of deliberate, free, heart-centered living.

Whether you envision situations connected to upset, anguish, suffering, fear, joy, love, or abundance, you are actively bringing more of what you envision to your life.

We now live in a society where MORE, BIGGER, FASTER, BETTER has become a complete mania and obsession. Marketing budgets are in the multiple billions and often intended to prey upon insecurities related to people's internal beliefs that he or she is not enough.

Take the cosmetic injectable market, for example. It preys strategically upon people's fear of aging and changing appearance and attempts to connect one's lovability and worthiness to physical appearance. Honestly, when did the beautiful and natural evolution of aging become a crime?

We are literally built to have increasingly wrinkly, saggy skin. Aging can signal wisdom, slowing down and sinking deeper into life, more meaningful creative expression, and the ability to enjoy more of what life has to offer. And yes, aging prepares us for the transition out of this worldly body and on to the next life... or wherever! Yet, somehow aging has become demonized.

In my "old life" of selling myself out to please others, I haphazardly created a vision and belief that "having the perfect body" would lead me to be loved, worthy, and complete.

I still find myself needing to sit and practice surrender in this arena at times. Being clear about unconditional self-love (and all other love) as my life's guidepost, I frequently practice surrendering attachment to this body and appearance because I, too, bought into the programmed belief that aging is bad or that aging makes you less lovable or worthy.

I am thankful that this belief has diminished greatly and continues to shrink. I am also thankful to have a partner who sees ME, my heart, my mind, and my spirit and sees my physical temple as perfectly imperfect at each stage.

Take Loving Action

Let us now take these self-love skills and put them into practice!

How to gain the courage to begin setting clear boundaries

Without boundaries, you will be inclined to feel like a victim or feel and be taken advantage of. Women who feel taken for granted are usually at the mercy of not having had experience setting strong boundaries and, in turn, interpret many situations as feeling powerless and then resentful, which then often turns to anger or apathy.

One begins setting boundaries simply by starting! You can begin looking for places where you feel angry, left out, rejected, resentful, taken for granted, and victimized. Sometimes you will need to set boundaries even with yourself and then with others as well. The goal is just to start and to start small. Begin to dip your toe into the water and test it out. Like anything new, practice is key. You should expect to experience resistance and pushback from others and from yourself. This is okay and expected—continue anyway.

Setting boundaries teaches you that you are worth advocating for and teaches others how they are permitted to interact with you. Certainly, others do not always comply with your boundaries, nor do you always comply with self-boundaries. But with practice, all situations will improve.

How to begin to speak your heart

As with all things, it begins with testing the waters! Self-love skills, by nature, bolster self-love, self-trust, self-compassion, and perceived deservingness. You can start by practicing self-eye-gazing for two minutes daily when you wake up in the morning or go to bed at night. With daily self-eye-gazing, you can begin breaking down the barriers where you judge yourself and others based on appearance and start "seeing into" others, into their spirits, into their hearts—a place where you can marvel at the entirety of life. And while you are not talking to another person, you will be speaking (or thinking) your heart to yourself, the starting point of all healing and growth!

Speaking your heart is a beautiful and vulnerable habit to develop. It is done with tons of kindness, sweetness, and humility, even when it feels unbearably difficult to share. This skill is a gift to all and not one to be avoided!

How to begin asking for what you want

This is a great time to start *small*, with baby steps. You could perhaps even put yourself on a schedule of sorts. Typically, I encourage clients to ask for something small every day for two weeks. This builds the asking muscle slowly and gives you time to get used to receiving, which can be quite difficult, even seemingly painful, for some.

If you are particularly challenged in asking for support, you might simply practice asking for things like a cup of water or the salt shaker. If you have some practice but not much and want to strengthen this muscle, ask someone to stop on their drive to pick something up for you, like lunch. It really only matters that you stretch a bit into a zone of slight discomfort. Here lies boundless opportunities for growing courage, a gateway to higher energy and happiness.

How to begin saying no!

Just say no!

No making excuses. No explaining why you need to say no like you are a small child who is about to get in trouble. You get to say NO just because you want to!

I don't know about you, but saying NO used to be a big issue for me. For the longest time, I was unable to say no, even when I really, really wanted to. I was far more interested in pleasing, not losing others' approval, or not disappointing other people than I was in honoring myself, my heart, my energy, or my own time. Yuck!

How many times have you said yes to something that you later (or instantly) realized you wanted to say no to? Life is super busy, and for many, it seems to get busier each year, especially when we consider our family, health, work, and...enjoying this thing we call LIFE and LIVING.

So, why do you let your free time get filled up with obligations you do not want? Especially at the expense of your health, family, rest, and FREE TIME?

Here are some examples of saying yes when you mean no.

Example 1: Your boss (client or colleague) wants you to stay late to work on an upcoming assignment. You say yes. Then, a month later, you realize you have had more dinners at work than you have had with your family.

Example 2: A family member asks you to watch a child, pet, house, etc. Of course, "anything for family," you say. Who would not say yes to helping family? So, you agree. Then you spend the next three days wishing you had said no, not because you don't want to help, but because you need to prioritize your health, your kids, and/or your husband. After all, you have not had a date night or consistent workout week in weeks, maybe even months.

Example 3: At your child's school, you are asked to help with a bake sale (or a class event). Yes, you would love to help your child's school. Only now you realize you are one of the only parents who constantly says YES. And while you LOVE to be present for your little darling, it's not your job to do it all!

Why does this keep happening to you?

It really is just one magic word...NO. It is all too common, and we are all guilty of saying YES when we mean NO.

You can stand in deep, unconditional love and compassion by practicing these four self-love skills!

As you can see, clarity in and around the self is abundantly important. It is a worthy endeavor to seek clarity for yourself in any and every arena.

Body image is not the only place we lack clarity and become unconsciously programmed into limiting beliefs and actions that do not align with self-honor and love.

We can look at the vast number of possible daily decisions and choices we make and how the evolution of technology, media, social media, and huge quantities of data has led us to become poor self-managers, scattered leaders, and frustrated parents and spouses who are untrustworthy to ourselves and desired commitments.

In my experience, "more, bigger, faster, better" is usually an illusion.

What this programmed belief leads to in so many people is an active practice of chaos, chronic busyness, overspending, overdrinking, overworking, overwhelm, feeling far too stressed, and wanting or craving to the point where nothing seems to be enough.

The feelings that are left without clarity are anger, fear, anxiety, frustration, and loneliness. Rarely are people satiated by seeking "more, bigger, faster, better."

Contentment is but a phantom ghost.

Life is practiced to the exclusion of actual sustained joy and happiness.

In addition to business owners and couples, I work with many single and dating ladies. Like I once did in my own relationships, they often come to me with many "foggy glasses" ways of showing up in relationships, like these examples:

- They might not be clear about sexual boundaries or speak those boundaries.
- They might not be okay with the casual asking out on a date by text but do not communicate this valuable and key desire.
- They might not be clear on character traits, integrity traits, or deal-breakers.

They often navigate in an unclear, foggy way that feels like they are accepting sad, spoiled leftovers.

But when each woman gets crystal clear about the following things:

- The strong, caring, self-honoring woman she wants to be;
- The specific kind of relationship she wants, including details like communication style, care, values, affection, and so forth (the clearer the better!); and
- How she wants to be treated...

...and, when she conveys these visions lovingly and courageously without side-stepping her own innate value and worth, she ALWAYS finds (or co-creates) the relationship of her dreams in a fairly short period of time.

In fact, I have singles and married people alike create a very detailed "relationship profile" in order to support and guide their hopes and dreams for a relationship.

In place of clear focus, you will fall prey to participating in societal norms, trying to measure up to others' expectations, approval seeking, unwanted obligations, perfectionism, pleasing, or other opportunities for selling yourself to self-betrayal.

The bottom line is that without connection to clarity, everything in life, business/career, and relationships can and will go haywire in ways that bring needless pain and suffering.

This is the power of clarity. When you are clear, life moves fluidly.

Key Takeaways

- The development and practice of self-love skills are deeply transformational. These skills demonstrate to yourself and others that you find yourself worthy, valuable, and deserving of love, care, and kindness through your own courageous actions.

- Boundaries are all about determining what you will and will not give or receive or what is related to your expectations of others and yourself. Defining clear boundaries is a loving action toward yourself and others.

- Speaking your heart first requires you to know your own heart, which encourages vulnerability and radical honesty. Without being tuned into the nuances of your own preferences, it is quite difficult to speak your heart intimately, deliberately, and lovingly.

- Speaking your heart comes from a deep softness, self-compassion, and unbridled humility—the trifecta of LOVE.

- Saying no often means taking a bold stand for yourself, your time, your energy, your contribution...and even your sanity! You are allowed to say NO, to anything, anyone, anywhere, anytime, simply because you want to say no or do not want to do what is being asked or expected of you.

- Visualization supports bringing what you desire into fruition more effectively and efficiently. When you visualize an intended outcome over and over, the brain starts building neural pathway "bridges," giving the illusion of actual experience and therefore growing confidence.

- You can stand in deep, unconditional love and compassion by practicing self-love skills!

CONCLUSION

Hooray!

High five!

You did it!

Congratulations on taking such a powerful stand for your happiness, growth, and spiritual evolutions! Living for love is a lifestyle and a daily practice that you have stepped into. Are you celebrating yourself along with me? By this point, you have gone through all of the homework and are building some incredible new habits and undoubtedly seeing joyful and profound shifts in multiple areas of your life.

Next, I want to invite you to continue your journey to living for love, honor yourself, let go of the sources of negativity in your life, and liberate yourself to live a life of true joy. I encourage you to revisit this book often as you venture through the experiences of life that test your new outlook. In a world where most people so often feel desperate, alone, resentful, never good enough, overwhelmed, and disconnected, this book promises a pathway to begin experiencing calm, joy, and a deep connection to all, starting from the inside out. This book will continue to be a beacon of light as you travel this path to living for love.

Remember, you are not alone. You do not have to go it alone either.

My team of expert coaches and I have traveled this path for decades and would love to guide you along your personal journey. If you are ready to take your learning to the next level, I invite you to consider exploring an individual coaching relationship with me and my team. To learn more about or apply for our programs and personal coaching and mentoring, please email us at drhaywood@reimaginelove.com.

You are one hundred percent responsible for your experience of life, but you are NOT your thoughts, habits, roles, or career. You are a child of God. You are imperfectly perfect in your humanness, and you deserve to live for love and be embodied by love. Commit to this journey and continue to do the work each day. I am here to support you.

Additionally, I invite you to reach out to me by email to share your transformation story. The more we share, the more we are able to spread light and love and show others that it's possible to live a life of true mental, emotional, and spiritual freedom. Find me at drhaywood@reimaginelove.com.

Bye for now, Shawn

Resources to Continue Your Learning

The following is a list of resources that live close to my heart. Several of them were referenced throughout the book.

Letting Go by Dr. David Hawkins

Healing and Recovery by Dr. David Hawkins

Transcending the Levels of Consciousness by Dr. David Hawkins

Truth VS Falsehood by Dr. David Hawkins

The Alchemist by Paulo Coelho

Manuscript Found in Accra by Paulo Coelho

Peaceful Warrior by Dan Millman

No More Mister Nice Guy by Robert A. Glover

Passage Meditation by Eknath Easwaran

Grant Fieldgrove lives in Bakersfield, CA, with his family and a bunch of dogs that annoy him. (The dogs, not the family.)

He has a TV that hangs out four-inches into the hallway and has been spotted driving a truck with a duct-taped dash.

You can see him in the upcoming films *Time's Up* and *Good Side of Bad*, with more to come in the near future.

If you have a child, or know of one, that is struggling to reach milestones and would like more information about early intervention screenings for autism, please visit **Autism-Society.org**